Norway

Nations of the Modern World: Europe

edited by W. Rand Smith and Robin Remington

This series examines the nations of Europe as they adjust to the changing world order and move into the twenty-first century. Each volume is a detailed analytical country case study of the political, economic, and social dynamics of a European state facing the challenges of the post–Cold War era. These challenges include changing values and rising expectations, the search for new political identities and avenues of participation, and growing opportunities for economic and political cooperation in the new Europe. Emerging policy issues such as the environment, immigration, refugees, and reordered national security priorities are evolving in contexts still strongly influenced by history, geography, and culture.

The former East European nations must cope with the legacies of communism as they attempt to make the transition to multiparty democracy and market economies amid intensifying national, ethnic, religious, and class divisions. West European nations confront the challenge of pursuing economic and political integration within the European Union while contending with problems of economic insecurity, budgetary stress, and voter alienation.

How European nations respond to these challenges individually and collectively will shape domestic and international politics in Europe for generations to come. By considering such common themes as political institutions, public policy, political movements, political economy, and domestic-foreign policy linkages, we believe the books in this series contribute to our understanding of the threads that bind this vital and rapidly evolving region.

BOOKS IN THIS SERIES

Norway: Elites on Trial, *Knut Heidar*

The Netherlands: Negotiating Sovereignty in an Independent World,
Thomas R. Rochon

The Czech and Slovak Republics: Nation Versus State,
Carol Skalnick Leff

The Politics of Belgium, *John Fitzmaurice*

Great Britain: Decline or Renewal? *Donley Studlar*

Denmark: A Troubled Welfare State, *Kenneth E. Miller*

Portugal: From Monarchy to Pluralist Democracy, *Walter C. Opello, Jr.*

Norway

Elites on Trial

Knut Heidar

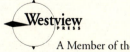

Westview
PRESS

A Member of the Perseus Books Group

Copyright © 2001 by Westview Press, A Member of the Perseus Books Group

Published in 2001 in the United States of America by Westview Press, 5500 Central Avenue, Boulder, Colorado 80301-2877, and in the United Kingdom by Westview Press, 12 Hid's Copse Road, Cumnor Hill, Oxford OX2 9JJ

Find us on the World Wide Web at www.westviewpress.com

Library of Congress Cataloging-in-Publication Data
Heidar, Knut, 1949–
  Norway: elites on trial/by Knut Heidar.
    p.   cm.— (Nations of the modern world, Europe)
  Includes bibliographical references and index.
  ISBN 0-8133-3200-1 (pbk.)
  1. Norway—Politics and government—1945– .   I. Title.   II. Series.

JN7461 .H45   2000
320.9481—dc21

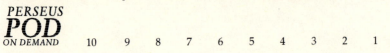

PERSEUS
POD
ON DEMAND   10   9   8   7   6   5   4   3   2   1

Contents

Preface

Curiosity is crucial in science in general and in comparative politics in particular. Having spent several years as both a student and a researcher in the United States and in Britain, I believe that an inquisitive mind is indispensable as a force for experience and learning. My hope is that readers will approach this book with their heads full of questions: What makes politics tick in a small country like Norway? Why is it a peaceful, quiet, and—now—rich country? And why is this country not a member of the European Union?

This book has been underway for a long time. There have been many interruptions—some of them quite fruitful—but during 1999 I finally got down to the writing and rewriting necessary to finish. Many people have helped along the way. Colleague and friend W. M. Lafferty got me started. The series editor Rand Smith provided encouragement at critical junctures. Another colleague and friend—Øyvind Østerud—gave me much valuable advice, most of which is reflected in the text. Fellow "party watcher" Jo Saglie also offered detailed and constructive advice.

I also received solid institutional and financial support. The department of political science at the University of Oslo provided support for my research, and I received a grant from the Association of Norwegian Nonfiction Writers and Translators to get started. Four institutions, in particular, were instrumental in shaping my perspectives on Norwegian politics as seen from abroad. In chronological order, these include Brandeis University, the London School of Economics, the University of Warwick, and Denver University. In the autumn of 1998, I visited the political science department at Denver University with the support of the Fulbright Foundation. Exploring Coloradan life gave me the opportunity to discover even more similarities and differences between Norway and the United States. Also the "Starbruck seminars" with Spencer Wellhofer deepened—I believe—my comparative perspectives. Numerous discussions with colleagues in Oslo and Bergen have also found their way into these pages. But, of course, the final responsibility for the text rests with me alone.

Finally, my thanks go to my family: to Kari who accompanied me on—or tolerated—most of my travels and to my three children who helped keep my curiosity alive.

Acronyms

AF	Federation of Norwegian Professional Associations
EC	European Communities
EEA	European Economic Area
EEC	European Economic Community
EFTA	European Free Trade Association
GATT	General Agreement on Trade and Tarrifs
IMF	International Monetary Fund
INGO	International Non-Governmental Organization
KS	Association of Local Authorities
LO	Norwegian Federation of Trade Unions
NATO	North Atlantic Treaty Organization
NHO	Norwegian Employers Association
OECD	Organization for Economic Cooperation and Development
OEEC	Organization for European Economic Cooperation
OSCE	Organization for Security and Cooperation in Europe
PLO	Palestine Liberation Organization
SDI	Strategic Defense Initiative
WEU	Western European Union
YS	Federation of Vocational Unions

1

Small-Scaled, Egalitarian, and Territorially Based

But it still lies there. Huge Norway,
sea washed and grand, with business and peaks.
If you seek them—the round views and the sky light—
don't stay up there, or let dreams carry you away.
There is a time of need and we are part of the world,
But from a different country
that the noblemen did not quite conquer
So we don't bow as deep as the neighbors do,
it was too steep up here.

—*Rolf Jacobsen, from the poem "Annerledeslandet"*
("Different Country"), translated by the author

On May 1, 1960, the U.S. Air Force pilot Francis Gary Powers was shot down in a U-2 spy plane over Sverdlovsk in the Soviet Union. His destination was Bodø, Norway. Global cold war logistics had placed Norway centrally on the United States–Soviet Union axis, as Norway bordered some of the most sensitive U.S.S.R. military areas on the Kola Peninsula. Membership in the North Atlantic Treaty Organization (NATO) has been the main pillar of Norwegian security policy since 1949. Within the NATO alliance, however, Norway has been both at the center and at the periphery: It was centrally located on the global map of cold-war nuclear missile strategies, but it has resided on the geographic flank of the "European theater." Among its continental allies, Norway's Atlantic, Anglo-American leanings placed the country at the periphery—at least in political terms. The feelings have to some extent been mutual: Twice Norwegian voters have rejected membership in the European Union (in

1972 and in 1994). After heated debates, including stern warnings about isolationism, economic failures, and loss of political influence from the Norwegian "establishment," the voters nevertheless decided (like the Swiss) that Brussels was too far away.

Norway has been a quiet corner in postwar European developments with few dramatic appearances in the international arena. During the 1990s, its presence was only sporadically noted in the global media, for example, at the height of the Middle East peace process, during the 1994 Winter Olympics, and when resuming commercial whaling. "The Oslo channel" hit the international headlines in August 1993. Secret as well as semiprivate diplomacy had produced an agreement between Israel and the Palestine Liberation Organization (PLO) about a gradual development toward mutual recognition and peace. The accord was signed at a White House ceremony in September of the same year. During the Lillehammer Olympic Winter Games in 1994, Norway was again in the media; these were, according to the chairman of the International Olympic Committee, Mr. Samaranch, "the best winter Olympic games ever." The praise was greeted with immense pride. With less pride, however, but with all the more stubbornness, the Norwegian government made international news in the early 1990s–especially in the United States–with its decision to resume whale hunting, defying the ban imposed by the International Whaling Commission. Norway argued that the whale population was not threatened and that responsible hunting was a question of biologically sound harvesting—a decision that no doubt reinforced a view of the cruelty of Norwegian huntsmen.

A Small Country

Size matters when it comes to visibility on the world stage. It will be argued in this book that it also matters in shaping political systems. This is both a question of what external dependency does to shape internal political processes and of what population size—combined with geography—does to mold the structure of internal politics.

Norway is undoubtedly a small country. With a population of just over four million, it is about the size of Minnesota, incidentally a U.S. state hosting many inhabitants of Scandinavian descent. Geography is also important. Norway is situated at the European flank. It is sparely populated and has a very long coastline and a mountainous inland terrain, making it difficult to establish and maintain lines of communications. The country faces the Atlantic Ocean, and Norwegians have historically been very dependent on the sea for communication and commerce. The logistic "stretch" of the country made strong local government a political necessity. The periphery remained strong throughout the process of nation-building. The center was a necessity, not a national pride.

Norway is both an old and a young nation. The old Norse kingdom was founded during the age of the Vikings in the eighth to the tenth century but vanished under Danish rule during the "national decline" in the fourteen and fifteenth centuries. National revival came in the century between 1814 and the declaration of independence in 1905. In 1814, Norway, in the post-Napoleonic turmoil, broke free from the union with Denmark, then saw its notables create the nominally still effective Constitution, and finally was forced into a union with Sweden.

Norway is by history and culture very much a Scandinavian nation. Not only is Norway historically bound to both Denmark and Sweden, but the culture and society of all three countries have been shaped by similar forces: a Protestant state religion and languages that are mutually understandable.

Historical Background

State power and political processes have played a crucial role in shaping the sociocultural fabric of Norwegian social life. This is illustrated by Norway's birth as a modern nation. The Constitution of 1814 was the operative instrument by which Norwegian independence from Denmark was sought. The Constitution—celebrated by Norwegian school children on May 17—was based on principles borrowed from the American constitution, British political practices, and French Enlightenment thought. It is still operative, although with numerous amendments, and plays an important role in government (though not as important as in the United States). One example is the rule that makes representation to Parliament from peripheral districts disproportionately strong. Norway has no commission to adjust constituency size or its number of representatives according to population changes. In this respect the Constitution violates the "one vote, one weight" principle.

In Chapter 2, I briefly present the historical background of nearly four centuries of Danish rule and the confederate union with Sweden from 1814 to 1905. In 1905 Norway gained full independence and shipped in a new monarchy from Denmark (prince) and the United Kingdom (princess) to secure international credibility and support. Prince Carl of Denmark was renamed Haakon VII. There had been six previous kings named Haakon in the old Norse kingdom, and it was hoped that the renaming of the new king would lend credibility to the new state. The forces of nationalism and the late independence were important factors in shaping Norwegian political culture in the twentieth century.

Since 1814 successive waves of peripheral political movements have captured state power. First, the liberal peasant movement of the late nineteenth century toppled the "public official's state" in 1884. They forced parliamentarism on a belligerent *ancien régime*. The second wave came with the workers' movement when the Labor Party entered government in 1935. Both peasants and workers were political armies of the periphery—in social as well as geographical terms. The political turbulence of the interwar period reflected not only the international economic crises but also a fundamental change within Norway from an agrarian to an industrial society. One might also include a third peripheral rebellion against the political center—the issue of membership in the European Union, which was debated in the 1970s and again in the 1990s. On both occasions, a broad alliance of central elites were voted down in a national referendum.

Current Setting

World War II changed important parameters in Norwegian politics. From the interwar policy of neutrality, Norway in the late 1940s became fully integrated in the Western bloc. The implicit reliance on British military forces before the war was changed into an explicit military alliance with the United Kingdom and, more importantly, with the United States through NATO membership in 1949. The economy was strongly dependent on shipping services and on the export of raw materials and semi-finished products to other OECD (Organization for Economic Cooperation and Development) countries. This made Norway's economy vulnerable to fluctuations in world markets. Norway, however, evolved from one of the poorest nations of Western Europe in the early nineteenth century to one of the riches countries in the world in the late twentieth. Discoveries of large oil and gas reservoirs in the North Sea in the 1970s only partially explain this development.

Politically, Norway is, in comparative terms, a very stable country by any indicator. The Labor Party (which controlled government in 1945–1965, 1971–1972, 1973–1981, 1986–1989, 1990–1997, and again from 2000) created, during its first twenty years in power after 1945, the institutional, economic, and cultural infrastructure for what has been labeled the "social democratic state" or more broadly the "social democratic order." The major pillars of this order were strong state presence in the economy, state redistribution of wealth to the benefit of the social as well as geographical peripheries, a welfare state caring for citizens from cradle to grave, and a uniform and almost universal state educational system. The culture of egalitarianism surviving from the old Lutheran peasant society was reinforced in this period.

During the decade of the 1970s, with its oil shock and the political "earthquake" triggered by the first European Union referendum, this social democratic order was challenged. The politics of the 1980s and 1990s have in general been variations over the battle between domestic "tradition" and international "modernity," between social democratic egalitarianism and the new liberalism. The center-right parties took over government from 1981 to 1986 and placed—in a modified form—elements from Thatcherism and Reaganomics on the political agenda. This government's major goals were to create a more "open society" and to "roll back the frontiers of the state." The inertia of Norwegian politics moved toward the liberal right during the 1980s, but the referendum over EU membership in 1994 also showed that at least some of the new winds had affected the center more than the periphery. In the referendum of November 1994 in which 89 percent of the electorate participated, 52 percent voted "No" to the European Union. Geographically, the strongholds against EU membership were astonishingly similar to the "No" areas in the 1972 referendum. The situation after 1994, however, was different from 1972, as Norway now was part of the European Economic Area (EEA), which opened the EU "single market" to the EFTA (European Free Trade Association) countries. (See Chapters 4 and 5 for more on the European Union issue.)

Three Themes and One Proposition

Government in Norway shares many characteristics with that in other small West European countries, particularly, Norway's Scandinavian neighbors: It is a stable parliamentary, multiparty system with a strong social democratic tradition. But Norwegian politics has its own profile, which is brought out by three central and persistent themes: Norway is a small and young state in the European periphery; its politics operates within an egalitarian social structure; and it is marked by the political strength of the periphery.

The first theme developed throughout this book is that the politics of Norway is characterized by Norway being *a small state in the European periphery.* Norway's history as a sovereign state has to a large degree been decided by European developments in war and diplomacy—in 1814, 1905, and 1940–1945. As a small country in the Nordic region, Norway has been an object rather than an initiator of change. This goes for the economic, cultural, and political matters alike, although there clearly are significant national adaptations to international trends. Openness and dependency have long characterized Norwegian society and politics, and this dependency has become even stronger since the 1970s due to the oil economy, the general liberalization of world markets, and the impact of the European Union's single market. This openness has in important respects made an impact on the political process, as reflected in Norway's strong corporatist structures and sensitivity in matters of national security.

The second theme is focused on *the egalitarian culture.* In a European as well as a Scandinavian context, Norway was unique in not having a viable aristocracy and in keeping a free peasantry all through the Middle Ages. The political mobilization of the peasantry in the nineteenth century as well as the socialist workers' movement in the twentieth both emphasized egalitarian values and goals. A Protestant state religion coexisted with a strong Christian lay movement that reinforced egalitarian cultural traits. Until the late nineteenth century, Norway was also—as argued above—a comparatively poor European country with an economy that did not provide a foundation for a substantial upper class.

The third theme characterizing Norwegian politics is the *struggle between the center and the periphery.* The issues related to this theme have two dimensions, the first stemming from Norway's position as a nation of the European periphery. These issues are reflected in domestic politics like the European Union issue. Another cluster of issues is generated by the topographical/cultural nature of a country with a long coastline, difficult communications, varied regional economies, and a strong egalitarian culture. The decisionmaking elites at the center of the country have regularly provoked peripheral reactions based on mixed feelings of resentment and dependence. Opposition toward the center, the Oslo elites, has indeed been crucial in shaping institutional structures and practices, giving Norway's polity and politics their character. It is not surprising that two of Norway's best-known political scientists/sociologists abroad, Stein Rokkan and Johan Galtung, both made the "center-periphery" analysis the cornerstones of their analyses.

In addition to these three themes, I am putting forth a proposition for further discussion: *the primacy of politics.* Historically, politics and policies have been crucial in developing Norwegian society. As a theme to characterize contemporary Norwegian politics—in contrast to the politics of other countries—it is perhaps dubious. But in part as a consequence of the three themes characterizing Norwegian politics, social and economic change has often been initiated within the political sphere.

One of Norway's "good kings" was Magnus the Lawmaker (1263–1280). During his reign, the laws were improved and extended to benefit the whole society. Similarly, the state has played a decisive role throughout Norway's modern history in shaping society. During the period historians label "the public official's state" (1814–1884), public officials vigorously advocated and put in place the vital institutions of a modern capitalist economy, such as banks and credit institutions. Bureaucrats and politicians, not entrepreneurs, created the foundations for private enterprise in Norway. Arguably, there is a link between this state-driven capitalism in the nineteenth century and the state-driven welfare state of the successive social democratic governments in the post-1945 era.

The primacy of politics does not mean "command politics," where absolutist rulers decide what is in the best interests of the country.[1] Rather my proposition emphasizes the importance of negotiated settlements between the various political forces in explaining change, possibly more important in Norway than in countries with a broader-based, more robust civil society.

However, as an early recipient of U.S. Marshall aid (1948–1952) and a founding member of the OECD (1961), postwar Norway developed an economy with a "balanced" public-private mix. Elections were free and human rights respected. The even greater integration of Norway into the world economy since the 1970s and the growing complexity of Norwegian society make the primacy of politics argument less convincing. The proposition assumes that the state/society mix of Norway is somewhat more "state biased" than most other West European countries. Norway's policy of "state feminism," that is, rules and practices established by the state in order to improve the position of women in society, illustrates this bias. In 1981, the Labor Party established binding rules that set gender quotas for party officials requiring a minimum of 40 percent of either sex in all elected bodies of the party. This decision had a strong impact on the recruitment of politicians and later on important aspects of public policy.

Approach

The general approach guiding this book is that of political sociology. This means that politics is not a game played in virtual reality but the struggle between diverging material and ideal interests—anchored in society and promoted by social actors. Political interests, political movements, politicians, institutions, and policies are at the same time products of social processes and producers of change in society. It does not imply a "sociology of politics" perspective in which politics merely mirrors class structures. The dynamics of politics certainly does not rely only on social structure; political processes are also triggered by forces integrative of the political sphere itself—by ideas, institutions, personalities, and organizational and persuasive qualities. Political analysis will always have to cope with indeterminate processes, including the occurrence of unexpected and random events.

The discussion is also based on the premise that politicians are rational beings. Their policies and actions are means to achieve particular goals.

The means may not always turn out to be the best ones, but they are striving, like everybody else, to find the best way. And politicians certainly have goals. Some are open and declared, presented in statements and programs; others are covert and implicit, to be sought behind closed doors and through hidden agendas. Politicians are certainly human in the sense that they sometimes promote conflicting goals and that they have goals with varying priorities. One goal may be to redistribute wealth in society, another to do this while adhering to democratic norms. Which goal is given the highest priority can vary over time and within the same political movement. In the European socialist parties, the turn-of-the-century debate about reform versus revolution focused on this. The social democrats chose democratic norms over redistribution, the communists reversed the priority. The general point is that modeling that choice of goals a priori on behalf of the actors and being closed to the dynamics of change impairs description as well as understanding.

The third general comment is that institutions as well as ideas matter. Undoubtedly, institutions establish a setting for the political forces and the political game. How does one make legitimate decisions about law and the employment of public resources? Most democratic actors go by the book (often broadly interpreted, of course) in competing for power and implementing policies. It tells one a great deal about the politics in a country if one know whether they have a presidential separation of powers system or a parliamentary government. But I are talking here about both the producers and the products.

Political institutions certainly shape the political process, but they are also shaped by it. The standard argument against the view that majority electoral systems create two-party systems is that causality is the reverse: Two-party systems create majority electoral systems in order to reproduce themselves. Institutions are indeed important, and institution making is part of the political strategy for the winner to perpetuate his interests. In the same way, ideas are Janus-faced: They may both rationalize material interests and be autonomous movers in their own right.

Structure of the Book

In Chapter 2, the basic information on social and historical background is presented. This is very selectively done, and the criteria for selection are to make the basic cleavages intelligible to the reader not familiar with Norwegian history and society. The political parties and the process of democratization is discussed as an integral part of this historic evolution of the major political forces. Politics and institutional arrangements are both cause and effect in historic evolutions, and Chapter 3 focuses on the background and current operation of basic political institutions, such as elections, the parliament, the government, the civil service, and major institutions in international cooperation. In Chapter 4, the theme is life within these institutions. The political parties are discussed in some detail—both in terms of organization and ideology. The process of selecting candidates for parliamentary positions is described along with the process of forming governments. This chapter also deals with the major channels of influencing policies and the level and type of participation found among Norwegian citizens. The economy and economic policies are taken up in Chapter 5. This is the basis of the "left-right dimension" so central to Norwegian politics. The role of the state in economic activities is at the core of much political debate. But the strong district dimension that permeates Norwegian politics in general also marks discussions on economic policies. This multidimensionality of the political "space" is evident in the chapter that follows dealing with several public policy areas. Chapter 6 looks into three such areas in particular, namely the policies making up the welfare state, the green policies, and the policies on gender equality. Changes in Norwegian foreign policies are discussed in Chapter 7. This chapter also presents the major structure of decisionmaking in this field. Finally, Chapter 8 summarizes the various discussions on the themes and the proposition on Norwegian politics presented in this introduction.

Notes

1. During the merger discussions between the state-owned Norwegian and the Swedish telecommunications companies in 1999, the Swedish minister in charge claimed Norway to be the last Soviet state. His outburst came in frustration over what he considered to be improper political interference in market issues.

2

People, Society, and History

The political restoration of Norway in 1814 was not simply a coincidence, even if the forces initiating it came from abroad. Freedom was not simply found. Freedom and independence can by their very nature never be won by finding them or receiving them as gifts—it can only happen by work and struggle.

—*Ernst Sars*

The population of Norway today is about 4.4 million. In Western Europe only Iceland and Ireland are smaller–disregarding geographical mini-countries like Luxembourg, Malta, and San Marino. The land area belonging to Norway (324,000 square kilometers) is larger than both Italy's and Great Britain's, making the country one of the most sparsely populated in Europe. At the time of American independence, Norway had about 750,000 inhabitants, about one-quarter of the population in the thirteen former British colonies. The population reached 1 million in the 1820s, doubled in the following seventy years and passed 4 million in 1975.

Decreased rates of infant mortality in the nineteenth century contributed much to population increase. However, this increase was tempered by Norway's high rate of emigration in the latter half of the century. Only Ireland had more emigrants than Norway relative to population size. Close to 1 million Norwegians went overseas between 1825 and 1930, and about 850,000 moved to the United States alone between 1820 and 1981.[1] The Nordic countries and the United States dominated Norway's statistics on emigration and immigration after 1945. Until the late 1960s, more people moved out of Norway than entered. But in the 1960s, immigration increased from Southern Europe and later from countries in Asia (for example, Pakistan). In the beginning, these immigrants were mostly people in search of work; refugees and asylum applicants came later. In the 1990s, a large contingent of Bosnians sought refuge in Norway, fleeing from the war in the former Yugoslavia. Immigrants—without any Norwegian background by way of parents or grandparents—in 1995 made up 5 percent of the population. About half came from countries outside of Western Europe and North America. As a result the Norwegian population is, in ethnic terms, still comparatively very homogeneous.

There are, however, several small ethnic minorities within Norwegian society: Sami (Lapps), Kvener (of Finnish origin), Romanis, and Jews. The largest group, and the only one with official status as an indigenous people, is the Sami population (see Chapter 3). The last census to include the Sami as a particular category (1930) registered 20,000 persons, and they were mainly living in North Norway. Today there is no reliable estimate, and with the Sami's high degree of assimilation, the number will very much depend on the definition employed. The most common estimates, however, range from 20,000 to 30,000. Only about 10 percent of these, however, are still active in the traditional reindeer trade. Compared to this, in 1995 there were more than 80,000 immigrants from Asian countries living in Norway. Although the numbers of these so-called long-distance immigrants are small, both in absolute and relative terms, compared to those emigrating from neighboring Sweden and other West European countries, these Asian and African immigrants are very visible in some of the major cities, particularly in the capital of Oslo.

Social Change, Civil Life, and Cultural Background

Social change in Norway parallels the familiar story from throughout Western Europe: In less than 150 years, Norway has been transformed first from an agricultural to an industrial society and then from an industrial to a service society. Norway was basically an agricultural society throughout the nineteenth century. In contrast to most countries at the time, however, the rural social structure was relatively egalitarian and the share of freeholders large. Relatively little land belonged to the few large estates, and the minute aristocracy had their titles abolished in 1821. Norway went through a period of rapid industrialization in the late nineteenth and early twentieth century. This happened comparatively late and accelerated after national independence had been won in 1905 (see below). Finally, the service sector gradually came to dominate the occupational lives of the economically active population during the last part of the twentieth century. Simultaneously women more frequently sought employment outside the home. Whereas less than 10 percent of married women were economically active in the 1950s, over 70 percent of married women were employed in 1990.[2]

Agriculture and fisheries dominated the old society. The census of 1900 showed that 41 out of 100 employed persons worked in the primary sector. Of these, 33 were in agriculture, 6 in fishing, and the rest in forestry and hunting. Fifty years later, the primary sector had dropped to 26 persons out of 100 and in the late 1990s to 5 out of 100. In economic life, agriculture had now become a marginal factor, even though it took its share of the state budget. Even fewer people were occupied in the fisheries, but fish remained an important and profitable export commodity. "Modernity" was for the first sixty years of the twentieth century identified with industrialization—with black smoke from chimneys and, increasingly, the white heat of electricity. In 1900, 26 percent were active in the industrial sector, a figure rising to 37 percent in 1950. In the next two decades, the rate of those employed in industry remained about the same before starting to drop around 1970. In 1994, 23 percent of the workforce was active in industry. Finally, the rise of the service sector has been substantial throughout the second half of the twentieth century. In 1900, the service sector employed 33 percent of the workforce. This increased to 37 percent in 1950, and by 1994, 71 percent of the workforce had an occupation classified within the service sector.

The great transformation toward a market economy was particularly noticeable in the years when the nineteenth century turned into the twentieth, especially in the countryside. From the 1870s onward, cheap grain flooded the European markets from the opening up of the American Midwest, and this caused changes in the agricultural production among Norwegian farmers, for example, toward more livestock husbandry. During this period there was also increased commercialization of landed property, and the market intrusion was an important factor behind the huge emigration to the United States. The increased presence of the outside world lowered the threshold for individuals and groups to break out of their traditional place in society. The first large-scale wave of emigration peaked around 1870, the second in the early 1880s.

However, the impact of international markets was nothing new to the main actors in the Norwegian economy. Trade and shipping had for centuries been integrated in European markets in fish and timber. In the late Middle Ages, the Hanseatic League was strongly involved in the fish trade on the west coast, and the demand for timber from Dutch and British consumers expanded during the sixteenth century. Mining, traditionally the prerogative of the crown, became increasingly important in the seventeenth century. Demands for metals were, of course, also much affected by international demands, and the mining industry in Norway was, in addition, very dependent on international, particularly German, expertise. After the British opened their trading routes to ships from other nations around 1850, Norwegian shipping grew in size and economic importance. The merchant marine became a crucial sector in generating capital for further industrial investment.

After the end of World War II in 1945, it was a common goal for all political parties in Norway to rebuild and to expand industry. The success of this strategy, however, reinforced at the same time the ongoing processes of internal migration leading to increased centralization and urbanization. During the years from 1875 to 1990, the share of the population living in the capital and the surrounding county (Akershus) rose from 10 to 21 percent.[3] Since 1950, the share living in North Norway has decreased. Also within regions and counties, there has been an increased concentration of people in urban areas. In the 1870s, 24 percent of the population lived in cities and urbanized areas; this share increased to 52 percent in 1950 and to 72 percent in the early 1990s.[4]

Family and Leisure

During the latter half of the twentieth century, enormous changes took place in how Norwegians live. Family patterns are very different today compared to thirty years ago. During the 1970s and 1980s, the two-income family became common, although the share of single-parent families also rose considerably. It became clear that marriage was not the only way to start a family, as the number of cohabitant couples increased. Statistically, the share of children born "outside marriage" was 41 percent in 1991, but it is such an integral part of cultural change that the term today is practically devoid of any connotation of social stigma.[5] Rates of divorce have increased. In the early 1970s, 5 of 1,000 existing marriages broke up every year; in 1991 that figure had more than doubled.

It is much more common to acquire higher education today than in the early postwar period. The great expansion in higher education came about when the huge postwar baby boom cohorts entered universities in the late 1960s. In 1952, 14 percent of the total population was registered in some form of education; this had increased to 21 percent by 1991.[6] The number of students registered in 1991 was twelve times larger than the number registered in 1952. Close to one in five (over the age of sixteen) had completed some form of university education in the mid-1990s. And in 1991 about one-third of those finishing high school went on to universities or colleges. During these years, there was also a near revolution in female education. Today women are a clear majority among students, whereas in the early 1950s they made up only 15 percent of this group. The choices of subjects, however, are still very different for women and men, very much reflecting the traditional sex roles.

Work and leisure have changed considerably over the past fifty years. In 1950, the standard work week was 48 hours, and employees had been granted three weeks vacation with pay (by law). In the 1960s, this was extended to four weeks, and the work week was gradually reduced to 37.5 hours by 1987. It follows that the opportunities for leisure activities have increased and that the pattern of vacationing has changed considerably. For example, people travel abroad much more frequently.

Religion and Culture

Norway has a Protestant state church, protected by the Constitution. However, although about 94 percent of the population nominally are members, only a minority of members practice their religion.[7] Less than half the population attends church at all, and surveys find that around one in four claim a personal belief. Obviously these are difficult things to measure.[8] The largest organization of religious beliefs or "life philosophies" outside the state church is the Norwegian Humanist Association, followed by the Islamic congregation. Historically, the Norwegian State Church has been torn between "high" and "low" tendencies. The Christian lay movement worked mostly inside the church, but often in opposition to the theologically educated clergy. They have built their own religious meetinghouses and organized campaigns for religious awakenings and for missionary activities. In the late 1970s, these organizations financed about 2,000 missionaries in forty-five countries.[9]

Three cultural movements operating at the grassroots level have traditionally been extremely important in confronting the dominant high culture in Norwegian politics. The Christian lay movement is one of the so-called countercultures and has support predominantly in peripheral regions of the west and along the southern coastline of Norway. This "low church milieu" challenged the official church and the cultural liberalism of the urban elites. Close to these groups, but organizationally separate, was the Norwegian temperance movement. Politically, this was most important at the time of Prohibition (1919–1926), but it continued to have an impact on public policies, in spite of declining membership in the postwar period. Also in decline, but still important, are the organizations supporting what in Norway is called the "New Norwegian" language. This alternative Norwegian language grew out of the cultural awakening, coinciding with European romanticism and the 1848 "springtime of the peoples." In Norway this movement expressed itself in the rediscovery of the original Norwegian, which had been distorted by the four-centuries-long Danish "occupation." The new language was a construction of the mid-nineteenth century, based exclusively on West Norwegian dialects. The claim was that these dialects were less diluted by Danish influences than those found in Eastern Norway. The language was sufficiently close to the eastern "standard" language for people to understand both without difficulty. The New Norwegian was made an official language on equal terms with the "standard" language (bokmål) spoken by the traditional elites in the capital. This was done in the 1880s as part of the political victory of the Liberal Party when the periphery-based opposition captured state power. The post-1945 decline in the use of New Norwegian has been marked. The share of pupils taught in New Norwegian has been about halved from 1950 to 1990. Today around 17 percent of parents choose this as the primary language for their children.[10] But part of the development has also to some extent been a reciprocal influence of the two languages on each other.

Political History and the Struggle for National Independence

"Norway" literally means "the way to the north" and was possibly coined by people living further south in Europe. The future Norwegians were outside the direct impact of the Roman Empire, and Christianity took root in as late as the eleventh century. Earlier, the Scandinavian tribesmen had been part of "the hordes" attacking the regions left by the Roman legions some centuries earlier. The attack on the Lindisfarne monastery at the east coast of (now) northern England in 793 is usually taken as the beginning of the Viking Age. Less than one hundred years later, the Kingdom of Norway was created by Harald Fairhair, based on the small coastal fiefdoms of the West and the Southwest. The kingdom was consolidated and extended to the inland areas, particularly during the first part of the eleventh century under the reign of St. Olav, when it came to cover the Norway we broadly know today, including some parts of today's Sweden. The efforts of King Olav II to christen the country—and his later martyr death in 1030 and subsequent canonization—made the Christian church an important contributor to the consolidation of national rule. The country grew to its largest size during the thirteenth century, comprising not only Iceland and Greenland but also possessions on the British Isles. In the late Middle Ages, however, the country went into decline and eventually fell under Danish rule in the fourteenth century.

Under Danish Rule

Norway was the subordinate part in the Danish-Norwegian union and eventually came, especially after the Reformation in 1537, close to extinction as a separate country. The king lived in Copenhagen, and Denmark was the stronger country in all fields–militarily, economically, and culturally. All state officials were educated in Denmark, and most officials sent north to administer and to preach were Danes. Norwegian historians, particularly in the nineteenth century, have presented this period as the four-hundred-years-long "Danish Night" in Norwegian history. Danish wars against Sweden also became Norwegian wars, and during the seventeenth century, significant old Norwegian territories were lost to Swedish kings. Later historians have emphasized, however, that the Danish rule also was a period of growth in Norwegian history. And in practice Norway kept some of its old autonomy within the union. Even after absolutist rule was introduced in 1660, Norway had some special treatment within the twin kingdoms, at least during periods of war when communications were difficult or completely cut off.

Following the Reformation in 1537, monasteries were closed and church lands were confiscated on behalf of the monarch. Old loyalty to the Catholic Church and the pope was broken, and the new Protestant state church became an active partner in securing internal peace, centralizing power, and, later, building a nation. The importance of Latin as the language of the selected few declined, and Danish-Norwegian became the language of the authorities, secular as well as clerical. Control over education was centralized and served the needs of the state, creating over time a relatively unitary culture. Economically, there was slow but steady growth, and during the eighteenth century an increasingly self-confident urban bourgeoisie—basing their position on increasing trade and shipping—grew in number and wealth.

In 1814 a group of representatives came together to make a constitution for an independent Norway. They also elected the Danish crown prince to be Norway's new king. The political background was that the defeat of Napoleon had forced his ally, the Danish king, to surrender Norway to Sweden and to accept as new king of Norway the Swedish King Karl XIV Johan, a former French general. The European turmoil had created a "window of opportunity" for the growing class of officials and bourgeois who wanted to create an independent Norway. This almost succeeded, but in the end the Norwegians were forced to accept the reign of the Swedish monarch. They had, however, won the right to home rule as well as to keep most of the new constitution. According to the "nation-building" historians of the nineteenth century—such as Ernst Sars—Norwegian freedom was not "found" but won by "work and struggle."[11]

Nation-Building and Independence, 1814–1905

"Nation-building" describes a policy to create a common identity for the population living within the territory controlled by the state. In practice this generally takes place through the twin processes of the penetration of state power into society, on the one hand, and the integration of society into the realm of state decisionmaking, on the other.[12] The short century from 1814, when Norway achieved home rule, to when it won full national independence in 1905 was marked, first, by an effort to build a unitary, mass-based culture and, second, by a stepwise broadening of political participation.

The first university in Norway was founded in Oslo in 1811. Prior to that Norwegians had to go to Copenhagen to get higher education. In all fields of Norwegian culture, the "national awakening," alternatively "the construction of a national past," was a distinctive effort on the part of the national movement, and this became particularly important during the second part of the nineteenth century. The claim to a national continuity from the Old Norse Empire in the High Middle Ages throughout the period of Danish domination to the semisovereign status of the nineteenth century was crucial to nationalist historians. Many artists of this period, inspired by romanticism, sought the original, unspoiled, and partly hidden Norwegian culture in the peasant communities. Edward Grieg collected old folk music and used it as a basis for his compositions, and the painters took the natural scenery and the old, "unspoiled" peasant way of life as motifs for their images of Norwegian society. Cloth designers used the rural clothing as models for the new "folk costumes," and Danish influence on the language was played down in the construction of the New Norwegian language. The aim was to present and recreate Norway as an old nation and to point out that the four hundred years under Danish rule was a breach in continuity—a parenthesis—not an integrated part of Norwegian history. The movement toward national resurrection gained additional strength from the resentment created by the union with Sweden, where Norway was subordinated in, for example, matters of foreign policy. During the nineteenth century Norway became a nation, but not a sovereign nation.

The political power of the citizens increased markedly in the period. The Constitution of 1814 was extremely liberal for its time by giving the vote to not only the upper classes but all owners of land, making about 45 percent of males above the age of twenty-five eligible to vote.[13] The power of parliament was nevertheless restricted. In the years after 1814, the King's personal power was significant, and in many ways the struggle was intense between the Swedish king on the one side and his ministers and parliament on the other. The MPs were in the early years mostly recruited from the class of state officials and the urban bourgeoisie. As the personal power of the king decreased, however, the principle of separation of powers gave the executive, headed by the government of officials, a much stronger political position. From about the 1850s onward the liberal intelligentsia in the cities increasingly joined forces with the peasant groups in parliament in order to make government more responsive to parliament—at the expense of the old class of state officials. Finally, in 1884, they succeeded in toppling the old government, making way for a parliamentary form of relationship with the executive. This new parliamentarism was based on the principle that the government could not continue in office against the expressed wishes of a parliamentary majority.

The franchise was gradually broadened throughout the century. In 1898 all men were given the vote, and in 1913 this was extended to all women on an equal basis. Local government was an important part of the nineteenth-century political system. In the 1830s the peasant opposition in parliament championed local self-government, and in 1837 new legislation established elected, representative municipal institutions, which restricted the local power of the state officials. This local political autonomy was extremely important in preparing for later national democratization.

During the 1890s tension rose between the Norwegian and the Swedish governments. The reason was a growing national resentment in Norway coupled with conflicts of interest over the common foreign policy, which was led by a Swedish minister. The leftist liberal party, Venstre, demanded an independent Norwegian consular service in order to help Norwegian shipping abroad and to secure national self-respect. The Swedish government refused, however, and the Norwegian authorities started to prepare for a military conflict. Norway strengthened its marine forces and built some new fortresses close to the Swedish border, raising tension even further. The parliament voted repeatedly for consular services, and in 1905 when the Swedish king again vetoed the decision, the Norwegian government refused to accept his veto. Negotiations broke down, and in the ensuing constitutional crisis the Norwegian parliament unanimously declared an end to the union with Sweden. A national referendum overwhelmingly supported this action, and after some rattling of sabers and subsequent negotiation, Norway's independence was reluctantly accepted by the Swedes.

After first having offered the Norwegian crown to a prince of the Swedish royal family—which was (as expected) turned down—the Danish prince Carl accepted after changing his name to Haakon VII. The royal name, Haakon, was the most frequent among the Old Norse kings. Haakon therefore was chosen in order to present the image of the reemergence of an old, historic kingdom. Also the fact that Carl was married to the daughter of the British king made his selection a diplomatic move aimed at securing international acceptance and support, which it did. Norway's late national independence has been claimed to be one reason why Norwegian voters in two referenda (1972 and 1994) rejected membership in the European Union. The argument is that Norwegians still see supranational rule as a potential threat to national independence.

Industrialization and Economic Development

At the turn of the century, the most dynamic sectors of the economy were industry and shipping. The first large-scale factories came with the textile mills in the 1840s. Later other consumer industries followed, including shoe manufacturing, tobacco processing, and the production of canned food. The heavy construction industry and shipbuilding developed to serve the fisheries and the merchant marine. The modernization of communications and transportation, particular railway construction, also created demands for products from mechanical industry. The largest sector in terms of employment was in wood products. This included the traditional sawmills and from the 1870s onward the new pulp factories. The sector generating most capital for investment, however, was probably shipping.[14]

After 1905 new markets and technological inventions combined with the optimism following national independence to create the so-called "new working day" for Norwegian industry. The mechanical industry was by now the largest in terms of workers. Hydroelectric plants were built next to large waterfalls, and these gave energy to new chemical and electrometallurgical processing plants. These new industries were situated in peripheral places with little previously established infrastructure. The joint number of jobs in industry and services now exceeded the primary sector. Large groups of construction workers were engaged in building the new industrial plants and the railroads. The construction worker or *rallar*—after a Swedish word for wheelbarrow—became the basis for political radicalism among the workers. This put its mark both on the trade union and the growing socialist Labor Party. The industrial breakthrough in Norway was based on natural resources combined with cheap electricity, a combination that remained a comparative advantage for Norwegian industry in international markets for the rest of the century.

Interwar Crisis

The "good times" came to an abrupt end in 1921 when the boom generated by World War I was over. The world recession of the early 1920s was reinforced by a national deflationary policy pursued by the Norwegian national bank. Unemployment increased and stayed at a high level throughout the interwar years. It was the German occupation in 1940 that finally "solved" the unemployment problem endemic to the Norwegian economy.

In spite of industrial setbacks in the early 1920s and continued high unemployment, the economy (as measured by the GNP) continued to grow slowly during that decade. In the autumn of 1930, however, the effects of the Wall Street crash hit Norway. Production declined and did not recover until 1935. In 1933 about one-third of all trade union members were out of work. It has been estimated, however, that just above 10 percent of the total workforce was unemployed.[15] Severe industrial unrest followed. In terms of working days lost to strikes, 1931 was the worst year in Norwegian history. But in spite of the lean years of the early 1930s, the interwar years as a whole were a period of growth, albeit uneven and sector-specific growth. Shipping, whaling, and consumer industries expanded substantially. Norwegian industry, as such, experienced a structural crisis of transformation. Industry needed to be more in line with national consumer demands. During the 1930s, the state increasingly tried to protect home industries, and the companies producing consumer goods for the home market grew markedly. In 1939 employment in industry had risen to 26 percent of the workforce, compared to 20 percent at its lowest point in 1931.[16]

War and Postwar Reconstruction

With the German occupation came the closure of most traditional external markets to Norwegian industry. Shipping escaped German control and became part of the allied war effort, while the Norwegian land-based economy was redirected to serve German war needs as well as internal consumption. Large construction works ordered by the *Wehrmacht* in order to strengthen defenses and improve communications gave work to large numbers of people. Many of these investments, however, were not particularly useful after the war ended in 1945.

The postwar economy grew rapidly carried along by state planning, foreign aid, and market adjustments. The immediate postwar effort was directed at rebuilding the country. In Northern Norway, the retreating German army had burned down many of the settlements, and industrial machinery had deteriorated all over the country. Strong state initiatives and tight controls were supposed to stabilize the economy. It was not possible, however, to subsidize key commodities sufficiently to keep stable prices, and in 1949 the government had to devalue the Norwegian krone (following Great Britain's devaluation of the pound). Between 1949 and 1953, most postwar price and quantum regulations were removed. Norway had in 1947 accepted the American offer of Marshall aid and became party to the international agreements and organizations working for freer world trade. This included the so-called Bretton Woods system (1944) to stabilize national currencies and the OEEC (Organization for European Economic Cooperation, 1948) to coordinate trade (see Chapter 7). The Norwegian postwar economy was based on natural resources, cheap energy, and sea transport. Shipping became extremely important not only for the many new jobs it created but also for the valuable foreign currency it earned.

Even though state regulations controlling industry were scaled down after a few years, the state continued to take an active part in economic activities. New state industries were created, particularly in the strategically important areas of metallurgy and electricity production. New public credit institutions were set up to channel fresh capital into the preferred sectors. Hydroelectrical power plants generated seven times as much electricity in 1970 as in 1946, and cheap electricity was used in more or less open support of the export industry. Both electrometallurgical and chemical companies greatly expanded in this period. In 1970 Norway was the largest exporter of aluminum in Europe and the world's largest exporter of several alloys of ferrous metals,[17] although all the bauxite needed for the production of aluminum had to be imported. For a small country like Norway, it was natural to continue the strategy of export-led growth, which had been the tradition since the 1840s.

Growth and Prosperity

Between 1946 and 1973, GNP tripled in real terms. The enormous growth was not exceptional, however, compared to Norway's trade partners in the OEEC/OECD.[18] The statistics show that West Germany was ahead of average, whereas Great Britain lagged behind—with Norway somewhere in the middle. In the early postwar years, it was also crucial to support the production of goods and services, such as shipping, that had the potential to bring in foreign currency, particularly the dollar. This was needed to finance further industrial development and to build a modern infrastructure. The transformation of the Norwegian society was formidable. The share of the workforce occupied in the primary sector decreased dramatically, and the population became much more urban.

Some public industrial policies were directed at countering the centralizing tendencies created by modernization processes. The state tried to create new industries in the outlying districts. In 1946 the state decided to build a large iron plant in Northern Norway. This required a huge amount of investment; its production exceeded Norwegian internal demands, and much of the output was exported. Over the years, however, the huge public subsidies became the focus of strong political contention until the company finally was shut down in the late 1980s. Other state enterprises, for example, in the areas of defense and electricity generation, were more successful.

Even though the ambition of successive postwar Labor governments was to establish more effective political control over industry—the ideological key word was still "socialization"—the outcome was a "mixed economy" rather than anything even close to unilateral state control. Actually, the public share of investment in the immediate postwar years was less then one-fourth of the total and remained roughly at this level during the 1950s and 1960s. Public expenditures as a percentage of GNP, however, increased from 16 percent in 1938 to 51 percent in 1977, indicating a much broader economic role for the state during this period.[19] The figures reflected not only large transfers between sectors in the economy but also a growing welfare state.

In the 1950s and 1960s, industry gradually changed from production at a low level of processing to an output consisting of increasingly sophisticated products. The aluminum production was based on imported ore, which was melted down and refined with the use of cheap electricity, and in the pulp factories, timber from the Norwegian forests was the most important factor in production. Over the years, shipyards and manufacturing plants producing more advanced products for international markets increased their share of the total industrial output. Technological changes were important to all sectors, and this made production less labor intensive. In the fisheries, for example, the workforce decreased from 110,000 jobs in 1945 to 37,000 in 1973, while the total catch of fish more than tripled during the same period due to more efficient boats and equipment.[20] In the early 1970s, fish made up about 7 percent of all exports.

When six nations created the European Economic Community (EEC) in the late 1950s, Norway's traditional west-bound trading profile—with Great Britain as its largest market—made it an easy political decision to follow the British instead into the EFTA (European Free Trade Association) in 1960. More difficulties, however, were associated with the decision not to follow Britain and Denmark into the European Communities (EC) in 1973. This I will return to in more detail later (see Chapters 5 and 7).

Several events occurred in the early 1970s that signaled the end to the almost "automatic" economic growth rates of the postwar era. The first was the 1971 devaluation of the U.S. dollar; the second was the international oil crisis of 1973. A general slowdown in the world economy followed. The subsequent "stagflation" of combined stagnation and inflation was something new and a sign of the underlying structural problems in most Western (OECD) economies. Another and more positive event for the Norwegian economy was that, by a strike of luck, the Phillips oil company discovered oil in the North Sea in 1969. From 1973, Norway became an oil-exporting country with rising revenues pouring into the state coffer. This made the economic development in Norway very different from that of its trade partners in the OECD (see Chapter 5).

Parties and Cleavages

The struggle for national independence to some extent subdued the different party political tendencies from the 1890s onward. These differences, however, became more distinct in the years following national independence in 1905. The liberal "Left," Venstre, and the conservative "Right," Høyre, had alternated control of government since they came to dominate parliament in the 1890s. The Labor Party, Arbeiderpartiet, was founded by the trade unions in 1887 but did not get its breakthrough at the parliamentarian level until 1903, after the introduction of universal male suffrage in 1898.

From 1905 to 1928, the liberals and the conservatives continued to alternate in government—with the liberals closest to status as "the natural party of government."[21] The Labor Party grew rapidly in terms of membership, votes, and—particularly after the introduction of proportional representation in 1921—parliamentary seats. The change of electoral system made representation in parliament fairly proportional to the share of votes. The lowered threshold for entry into parliament also had an impact on the founding and later success of the agrarian Center Party, Senterpartiet, which was created in 1921.[22] Subsequently it also affected the Christian People's Party, Kristelig Folkeparti, founded in 1933, with a national breakthrough at the Storting election in 1945.

In 1928 the Labor Party controlled government for a very short period (18 days!), but for most of the interwar period, the liberals and the conservatives still controlled executive power. In 1935, however, Labor won executive power for the second time, and this time they managed to stay in office for thirty years, although their term was interrupted by war exile. The Labor Party at first formed a single-party, minority government supported by the Center Party in parliament. During the whole period from 1918 to 1940, Norway had no majority, single-party government, and historians have labeled these years the age of the "multiparty state."[23] The Labor government in power from 1935 up to the German occupation in 1940 was, however, a harbinger for the majority Labor governments to follow after 1945.

The Social Democratic Order

The Labor Party that entered government in 1935 was, contrary to much "socialist" party rhetoric, a pragmatic social democratic party. It was also a party with a revolutionary past. From 1919 to 1923, it had been a member of the Komintern, the Moscow-based communist international organ advocating armed revolution by the working-class avant-garde to create a true people's democracy. In 1921 a social democratic party split off to the right, but this was reunited with Labor in 1927—after Labor had left the Komintern. The break with the Moscow communists in 1923, however, led to a party split and the founding of the Norwegian Communist Party.

The Labor Party became the hegemonic party in Norwegian politics for more than thirty years after 1935. From 1945 to 1961 it commanded a majority in parliament, and a "parliamentary situation" could only arise—according to an explicit statement from the leader of its parliamentary faction in the late 1950s—if the Labor Party itself so wished.[24] And even when the coalition of center-right parties took over from 1965–1971, the change in political direction was not great.[25] The war experiences and the moderation of the Labor governments of the 1950s had prepared the ground for increased political convergence of the major political parties. A corporate mode of decisionmaking, including private industry and special interest organizations outside the "Labor family," contributed also to a low-conflict political system, a new "social democratic order."[26]

This social democratic order from the early 1950s to the late 1970s was characterized by several distinct political and social qualities. Labor was the "natural party of government" in the period. During the thirty years from 1950 to 1980, the Labor Party was out of office for less than eight years, and Labor never ruled in a coalition with other parties. Social progress was founded on more or less continuous economic growth during this period. The state gave priority to industrial development, and a strong belief in progress, as such, permeated society. Planning was a central instrument in state economic policies, and sectors like agriculture, fishing, and transportation were all strongly state regulated. The social democratic order was also marked by a belief in a strong state. Primary public goals were full employment, social equality, and a high level of welfare. Accordingly, redistribution of resources was a major objective, and it was considered the responsibility of the state to provide free education and free health care and to look after important cultural institutions. In short, markets were to be guided, private solutions were eschewed, and the chances for "opting out" were restricted.

Political Cleavages

Parties reflect different periods of historical development; they are organizational sediments of past struggles. The Norwegian social scientist Stein Rokkan coined the term "political cleavage line" to identify the major effects of decisions at critical junctures in the history of nation-building.[27] Inspired by the functional approach of Talcott Parsons, he identified four critical "lines of cleavage" in the modern political history of

Western Europe: first, between subject and dominant culture; second, between church and government; third, between primary and secondary economies; and fourth, between workers and employers. This general version was based on his empirical studies—with Henry Valen—of the Norwegian conflict system.[28] They argued that in the history of "Norwegian mass politics there emerged seven cleavage dimensions that were crucial in the structuring of the party alternatives and in the alignment of the electorate."[29] One such cleavage was based on geography, three on culture, and three on economy.

First, there was the *geographical cleavage* between the eastern center in and around the capital, Oslo, and the two peripheries: one in the "countercultural" southwest, the other in the "class-polarized" north. This center-periphery cleavage was particularly important during the struggle between the Left and Right parties when they were founded in the 1880s. An important sentiment in the leftist party movement, which won over the "official's state" in 1884, was the feeling—strongly present in the peripheral constituencies—that their values and interests were not properly represented in or accepted by the state. Even today any large Norwegian party has an internal element of this cleavage. What made the Labor Party so successful in the 1930s and later so dominant in the electorate was precisely the fact that the party managed to forge an alliance between the rural underprivileged and the urban working class. In Chapter 4, we shall see that this was one reason why the question of membership in the European Union became so difficult to handle within the Labor Party: The center was up against the periphery inside the party itself.

Three cultural cleavages have been formed over language, alcohol, and religion. First, the *linguistic cleavage* is rooted in the fact that since the late nineteenth century, protagonists of the rural Nynorsk ("New Norwegian") have antagonized the defenders of the established central standard, the Riksmål. The second cleavage arose from recurring struggles over *moral issues,* foremost among them the question of alcohol. There have been various positions in the continuous debate—from banning all sales, to controlled sales and/or increased prices, to the position that alcohol should be treated like any other commodity in the market and with a minimum of state interference. The third cultural cleavage has been over *religion.* Central elements in this cleavage have been who should control the state church and what should be the impact of Christian values in state affairs. How to teach religion in the public schools, for example, has been a recurrent theme in the debate, and from the 1960s the issue of abortion has been extremely important. Historically, this was a conflict mainly within the church itself between the orthodox Lutherans organized in lay movements and the more liberal university-trained clergy. Today—although the questions concerning the state church are still on the agenda—this is more a conflict between the active, practicing Christians and the secularized majority of nominal church members. These "countercultures" joined the center-periphery cleavage as an integrated part of the conflict between the liberal Left and the conservative Right during the formative years of the party system in the 1880s. Also the founding of the Christian People's Party in the 1930s can be seen as based on these cultural cleavages.

Three economic cleavages have their origins in the markets for commodities and for labor respectively. In the commodity market there has been the old *urban-rural conflict* between producers and consumers. This materialized in "the battle between market farmers and the various urban interests over the control of prices and subsidies."[30] The cleavage was operative at the time when parties were first founded in the 1880s. The liberal Left party was predominantly a rural peasants' movement, challenging the illiberal privileges and state control of the urban elites. The second economic cleavage sprang from the *rural class struggle* between laborers and smallholders in the countryside on the one side and the peasants/farmers who controlled land and capital on the other. This cleavage contributed to party splits in the Left party at several points in time. It was also important in giving the Labor Party political capital to recruit voters outside of industrial areas. Third, there was the *industrial class struggle* between owners/employers and their workers. This has unquestionably been the dominant cleavage in twentieth-century Norwegian politics, giving rise to the division between the "socialist" and the "bourgeois" blocs of parties. This divide placed the Labor Party (and its later offspring, the Communist Party and the Socialist People's Party/Socialist Left Party) on one side and the different nonsocialist or bourgeois parties on the other. Although still used in political debate today—mostly for polemical reasons—the socialist-bourgeois divide had its origin in the industrial age and is less useful when discussing the party system today. There is also a problem in that the Labor Party cannot meaningfully be described as "socialist" anymore. If "socialism" is taken to denote an ideology advocating the socialization of industry, meaning state takeovers, then Labor left the socialist path in practice in the early 1930s, and in its programs in the 1950s. The party itself, however, waited until 1981 to remove the term completely from its programs, but by then it had long described itself as social democratic.

Rokkan's cleavage approach served a double purpose. First, it provided a model for explaining variation in party systems in Western Europe. Second, it could be used to generate hypotheses about electoral choices today. Later debates have focused on how to revise the historical cleavage model to include a set of cleavages more fitting to describe today's electorate. Several new cleavages have been proposed to fill that need, such as the materialist-postmaterialist cleavage, the cleavage between public and private employees, between men and women, and so forth.[31] We shall return to this discussion in Chapter 4, particularly as it relates to the changing party choices of the electorate.

Four Thresholds for Democracy

Stein Rokkan also distinguished between four "thresholds" in the process of democratization. These he labeled legitimization, incorporation, representation, and executive power.[32] He used them to describe critical stages on the path toward a democratic polity. The first threshold a popular movement has to cross on its way to power is *legitimization*. This embodies the right to oppose the authorities, the right to petition, and the right to assembly; in short, freedom of expression. In Norway the right to oppose the authorities came gradually. Actually, the right to petition the king was ancient and was used repeatedly during Danish rule. Outright peasant rebellions were also met with relatively mild repression in the eighteenth and nineteenth centuries. The leader of the last large uprising of small peasants and workers in 1848—in the aftermath of the European revolutionary "springtime"—received a four-year sentence and later emigrated to the United States. Freedom of expression was officially first established in 1770, but later restricted again. It was included, however, in the Norwegian Constitution of 1814.

The second threshold of *incorporation* points to the people's right to influence in state affairs and concerns the process of transforming the state's subjects into "citizens," in practice, establishing elections based in the principle of one man (and later woman), one vote, one weight. The Norwegian Constitution of 1814 gave voting rights to state officials, urban bourgeois, and rural peasants owning land. This meant that 45 percent of all men above the age of twenty-five, or 10 percent of the total population, were allowed to vote (although only 7 percent were actually registered voters). These rules were adjusted in 1884 when the property requirements were relaxed. Significant extension of voting rights did not, however, take place before 1898, when all men above twenty-five years of age were granted the vote. In 1913 universal suffrage was granted, after some property-owning women had become qualified in 1909.

The third threshold to be passed to achieve a democratic polity is *representation*, or incorporating the opposition within the political system. This focuses on the barriers against fair representation in political institutions. In practice, the question concerns the rules for allocating seats in national representative bodies, such as parliament. The 1814 Constitution set the threshold relatively high. Election to the Storting at that time took place in two stages: First, the election of an electoral college was conducted by majority vote in the constituencies; second, the electoral college elected parliamentary representatives by a majority vote. In 1884 the secret vote was introduced, and in 1896 modified proportional representation was established for local-level elections. Between 1906 and 1918, a system of single-member districts with two ballots was in operation at parliamentary elections. To be elected in the first ballot the candidate had to get a majority; to be elected in the second only a plurality of the votes was needed. This system created a significant underrepresentation of the emerging Labor Party, which was a rising third party in the system. In 1921 the proportional system was introduced for parliamentary elections. This system lowered substantially the threshold for the number of votes needed to gain representation. However, the system used to translate votes into seats, the d'Hondt system, still produced marked deviations from the mathematical proportionality between the share of votes and the share of seats. This improved in 1953 when a new formula was introduced (modified Sainte-Laguë). This system will be discussed in more detail in Chapter 3. The crucial point here, however, is that by 1921 the barrier against representation had been lowered sufficiently for new and smaller parties to enter parliament.

The last threshold to achieving a democratic polity concerns the rules determining how to win *executive power*. Two opposition movements in Norwegian history have challenged established regimes. First, the peasant movement of the nineteenth century faced the "official's state" and organized the Left Party to fight it. The Left Party formed a government in 1884 amid intense political debate and rumors of an approaching reactionary coup. The former government had been impeached by the parliamentary majority and lost its position due to a constitutional court ruling. The second challenge came from the socialist Labor Party confronting the reigning bourgeois political powers. Labor formed a short-lived government in 1928 amid parliamentary disbelief, helped along by royal intervention,[33] although its days in office were few. The party returned, however, for a rather longer period in 1935. The political regime in place after the war in 1945 was by these standards a fully fledged democratic system without significant institutional barriers toward movements challenging the political order.

Conclusion

Norway today is an economically modern, affluent country. It has a stable multiparty democracy, is economically integrated into but not a member of the European Union, and is part of the Western defense alliance (NATO). Culturally, the country belongs to the sphere of American influence with American films, American advertisement, American music, and the American way of life as part of its popular cultural expressions. At the same time, the struggle for national independence still features prominently in the political history engraved in the mind of the average Norwegian citizen. Three critical junctures stand out: Winning political home rule in 1814, forcing the Swedes to concede national independence in 1905, and fighting the German occupation 1940–1945.

The road to national independence was also the road toward political democracy. In particular, this was the case in the rhetoric of the Left Party and, later, the Labor Party. The values embedded in "the nation," the flag, and (after 1905) the monarchy did not—as in most other European countries—exclusively become conservative icons. They were also a central part of the heritage of the liberal Left. And even though the socialist workers' movement for much of the interwar period advocated an internationalist, revolutionary ideology, this was definitely not a hindrance to the full acceptance of "national values" after World War II. An independent, national social democracy was, in the postwar Labor ideology, the final destination on the road toward a fully developed nation-state.

Notes

1. Ørjar Øyen, "Norges befolkning," in Natalie Rogoff Ramsøy and Mariken Vaa, eds., *Det norske samfunn*, vol. 1 (Oslo: Gyldendal, 1975), pp. 5–38. See also Fritz Hodne and Ole Honningdal Grytten, *Norsk Økonomi, 1900–1990* (Oslo: Tano, 1992), pp. 75–77. Estimates vary in different sources.

2. *Sosialt Utsyn 1993* (Oslo: Statistics Norway, 1993), p. 213; and *Fakta og analyser. Særskilt vedlegg til stortingsmelding, nr. 4 (1996–1997). Langtidsprogrammet 1998–2001* (Oslo: Finans- og tolldepartementet, 1997), pp. 24–25.

3. *Historical Statistics 1994* (Oslo: Statistics Norway, 1995), p. 63.

4. Ibid.

5. *Sosialt Utsyn 1993*, pp. 289–301, 313–323.

6. Ibid., pp. 117–170.

7. *Statistisk Årbok 1997* (Oslo: Statistisk Sentralbyrå, 1997).

8. Olaf Aagedal, "Religionen," in Hans Fredrik Dahl and Arne Martin Klausen, eds., *Det moderne Norge. Tro, tanke, form*, vol. 4 (Oslo: Gyldendal, 1983).

9. Aagedal "Religionen," p. 173. See also Chapter 7.

10. *Statistisk Årbok 1997*, p. 152.

11. Ernst Sars, *Norges politiske historie* (Kristiana: Oscar Andersens Bogtrykkeri, 1904), p. 1. Sars was the most prominent nation-building historian of the liberal Left party and published this work one year before independence from Sweden.

12. Stein Rokkan, *Citizens, Elections, Parties* (Oslo: Universitetsforlaget, 1970). See especially chapter three: "Nation-Building, Cleavage Formation, and the Structuring of Mass Politics," pp. 72–144.

13. Stein Kuhnle, "Stemmeretten i 1814," *Historisk Tidsskrift* 51, no. 4 (1972):373–390.

14. Fritz Hodne, *Norsk økonomisk historie, 1815–1970* (Oslo: J. W. Cappelen, 1981), ch. 5.

15. Ola H. Grytten, "Arbeidsledighetens omfang i mellomkrigstiden," *Historisk Tidsskrift* 71, no. 3 (1992):249–277.

16. Hodne, *Norsk økonomisk historie, 1815–1970,* p. 133.

17. Ibid., p. 567.

18. The Organization for European Economic Cooperation was created in 1948 to coordinate efforts to get the European markets to operate efficiently without too many hindrances. The OEEC was dissolved in 1961, but much of its work was continued within a new organization, the OECD, the Organization for Economic Cooperation and Development.

19. Knut Heidar, "Staten, politikken og det sivile samfunn," in Lars Alldén, Natalie Rogoff Ramsøy, and Mariken Vaa, eds., *Det norske samfunn,* 3rd ed. (Oslo: Gyldendal, 1986), pp. 112–142.

20. *Historical Statistics 1994,* pp. 347–348, 430.

21. The expression was used by the British prime minister Harold Wilson in the 1970s about the Labour Party. The subsequent Thatcher years revealed how inadequate notions about anything being "natural" in politics are.

22. The original name was Bondepartiet, the farmers' party. The change of name was done in 1957.

23. Jens Arup Seip, "Fra embedsmannsstat til ettpartistat," in *Fra embedsmannsstat til ettpartistat og andre essays* (Oslo: Universitetsforlaget, 1963).

24. Per Stavang, *Parlamentarisme og maktbalanse* (Oslo: Universitetsforlaget, 1964), pp. 144ff.

25. In Norway this was labeled a "bourgeois" coalition without any derogatory overtones.

26. Berge Furre, *Norsk historie, 1905–1990* (Oslo: Det Norske Samlaget, 1992), pp. 248–253.

27. Stein Rokkan, "Nation-Building, Cleavage Formation, and the Structuring of Mass Politics," ch. 3 in Stein Rokkan, *Citizens, Elections, Parties* (Oslo: Universitetsforlaget, 1970), pp. 72–144.

28. Henry Valen and Stein Rokkan, "Conflict Structure and Mass Politics in a European Periphery," in Richard Rose, ed., *Electoral Behavior: A Comparative Handbook* (New York: Free Press, 1974).

29. Ibid., p. 326.

30. Ibid.

31. Oddbjørn Knutsen, "Partipolitiske skillelinjer i avanserte industrisamfunn," *Tidsskrift for samfunnsforskning* 29 (1988):155–175, and Bernt Aardal, "Hva er en politisk skillelinje," *Tidsskrift for samfunnsforskning* 35 (1994):218–249.

32. Rokkan, "Nation-Building," pp. 72–144. The scheme has been employed by both students of the peasant movement and students of the labor movement; see Øyvind Østerud, *Agrarian Structure and the Peasant Politics in Scandinavia* (Oslo: Universitetsforlaget, 1978), and W. M. Lafferty, *Economic Development and the Response of Labor in Scandinavia* (Oslo: Universitetsforlaget, 1971).

33. See Rolf Danielsen, "Nye kilder til regjeringskrisen i januar 1928," in *Historisk Tidsskrift* 57, no. 1 (1978):93–102. See also Carl-Eric Grimstad, "Hornsrudregjeringer i 1928-kongemakt og mytedannelse," in Nytt Nork Tidsskrift 17, no. 2 (2000): 205–216.

3

Political Institutions

I love Parliament. The public life. Foes as well as friends. The building where we sit. The benches. The facade. . . . Parliament itself, think about the long months full of light when Parliament is in session. Lavinia, Lavinia—that is a good place to be.

—Nils Kjær, **Det lykkelige valg** *("The Fortunate Election")*

The sentiment that politicians are encapsulated in partly irrelevant, partly vicious power games, staying aloof from the ordinary lives of their electors is not a novelty, a discovery of the late twentieth century. Politicians have always been the targets of public ridicule, as is evident in the quote from the play by writer Nils Kjær above. We hear the fictional MP after being defeated by his wife, Lavinia, in a still popular play about vanity, ambition, and politics in Norway before World War I. The other side of the coin is the politicians' prominent position—in the life of the nation as well as in local communities. State-building and the politicians to man public institutions figure prominently in the history of Norway. Knowledge of institutional structures and relations is imperative for understanding how politics and governance are conducted. The perspective adopted here is that these institutions both shape and are themselves shaped by political processes. Political institutions are both cause and effect. When the Norwegian Storting in 1919 changed the election law from a majority system to proportional representation, this undoubtedly had major effects on the party composition of the parliaments to come. An important political motivation for the change, however, was the desire to keep the revolutionary and rapidly growing Labor Party from reaping the full benefits embedded in the existing majority system of being the largest party. Political developments caused institutional change when the bourgeois parties altered the existing electoral rules in an attempt to keep their power.

In this chapter I shall not focus much on discussions about causes and effects, however. The task is to present the institutional framework of Norwegian politics in the late 1990s. I start with a discussion of the political role of the Constitution before moving on to the constitutionally prescribed structures: the legislature, the executive, and the public bureaucracy. Subsequently, I discuss the institutions set up to regulate regional and local government, briefly describe the new Sami Assembly, and end by considering the political impact of international regimes such as the European Economic Area (EEA) agreement regulating Norway's integration into the economic free market of the European Union (EU).

The Role of the Constitution

The primary importance of the Norwegian constitution lies in its symbolic value. It was adopted by the constitutional assembly on May 17, 1814, and is revered as the second oldest constitution still in force. This gives the basis for the annual celebration of the constitution. On the anniversary of its adoption, school children and citizens parade all over Norway (and even in New York!) to commemorate the founding fathers as well as to pay homage to the nation's freedom, independence, and democratic political institutions. Still, in particular instances the symbolic value can be transformed into political value and can become a major force in an ongoing political battle—as in the issue of Norwegian membership in the EU.

In the daily routine politics, however, as well as in much *realpolitik*, the constitution is not a viable force or is at least a fairly distant force. For example: According to the text, the King selects his ministers. This is definitely not the case, and it has not been true since the breakthrough for parliamentarism in 1884. Other significant changes took place in the postwar years without any constitutional amendments. First, the introduction of the enabling acts gave much discretionary power over the economy to the government and the central bureaucracy. Second, the practice of consulting special interests (companies, organizations, etc.) before decisions are made has gained increased prominence. This new "corporate pluralist" system was put in place without any constitutional change.[1] The director of the first Norwegian Power Study pointedly argued, that the constitution is the very last document one ought to read in order to learn how power is dispersed in today's Norwegian polity.[2] The reason for its inadequacy as a piece of description is that a widespread "constitutional conservatism"[3] has impeded efforts to revise the document so that it is consistent with practices. Politicians have likewise been reluctant to initiate any grand revisions like those found in neighboring countries. The enactment of new constitutions took place in Denmark in

1953 and in Sweden in the early 1970s. The other side to this reluctance toward change has been a creative capacity to accept a liberal interpretation of the existing paragraphs.[4] A constitutional lawyer has argued that the constitution today is primarily a symbol, and its importance is a myth that is "useful in the national folklore."[5]

This interpretation of the constitution's prime function, however, conceals the fact that inside its soft wrapping it also contains some hard elements. For example: New laws cannot be applied to past events; public expropriation of private property must be compensated; freedom of expression shall prevail; the actions of the government shall be controlled by parliament; at least half the government shall be members of the state church. A main point about these hard elements is that they cannot be changed by a mere majority in parliament, but only after a special procedure requiring two-thirds of the vote. The Supreme Court practices—not often, but increasingly throughout the 20th century—the right to judicial review.[6]

The recent debate on Norwegian membership in the European Union shows that there is still political ammunition in the old constitution. The issue was whether a yes-majority in the referendum in 1994—referenda are unknown to the constitution—would be morally, politically, or legally binding for the parliamentarians who later would make the final decision. The political point was that according to the constitution, a minority in parliament could block entry, even after a yes-majority in the referendum, and a heated debate took place over the fairness and morality of a minority among the elected representatives potentially turning down the people's choice.[7] Due to the no-majority vote, however, the positions were never put to a real test.

Another current effect of the constitution is reflected (but not mirrored) in the institutional design of the governmental structures and their relationships with each other. Although not guided in any detail from constitutional paragraphs, their development and division of labor must be understood as historical outcomes where constitutional rules were important elements. We start with the people's representatives in parliament.

The Storting

Representatives to the Norwegian legislative assembly, the Storting—literally "large assembly"—are elected in September every fourth year. The term is fixed, and the Storting cannot be dissolved before the end of the term. It is a parliament in the British way in the sense that a majority in the Storting can vote, at any time and for any reason, the current government out of office by expressing "no confidence." The main tasks of the

Storting are to enact laws, to decide the state's budget, to control the government, and to ratify international treaties.

Election and Composition

Today the Storting has 165 seats, a number that has increased gradually. At the turn of the century, there were 114 parliamentarians. All but eight MPs (members of parliament) are elected from nineteen multimember constituencies. The constituencies are identical to the nineteen counties, and each is represented by from four to seventeen MPs, as specified in the constitution. The variation is based on the counties' population size with a certain "district bonus" in addition. The eight remaining seats are used to adjust the overall distribution of seats in the Storting to improve the proportionality of the national vote. The adjustment seats are given to the candidates of nationally underrepresented parties. The chosen ones are the candidates on the constituency lists coming closest to winning an additional seat in the first round. However, only parties with a minimum of 4 percent of the national vote may take part in this additional distribution of seats.

The election system is proportional, meaning that the technical procedure to translate votes into seats aims at making the party composition of the Storting roughly similar to the parties' relative electoral support. When Labor in the 1997 election received 35 percent of the vote, it ought to have won, on a proportional basis, 35 percent of the seats. Actually it got 39 percent, which was due to an intended "large party bias." In contrast, the majoritarian systems of the United States and Britain produce much larger discrepancies. The British Labour Party won 43 percent of the vote in the 1997 election but captured—through the "first past the post" plurality system—64 percent of the seats in parliament. The proportionality of the Norwegian elections is technically arrived at by the modified Sainte-Laguë method.[8] Norwegian elections are based on political parties, more precisely on constituency party lists, not on individual candidates with a party label. The parties present a list with multiple, numbered candidates in each constituency where they choose to run. Most parties winning representation in the Storting are national parties presenting lists in all constituencies. It sometimes happens, however, that some people organize a list in one county only and occasionally win a seat. This was the case in the 1997 election when a whaling skipper resented the restrictive policies of the central authorities toward the hunting and export of whales and seals, and he organized the "Coastal Party" to fight for the interests of the population along the coast. He ran for election in one county (Nordland) and ended up in parliament. The nomination of candidates to party lists is decentralized, and attempts on the part of the national party leadership to influence the constituency parties in these matters is considered improper and may easily backfire for the preferred candidate. We shall return to how these party lists are put together in the next chapter.

Who are the parliamentarians? We know now that the MPs are fairly representative of the electorate according to their party support and in terms of geographical distribution. But socially? By gender and by education? Are Norwegian MPs mirroring the voters they represent? The answer is no, but the answer needs some qualification. The Storting representatives are a social elite, which is the case in all elected representative assemblies around the world.[9] A study of the 1993–1997 Storting showed that when looking at the standard socio-demographic characteristics, one of the largest discrepancies between the representatives and their voters was found in their ages. The age group of 45 to 54 years was more than twice as numerous in the parliament as in the voter population.[10] As far as gender, 38 percent of the representatives were women; only the Swedish Riksdag had a higher percentage of women among the Nordic parliaments. The public employees, the self-employed, and in particular the white-collar occupations were strongly overrepresented in the Storting—just as they had been in previous periods. But the largest discrepancy between representatives and represented was found in education.[11] It is important to note, however, that the Storting MPs, although definitely a social elite, are more equal to their voters in socio-demographic respects than parliamentarians in most other countries—the Nordic ones included.[12]

Internal Structures

The most important internal structures in the parliament are the committees and the party groups. The Storting is a so-called working parliament. This means that it not only says yes or no to government proposals but also gives the opposition a chance to criticize and present alternative policies; the MPs actively research the subject matter in committees to prepare the issue for the Storting at large. Often government proposals are reworked to fit the opinions of the parliamentary majority.

The major institutional (but politically trivial) internal division of the Storting is the two chambers—the Lagting with one-fourth of the MPs and the Odelsting with three-fourths. This division is activated only when the parliament debates new laws. But since the party composition is the same in both chambers, and—as we shall see below—the voting discipline in the party groups is extremely high, the same party majority rules everywhere. As a consequence, the semi-bicameralism does not have implications other than making the minimal time to adopt a law in

parliament three days—since this is the constitutionally required minimum interval between law debates in the two chambers.[13]

More influential to the way the Storting operates is the work of the
Speakers Conference. This group of six speakers and vice-speakers in the
three *tings* (Storting, Lagting, and Odelsting) is elected on a party proportional basis. The basis for their work is the Standing Orders, which gives
rules for the practical administration of the Storting work, such as the
composition of committees, the participation and speaking time in general debates, and so forth. Still there are questions that have to be settled
by the speaker or the Speakers Conference, for example, when alternative proposals are on the table and the voting order may potentially be
politically relevant. On the whole, however, the position of speaker is not
a politically important one, even if the formal protocol ranks it next to the
king.[14]

There are twelve standing committees in the Norwegian parliament.[15]
They are mostly set up according to subject areas, and these correlate
roughly with government ministers. For example, the Church, Education, and Research Committee covers the affairs of the Ministry of
Church, Education, and Research. All MPs are a member of only one
committee—multiple memberships are not allowed. The committees are
composed relative to overall parliamentary party strength, and the important positions of committee leader and vice-leader are distributed
among the party groups in the same way.[16] There are no "rights" on the
part of the individual MP to pick his or her committee or to get a leading
position within it. This is decided by the party groups and determined on
the basis of the party political "needs" and what the leadership can gain
acceptance for within the group itself. Individual qualifications and the
MP's own wishes and tenure are criteria considered important by the
party groups. The committee deliberations take place before the plenary
stage, and they are generally closed to the public. The committee may
call outsiders, for example, the minister, to give evidence and argue their
case before the committee. At present, there is also a limited experiment
going on in allowing the committees—if they so wish—to hold open
hearings, but so far this is not commonly done. The idea behind having
closed discussions is that it makes the discussions at this early stage more
substantive and open to compromise in a way that public meetings
would not allow. Whenever the committee cannot reach an agreement,
they present divergent proposals to the plenary *ting*. By and large, however, the real decisions are made at the committee stage. Naturally, lobbyists generally direct their activities toward the relevant committees.[17]

The committee members do not, of course, operate in splendid isolation. They are placed in the committee as representatives of their parties,
and for committee work to be of political value, the party representatives

must stay in close contact with the party groups. In controversial issues or when the party programs do not give any clear guidance, the MPs must have the support of their party groups to act effectively. The party groups are made up by all MPs elected under the same party label and party program.[18] Economic support for administration and research is given by parliament to the party groups, not to the individual MPs. The groups coordinate the political work of their members. Anything controversial in parliament—small or large—will (with a few exceptions) eventually be decided by a party political vote. This may be the assignment of office space in parliament, the national budget, or the life or death of governments. And the party group itself decides the stand taken in these issues. If the party program gives clear guidance, there is usually little debate within the party group. But if that is not the case, the MPs in the group will have to consider the opinion of the external party organization, their constituency parties, the voters' sentiments, and so forth before making up their minds. All groups elect a parliamentary leader, who need not be the leader of the external party organization, and a board to organize the work of the party group. The leader is also generally the major spokesperson for the party in parliament.

Parliament at Work

The party group is the political cement of all parliamentary work. A standard index for measuring the extent to which MPs of the same party vote together, the Rice Index, showed that around 1980, as well as in the early 1990s, the Storting parties scored an average of 97.5 on joint voting. The Rice Index is a scale from 0 (always evenly split) to 100 (always full agreement).[19] This is extremely high and reflects that the fact that MPs only vote differently from their parties when—on rare occasions—they are allowed to do so by their party group. A "free" vote—a vote without the party whip—is traditionally allowed in matters matching two requirements: It is not covered by the party program,[20] and it involves a matter of conscience (for example, religious issues). A free vote may also be allowed in a decision about where to locate important infrastructure or large public production plants. In these matters the constituency parties often have very strong opinions, and here the geographical dimension in Norwegian politics often collides with party politics.

A parliamentary debate most often starts with a proposition or a political statement issued by the government to the Storting, for example, the budget, a new law, new guidelines for a particular sector of public policies, an orientation from the minister for foreign affairs on the international situation, and so forth. If there are material decisions to be made, the proposals are first sent to a committee. After hearing the relevant evidence and discussing the matter in the committee, the various fractions present their recommendation to the Storting. In 80 percent of the cases—as measured during the forty years from 1945 to 1985—the committees are unanimous in their recommendations. In recent years, however, dissent has become much more common at the committee stage.[21] Proposals for new laws are, as mentioned above, sent to the Lagting and the Odelsting. Other issues go to the full Storting for debate and a vote. The final decision is nevertheless almost always ready when the committee fractions have tabled their recommendations. Still there is a plenary public debate where the parties present their arguments. At this stage, however, the purpose of the debate is to win the public, not the votes.

Norwegian governments do not need an investiture or a positive vote of confidence to continue; they stay in power as long as a majority does not actively seek to get rid of them in the Storting. Most governments resign in practice as a consequence of defeat in election, not through a loss of confidence in parliament. Up until the mid-1970s, the accepted truth was that parliament had lost power to the government, the bureaucracy, and the corporate channel. Since then, however, successive minority governments—which all have a strong political incentive for close cooperation with parliament—have gradually changed that, bringing back the old interwar fear of "assembly government" in the public debate.

There are various controls to ensure that governments actually follow parliamentary decisions. The Storting appoints a group of accountants who report on the way the executive has used appropriated funds. A special committee also scrutinizes the formalities around decisions made by the government. More important, however, is the control through debate and specific questions. The parliamentarians, predominantly MPs from the opposition parties, raise specific issues in question hour. Then the ministers have to defend their decisions as well as the activities—especially the lack of activity—of their departments.

The Government

The government is made up of about eighteen ministers, each in charge of a department, and headed by the prime minister. It is the duty of the Storting to secure that the country has a government, and the government is as strong in political terms as the Storting allows. The latter is not always evident in periods with strong government but becomes visible as soon as its political base in the parliament is weakened. A hostile parliament has ample means to frustrate the political ambitions of any government. On the other hand, if the government controls the parliamentary majority, it does not have to worry much about the Storting.

Two aspects of the government's work make it the central locus of power and attention in Norwegian politics. The first is its strong control over the political initiative; the second is its position at the head of the civil service. In relation to the parliament, the government is made the active party in the constitution. The government presents the budget to parliament every October and prepares proposals for new laws whenever deemed necessary. It has the power to appoint top personnel in the civil service and to set up state commissions to evaluate and propose action in any field of society. The government's right to initiate is not interfered with by the Storting, which can only "control" in hindsight or—in the extreme case—refuse to grant the necessary funds.[22]

Political power also flows from heading the state bureaucracy. The department bureaucrats are highly skilled experts who can assist the ministers in preparing their policy initiatives and manage the flow of information in ways beneficial for the government. The most experienced and professional "spin doctors" are probably found in the departments. The foreign policy prerogative also gives the government a special position in directing foreign policy issues. Traditionally this has been an exclusive, rather closed process, often involving only the Foreign Office and a few senior ministers around the prime minister. As we shall see in Chapter 7, this is opening up and these issues have become much more difficult to separate from domestic affairs. In sensitive matters, however, the government may consult the parliamentary party leaders in parliament or its ad hoc "enlarged" foreign relations committee. To keep the initiative in these matters is often a question of controlling the media and of securing tacit support in parliament.

Executive-Parliamentary Relations

However important relations with the media and with the public at large are for the long-term strength of the government, its position in the short term is determined by its relations with the Storting. In a parliamentary system, a strong government will emerge if it is backed by a cohesive majority party in the Storting. This was the situation from 1945 to 1961 when Labor ruled and the parliament was described as "exiled" from the process of real policymaking.[23] Taking the period from 1945 to 1970, the Labor one-party, majority government stayed in power for almost two-thirds of the time. Naturally this was a very strong government as decisionmaking in practice was confined to one party alone. If the government could control its parliamentary group, and it usually did, it had nothing to fear from parliament. In 1961, however, Labor lost its parliamentary majority, and since then Norway has had minority or coalition governments—sometimes both. In the period between 1971 and 1996, the comparatively rare construction of a minority, coalition government held power for 10 percent of the time.[24] After the 1997 Storting election, a new minority coalition was formed based on the three political parties "in the center." These parties together had the support of only 25 percent of the MPs in the parliament.

Although the parliamentary principle cannot be found in the constitution itself, it is part of constitutional prescriptive law. This means that the government has to leave office if parliament passes a "no confidence" motion. The mere existence of the parliamentary stick, however, means that parliamentary-executive relations in every detail are permeated by the knowledge that this could occur. Actually, since Norway became independent in 1905, the government has only twice been kicked out of office by a vote of no confidence in parliament. The two most common ways for Norwegian governments to leave office are, first, by defeat in election and, second, when one or more coalition parties chooses to leave the coalition. During the postwar years, however, the governments of Norway have enjoyed a fairly stable position, although change of government did become somewhat more frequent after 1970. More often than not, the same governments sit through the full four years' period. Altogether there have been thirteen parliamentary terms between 1945 and 1997. In nine of these, the same party controlled the position of prime minister throughout the full term. In the post-1945 period, the Labor Party has been to Norway what Harold Wilson wrongfully claimed about Labor in the United Kingdom: "the natural party of government." But nothing, of course, is "natural" in politics. Labor was in office roughly twenty years (out of twenty-five) in the 1945–1970 period and nineteen years (out of twenty-six) in the period from 1971 to 1997. Nevertheless, the "life expectancy" of Norwegian governments dropped by one and a half years from the third to the fourth quarter of the last century.[25]

The strength of governments relies on more than constitutional practice and stamina in office. Executive-parliamentary relations are the sum of numerous and delicate political mechanisms. What may look like strong governments may not be so strong in practice, and weak ones may sometimes be rather strong. For instance, the Labor government headed by Oskar Torp in 1951–1955 was a one-party, majority government and could apparently do whatever it liked. In real politics, however, the Labor Party chairman, who was also leader of the parliamentary group as well as former—and later returning—prime minister (1945–1951; 1955–1963; 1963–1965), Einar Gerhardsen, remained the strong man in the labor movement throughout the period. The Torp government always had to look over its shoulder to find out whether it had the party behind it. In this sense, it was a weak government. On the other hand,

Gro Harlem Brundtland headed a Labor minority government in 1990–1997, and this was fairly strong. This was due in part to her strong personal standing within her party but derived also from the political situation, particularly the role played in this period by the Norwegian EU membership issue. This required wide cooperation between old adversaries.

Government·Structure and Personnel

The ministers share collective responsibility for the government's decisions. In one-party governments, ministers are bound by these decisions; in coalitions, they at least cannot argue publicly against the policies of their own government—although they often make it known that they lost the fight. The internal work and the discussions inside the government are conducted behind closed doors. Coordination and decision-making take place through an elaborate arrangement of regular meetings (two or three per week), cabinet subcommittees, and bilateral contacts between the ministers, their state secretaries, and political advisers.[26] The political personnel of the government consist of altogether around sixty persons. In coalition governments where the need for political coordination between different parties is especially important, central departments, such as finance, foreign affairs, and the prime minister's office, often have undersecretaries from more than one party.

The role of the prime minister and his office is central to the efficiency and political efficacy of the government. He or she is not a "superstar" but the central organizer of the government team.[27] Apart from the exceptional situation in 1945, all prime ministers have held a central position in the Storting prior to taking office. It is also indicative of the role of parties in Norwegian politics that the prime minister—with two exceptions—also had been (or was at the time) the leader of the external party organization. In recruiting the ministers to the particular departments, the prime minister has an important, often a final, say in the selection. However, in coalition governments, he or she has to accept the appointees of other parties. Also in one-party governments, the prime minister has to get his candidates accepted by the party group and the central party organization, but this is more easily accomplished.[28]

Whatever the circumstances, all prospective prime ministers know that several norms guiding government-making must be observed for political reasons. First, the government must include ministers from most parts of the country. A government without any minister "representing" North Norway would be politically crippled at the outset, no matter its party base in parliament. Second, it would be very difficult today to form a government without a fairly even representation of women. The rate of political "necessity" changed quickly in Norwegian politics when Mrs. Brundtland "shocked" the world by bringing in nearly 50 percent women in her Labor government in 1986.[29] Third, the government's relationship with the Storting has to be secured by bringing in a number of experienced MPs. Post-1945 governments have varied, however, in their balance between the "external" experts and people with important positions in society, on the one hand, and the politicians in the Storting and the party organization, on the other. It would be wrong, however, to suggest a watertight division between those two groups.

Looking at the patterns of actual recruitment, the possession of political experience is obviously central. Although half the ministers serving in 1945–1979 did not have any previous experience in the Storting, almost two-thirds had served as a party representative on a local, municipal council.[30] Having held office in the party organization at the local or national level is also part of the background for many ministers.[31] The government ministers make up even more of a social elite than the parliamentarians. It is still notable, however, that careers in politics and organizational leadership are a major route to ministerial office even without high education and a distinguished professional career, whereas the latter is almost never sufficient on its own.

The Top Civil Service: Politics and Administration

Public administration and public services are established at different levels: The departments are the central staff serving the national-level ministers and the government. These are located in Oslo and have national goals. Other national-level goals are pursued by the directorates, which are designed to look after more routine tasks such as handling customs, managing the fishery regulations, and administrating a particular law or policy field. These are organized independently of the departments and are often asked to advise the departments on new policies affecting their field of work. The two main subnational levels of public administration are, first, the nineteen counties *(fylker)* and, second, the 435 municipalities *(kommuner)*. There is also an international bureaucracy to be considered, which administers the intergovernmental treaties and deals with the international organizations of which Norway is associated. Here I focus on the national-level bureaucracy and its relations with the government.

The Departments

The department is the minister's secretariat, which prepares issues for discussion in the government and in parliament. It also carries out the decisions made and ensures that they are properly applied.

The minister has to balance three tasks: He or she is the head of the department, is a colleague within the government, and is responsible vis-à-vis the Storting for everything done or not done by the department. To be a minister is a demanding job, which most find both exhausting and meaningful. It is often the ultimate aim of Storting politicians to become a minister. But among the experience reported by former ministers is that the bureaucracy sometimes resists new policies. Experienced ministers also admit, however, that it may be difficult for the minister to separate relevant problem discussions from politically motivated obstruction on the part of bureaucrats.[32] It is furthermore pointed out that the minister must know his or her objectives and priorities and must be explicit about them in order to make an impact on the department. The state secretary of state and the political advisors increase the political presence and potential impact in the department. Whether the minister becomes a departmental leader or a hostage to the mandarins, however, depends not only on his or her personal qualities and experience but also on the kind of department and the policy objectives pursued. Ministers from some of the fairly recently established departments, such as environment and children and family, reported more resistance to new policies than ministers in some of the old, traditional ones like foreign affairs and justice.[33]

In the late 1990s, there were sixteen departments—in addition to the prime minister's office—with responsibility for different policy areas. Both the departments of social affairs and health, as well as the department for foreign affairs, are led by two ministers each, which makes a government of nineteen ministers, including the prime minister. The departments are internally divided into sections and offices, and they are staffed with about 3,500 employees, of which roughly 1,600 work at the level of consultant or above. The departments vary much in size and character—the ministry of foreign affairs (from 1905) has a strong *corps d'esprit* among its diplomats, and the department of oil and energy (created in 1978) has highly specialized personnel in order to negotiate with multinational oil companies about economic and technological matters. The department bureaucrats work out in detail the position papers and political initiatives to be presented to the minister, the government, or— after adoption by the government—to the Storting. In more complicated matters, like proposals for new laws, the department conducts the work. The process usually starts with the government appointing a committee to work out a first proposal. Then interested parties are allowed a hearing before the government—after further preparation in the department— forwards its proposal to the parliament. Sometimes the government finds it opportune to first present a parliamentary report or discussion paper to parliament for general debate. This message presents facts and uncommitted options, and the purpose is to sound out the parties in parliament before the government commits itself. When a final decision has been made by the Storting, the law often needs to be supplemented by a set of regulations worked out in the department to identify the necessary administrative requirements.

Departmental work is organized around a moderate hierarchical structure with the minister at the top. A senior administrative employee heads the department staff *(departementsråd)*. Immediately below him or her are the section leaders *(ekspedisjonssjefer)* who direct the work in several "offices," each with a "head of office" *(byråsjef)* in charge. The number of departments, and the sections and offices grouped together, has changed substantially over the years. Reorganization often takes place with an incoming government in order to meet its political objectives.[34] Traditionally this is a matter of the government's "internal organization" and belongs to the executive prerogative, which is generally not interfered with by the Storting.

Another recent change is the rise in the number of departmental sections and the decline in the number of offices. This has been a policy to create more flexible units.[35] There has also been a trend toward more planning and research in the department at the expense of routine administration within standard procedures. In recent years there has been an emphasis on strengthening the international perspectives of the specific policy fields of the department.

Recruitment and advancement within the departments is strongly based on education and tenure. Traditionally, the civil service bureaucracy was the stronghold of lawyers, but after 1945 economists and other social scientists made their entry. In terms of most standard background characteristics—like region of birth, social background, and education—the bureaucrats differ from the population at large.[36] The most notable similarity shared with citizens is gender. Women constituted 43 percent of all bureaucrats in 1996. A substantial part of both sexes is recruited directly from higher education, and almost all making a career within the department start at the level of consultant and make their way up.

The Directorates

During the past few decades there has been an effort to reshape departments into organizations that focus more on policy development—ideally being the minister's secretariat. More routine work has been delegated to independent agencies, to the directorates, and to independent institutions. Historically there is no clear-cut division between departments and directorates, but today directorates are more hierarchically organized and generally designed to execute the laws and to apply the numerous public regulations of a modern society. Around 10,000 people work in the central civil service outside the departments, and almost all directorates are located in Oslo. The number of directorates has increased from thirteen before 1884 to between sixty and seventy today.[37]

An example of a classic directorate is the directorate of customs and excise; a modern example is the directorate of immigration. The tasks of these agencies differ, but all are organized to implement state policies—on a national basis—in their particular field. They are headed by a director and sometimes guided by a board, but subordinated to a department. They are usually free to make decisions within the general rules and principles given in the law or in departmental regulations. Studies of the personnel recruited show that these persons, more often than those in the departments, have a science background, reflecting the fact that specialists are needed for implementation and control.

The Ombudsman

The parliament oversees the political control of the ministers and their departments. In order to give the individual citizen an instrument, outside the courts, to complain about "unfair treatment" by public authorities, the *ombudsmann* was created in 1962, after Swedish and Danish models. The Storting elects the ombudsman for a four-year term. He can consider complaints on decisions made anywhere in the public bureaucracy (and even outside if a private agency is operating within the public domain). This includes decisions by municipal or county bureaucracies, but not the policies adopted by the elected assemblies at these levels. The ombudsman can, in addition, consider public practices at his own initiative. This is also the case with the various other ombudsmen appointed by the government to look after gender equality, children's rights, and the rights of army conscripts. These are intended as watchdogs guarding the rights of special groups vis-à-vis public authorities. They are also spokespersons for these groups in the public debate and voice their opinions about new laws and regulations. Operating close to these ombudsmen is Data Inspectorate, an agency that is responsible for the protection of individual rights in relation to data registers—public and private—on individuals.

Regional and Local Government

Norway is a unitary, not a federal, state (see Chapter 8). Nevertheless, local government has a long and strong tradition. Local government was introduced in the 1830s with the so-called Formannskapsloven (1837), which gave an elected municipal board the right to decide specific local matters like relief to the poor and the construction and maintenance of

roads and schools. In no other European state did the same degree of local government exist at that time.[38] Local self-government has enjoyed an
almost revered status in Norwegian political rhetoric. Over time, the
tasks given to this "close democracy" or "community democracy"—as
opposed to the national "distant democracy"—have been broadened as
well as deepened, and it has undoubtedly contributed to increasing the
general participatory practices and political skills in Norwegian politics.
Nevertheless, the degree of local democracy has often been questioned.
Compared to the importance attributed to local government at the level
of the municipality, the county government introduced in 1976 is considered both more marginal and more fragile.

Municipal Government

The 435 municipalities in Norway vary much in population—from about
300 to more than 480,000 inhabitants. Today they employ altogether
about 300,000 persons, and their number has been growing rapidly.[39]
Every fourth year the voters go to the polls to elect a local assembly *(kom-
munestyre)* to decide municipal policies during the election period.

The political parties are—just like at the national level—the major political actors in local politics. The local elections take place in September
two years after every parliamentary election. As in the parliamentary
elections, the election method is proportional, and the parties present
their lists of names to the voters. At the municipal level, however, the
voters are allowed to influence the selection of persons on the party lists
by putting up a name twice and by deleting others. In practice, this can
affect, and occasionally has affected, which representatives are elected
from the parties. Generally, however, the voters cause only a moderate
reordering of the parties' own choices. One reason for this is that the parties are allowed to place the names of their major candidates more than
once on the list. These practices do not normally influence the number of
seats achieved by a party, although particular groups may sometimes
suffer. Research on the 1991 election shows that although 39 percent of
the candidates nominated were women and 37 percent of the candidates
put up twice by the parties were women, only 29 percent were elected.
The only explanation for this is that voters favored male candidates.[40]
The share of women elected was over 30 percent in 1987 and a record 33
percent in 1995. Of the mayors elected after the 1995 local election, 16
percent were women.

An important difference from parliamentary elections is that immigrants without Norwegian citizenship can participate in both municipal
and county elections, provided they have lived in Norway for the past
three years. Participation in local elections is normally about 10 percent-

age points lower than in parliamentary elections, mostly varying between 65 and 75 percent. Local elections are supposed to focus on local matters, but increasingly they are taking on a national character. The national media, the national issues, and the national politicians figure prominently. Party swings at the election are also fairly uniform throughout the country, indicating that local issues as well as local politicians are less important to the voters' choice. There is a high turnover of representatives in municipal councils, and the delegates complain about their workload.

The local councils vary in size according to the size of the municipalities—with a minimum of eleven council members in municipalities with less than 5,000 inhabitants. The council elects the municipal board *(formannskap)*—which is the most important local political body—on a party proportional basis. Both the council and the board are headed by the mayor, who is elected by the council. Generally, this arrangement creates a system of interparty consensus or cooptation—depending on which way one sees it. There is the option for the municipality to drop the board and to choose a parliamentary method for running the municipality. Then the council selects a municipal "government" (one-party or a coalition), which is collectively responsible vis-à-vis the council. Only Oslo has been practicing this system, although it was introduced in Bergen in 2000.

The system of local government is based on ordinary law, which means that the Storting has decided to delegate public authority to the local councils. In theory the Storting could return that authority to the central state; in practice that would hardly be politically possible. The values enhanced by this system of local government are threefold: freedom, participation, and efficiency.[41] Traditionally, it was considered a system to channel the opinions of the layman in the governing of local communities. Increasingly, however, the municipalities have employed a huge, professional staff to implement policies.

The municipalities have several functions given by law but are otherwise free to take up whatever they consider necessary and beneficial for the local community. Municipal activity is mostly concentrated in four sectors: health and social services, preschool and primary education, construction and physical municipal planning, and culture. The freedom to take up new tasks is in practice restricted by state power to direct municipal activity through laws and regulations as well as through the transfer of money and the issuance of guidelines, that is, by exerting political and moral pressure. There is a continuous and politically important struggle over the degree of local democracy. The municipalities and their representatives complain regularly that the state undermines local freedom by constantly assigning new tasks to the municipalities without at the same time granting sufficient money to look after these tasks. The principle of local democracy often collides frontally with the principle of equality in these debates. If equality demands equal service throughout the country, this obviously restricts the freedom of the municipalities to do different things. Still, the central importance of the municipal level in providing public services is evident in the fact that municipal consumption as a percentage of total public consumption is about 60 percent. This is a standard Nordic level, but far above what is found in Western Europe in general.

In principle, the municipalities can raise money by increasing taxes. Because all municipalities are employing the highest rates allowed by the law, however, this is not a real option. In the mid-1980s, there was an attempt to curb the earmarked state support to the municipalities. Instead the municipalities received general support in order to increase local freedom. Since then, however, the state money with strings attached has tripled due to political pressure to "do something" about particular problems such as integrating psychiatric patients in local communities or improving services for the elderly. And it was felt that this "something" should not depend on the goodwill of the local council.

Another way to improve services is to make more efficient use of funds. A recurring theme in Norwegian political debates is whether to redraw the map over the municipalities in order to make them larger and more rationally organized. The number was cut from 750 around 1960 to 450 a decade later. A proposal for further reduction in the early 1990s—trimming them to about 200—was met by fierce resistance and got nowhere. The problem is an old one, familiar from democratic theory: Creating optimal-sized entities has to balance the economic efficiency of scale and the democratic potential of small units.

County Government

The first county councils were elected in the autumn of 1975. However, the counties were administrative units before that—partly made up by the office of the state representative in each county, the "county governor," and partly by compulsory cooperation between the counties. The counties of the 1960s had the responsibility for secondary schools and hospitals, and they grew in political and economic importance. Actually, the counties have been the fastest growing public sector since 1945, and particularly rapid growth took place from the mid-1960s to the late 1980s.[42] To make up for the "democratic deficits" of the old county, the politicians were to be elected by the voters and thereby made directly responsible to them. The voters in 1975 got two votes at the local elections—one for the municipal election and one for the county election.

The county councils were elected roughly in the same way as parliament; elections were proportional, and the voters did not have the option to influence which persons were elected (as in the municipal election). The parties decided a candidate's chance when they set up their county election lists.

The counties are organized in the same way as the municipalities. There is a small executive body, the county board, made up by party councilors in relation to party strength in the council. The council also elects a county mayor to lead and represent. The activities of the county are financed by a special county tax and—for the largest part—by state grants. About 90 percent of the money is used for three tasks: to construct and run the hospitals, the schools, and the county roads.

Since the mid-1980s, there has been a debate about the future of the county. Some argue that it is not needed because most jobs done at this level could be either taken over by the state directly or delegated to the municipalities. Besides, the citizens have not come to identify much with the county level, at least not the way they do with both the municipality and the nation at large. Others argue that institutionalized cooperation at this intermunicipal level is both more efficient and more functional. For the time being, practical needs make it likely that the county will stay on, possible in a reorganized form.

The Sami Assembly

The Sami Assembly first met in 1989. It does not have much power, but symbolically and politically it is important because the historic record of the treatment given to the Sami population and other ethnic minorities by the Norwegian state and the society at large is not a good one. There are thirty-nine representatives in the Sami Assembly, and it is led by a board and a president elected by the assembly. The Sami Assembly is located in the largest Sami municipality in the county Finnmark in North Norway where it also has a small administration. About two-thirds of the Sami population live in Norway; the rest live in Sweden, Finland, or Russia. The Sami Assembly does not have the power to make any decisions binding Norwegian citizens or authorities. It can only advise matters it considers relevant to the Sami population. The election of the assembly takes place jointly with parliamentary elections, and the voters must be registered in a Sami census compiled on an self-reported ethnic basis.

The "Sami question" arose on the background of the harsh treatment given to the Sami population in the past by Norwegian authorities. An early policy of "Norwegianization" discriminated against the Sami on the basis of language and culture. This became a public concern particularly around 1980. A debate was triggered by a national struggle over a new hydroelectric construction project that threatened to interfere with traditional Sami trades. This also coincided with an international trend in concern about the rights of indigenous peoples. A commission on Sami rights produced its first report in 1984. This report led to the passing of the Sami Act (1987)—creating the Sami Assembly—and to a special paragraph in the constitution protecting Sami language and culture (1988). Norway also ratified an international convention on the rights of indigenous peoples in 1990.[43]

There are also other ethnic minorities in Norway—descendants of Finnish immigrants, the Gypsies, and the Jews—but only the Sami population have been given a special protection in law. One reason for this is that the Sami have inhabited the same territory for centuries, beginning long before the Norwegian state claimed sovereignty over the same area. The Sami Assembly has opened up an arena for pressing claims toward the authorities. So far this has been most successful in connection with questions of language and culture, not with respect to control over "the water and land" in the traditional Sami territories. These are the most controversial ethnic claims—not the least because they affect the rights of the non-Sami Norwegian population living in the same area. The Sami Assembly has also brought into the open differences within the Sami population between traditionalists and modernizers and between men and women.

International Cooperation

The political institutions influencing the politics of a country—particularly a small country like Norway—are not found exclusively "inside" that country. One can perhaps speaks about a "fourth level of government," meaning that above the municipality, the county, and the national level there is an international level of decisionmaking institutions with national impact.[44] These are international organizations, intergovernmental conferences, and treaties. In the twentieth century, there has been a tremendous growth in the formal networking at this level: In 1910 Norway was a member of seventeen international organizations; in the early 1990s this had increased to around one hundred organizations. The growth since 1945 has been particularly steep.[45] It has been estimated that by around 1980 Norway had ratified and was bound by almost 2,000 international treaties.[46]

At the international level of government, there are regulations and guidelines of various degrees of legal force that national administrators have to take into account. The bureaucrats in the departments are using an increasing amount of their time doing this. From 1976 to 1996, the proportion of bureaucrats working at least some of the time with international issues increased from 24 percent to 33 percent.[47] Part of this is the traditional, almost routine business of unilaterally looking into the policies of other countries in order to learn from their experiences, as when the prime minister in 1988 asked all departments to go through laws and regulations in order to bring them into line with the standards of the European Union. But an increasing amount of time is also used to enforce decisions made by international organizations or in conferences where Norway has been a part.

European Economic Area

In the 1990s a treaty between the European Free Trade Association, EFTA, and the European Union, EU, created the European Economic Area, EEA. This clearly has been the most important "fourth-level" institution in its effects on Norwegian governance. In substance, it is the most far-reaching international agreement entered into by the Norwegian state.[48] During the first years after it came into effect in 1993, about 15,000 pages of Community (EU) rules were adopted into Norwegian law.[49] As a treaty it was a hybrid arrangement, trying to square the fact that formally it is an agreement between sovereign nations, but in reality it is an EU supranational arrangement, where Norway is not a member. Norwegian authorities are only allowed to influence the EU decisionmaking process by participating in the preparation of new rules with experts and at hearings, but they cannot participate in the final decisionmaking. However, these EU decisions become binding for Norway through the EEA—although the Norwegian authorities, in principle, could veto the decision afterward.[50] This is only likely to happen in issues of very high national significance.

The EEA agreement gave Norwegian industry full access to EU's single market—agriculture and fisheries were kept outside the treaty as were policies on tariffs and taxation (see Chapter 5). Norway had to accept all existing EU regulations of the free market. Enforcement was mainly left to national administrative institutions. The departments have, on the one hand, the main responsibility to apply EEA rules within their fields. On the other hand, they have the task of influencing the EU administration when new rules are prepared. Departmental work is here organized at three levels: the special committees on particular substantive areas, the coordinating cross-departmental committee headed by a foreign office representative, and the delegation to represent Norway within EFTA and the EEA.

The traditional distinction between foreign and internal policy is fairly blurred within this structure. By connecting to this "fourth level," the bureaucrats are also given a more important role in the de facto lawmaking relative to the politicians than they have in the non-EEA fields. In certain questions, such as subsidies and large public procurement projects, the central civil service also has increased its power to influence and direct the activities of municipalities and counties.[51]

New legislation on the single market comes mostly from the EU. The Norwegian Storting, in practice, has only the option to accept. The government consults the parliament through a special committee based in the foreign relations committee supplemented by the six Storting delegates to the EEA parliamentary committee.

Personnel from Norway, Iceland, and Liechtenstein man the EFTA institutions within the EEA arrangement. After one year, the old EFTA members—Austria, Sweden, and Finland—joined the EU, while the Swiss turned down the EEA agreement in a referendum. Coordination between the EFTA and the EU takes place through a two-pillar arrangement. The EU side is made up by the existing EU institutions, and the EFTA has created a (much smaller) pillar with a general committee, a surveillance organization, and a judiciary. Together with the matching institutions on the EU side, the three make up the central EEA institutions. In addition there is a parliamentary committee as well as a committee for the main actors in the labor market.

The EFTA surveillance organization is located in Brussels. Its job is to observe that the obligations incurred by the EFTA countries are not violated. It can summon the national authorities before the EFTA court and also issue instructions directly to Norwegian companies, directing them to observe the EEA rules on free competition. The EFTA judiciary is bound by the EU judiciary's interpretation of EU law made prior to the treaty. This was done to harmonize the single market regulations at work. The political problem, however, was and still is that the EU judgments made after the treaty could not be made part of the treaty itself without making the EFTA countries legally subordinated to the EU.[52]

The complex institutional structure of the EEA has not been tried in a crisis situation. If Norway vetoes an EU regulation—which it has so far not done—the EU is free to retaliate by withdrawing from parts of the EEA arrangement; that is, in practice it may ultimately exclude Norway from the single market.

Constitutionally as well as politically, the treaty created a difficult situation.[53] Norwegian voters said no to EU membership while the dominant political and economic cadres wanted and still want as close an integration into the EU system as possible. In practice, Norway will be bound by decisions that it cannot participate much in making. Regularly, new EEA laws are adopted without much internal preparation or debate in Norway or in parliament for that matter. In the spring of 1998, the surveillance organization ruled illegal the traditional investment support given to industry in Northern Norway. This traditional part of Norwegian district policy was seen as distorting the operation of the free market, and the system had to be changed. There is, in other words, no doubt that the fourth level of government in the shape of the EFTA/EEA institutions directly affects policies in the internal arena, and in this latter case it also bypassed both the Norwegian executive and the parliament.

Other Intergovernmental Cooperation

The EEA institutions are unique but obviously not the only international "regime" affecting Norwegian public policy. Other important intergovernmental organizations of which Norway is a member or treaties to which Norway is a party do not, however, have the elements of supranationality and/or one-sided adjustment that are found in the EEA treaty. Through international agreements among national governments, Norway is integrated into a large web of obligations, which legally and politically play an important part in shaping internal policies and laws. This ranges from the European Convention on Human Rights through membership in the NATO alliance to the 1997 agreement in Kyoto for reduction in the emission of greenhouse gasses. The latter agreement has recently fueled the Norwegian debate on energy questions in general and, in particular, discussion concerning a bid to build two new gas-based electricity plants on the West Coast. The issue threatened the voter support of the Labor Party in the Storting election in 1997, and the decision was postponed by the Labor government until after the election. In March 2000 it forced the center government out of office. I shall return to this issue in Chapter 8.

Norway's NATO membership is illustrative of these institutional linkages between the national and the international arenas. In effect, NATO sets national guidelines for military strategies and for levels of defense spending and gives strong incentives for particular priorities in Norway's own infrastructure programs. In terms of money, Norway—bordering the former Soviet Union and with a long North Atlantic coastline—receives significantly more than it puts into the NATO coffer. Making an impact within the NATO institutions—and in particular on the United States and other supportive allies such as the United Kingdom and, later, Germany—has been crucial to all Norwegian governments. Decisions made by NATO obviously are of central importance to the government's own economic, defense, and security policies. In 1948–1949, the very issue of NATO membership was about even more important issues: It was a choice between freedom and democracy, on the one hand, and submission and dictatorship, on the other.

Conclusion

Norway is a parliamentary democracy with regular national and local elections. It is also a constitutional monarchy, but for all practical purposes, the monarch is without political power. The parliament is the highest political authority with four main tasks: to give the country a government, to control the actions of that government, to provide new laws, and to decide the state's budget. The government has to leave office if met by a vote of no confidence in parliament. In daily affairs, however, the government has the political initiative and also has formidable administrative resources at its disposal.

Local politics has, since the 1840s, had a strong position in the system of governance in Norway. The municipality is led by an elected council and headed by a board composed in proportion to electoral strength. There is also a county level, which is a more recent construction. The county council is also popularly elected, but it does not enjoy the same popular support as the municipalities. The symbolic creation of a Sami Assembly gives the small ethnic minority with its roots in North Norway a political instrument at their disposal—so far used only to advise other public authorities.

The institutions found at the international level bind as well as guide the public policies of the Norwegian state. The ties are numerous and similar to what can be found in most other industrially advanced nations. The EEA agreement between the EFTA and the EU, in particular, has both precise and wide-ranging implications for public policies. This means that the "democratic deficit" of the EU countries—meaning the lack of electoral control of EU policies—is not exclusively an EU problem but also an endemic part of the EEA treaty.

These four levels of political institutions are central in shaping public politics in Norway. They have been the focus of some constitutional debates. From time to time, there is a call for a new constitution. The argument is that Norway needs an updated constitution that both accurately describes and usefully prescribes an institutional structure fitting our time. Parties and parliamentarians generally do not see the point, however. There is often acknowledged a need for minor adjustments, but rarely for a major overhaul. The politicians prefer to interpret the old constitution as they move along instead of embarking on the uncertain option of writing a new one. In operative practice, the Norwegian written constitution therefore does not differ that much from the unwritten constitution of Britain. But the Norwegian Storting would have to have a two-thirds majority to adopt a new clause, whereas the British parliament would have to wait until a new practice had settled.

Notes

1. Francis Sejersted, "From Liberal Constitutionalism to Corporate Pluralism," in Jon Elster and Rune Slagstad, eds., *Constitutionalism and Democracy* (Cambridge: Cambridge University Press, 1988), pp. 131–153.

2. Gudmund Hernes, "Hva styrer styrerne?" in Gudmund Hernes, *Økonomisk organisering* (Oslo: Universitetsforlaget, n.d.), p. 17. Also printed in *Samtiden*, no. 1, 1980.

3. See, for example, Torkel Opsal, "The Changing System of Social Values and the Written Constitution," in *The Role of the Constitution in a Changing Society. Joint Polish-Norwegian conference, Oslo, 14–16 May 1991*, published by the Norwegian Academy of Science and Letters, Oslo 1991, pp. 22–33, especially p. 29, or Johs. Andenæs, *Statsforfatningen i Norge*, 7th ed. (Oslo: Tano, 1990), pp. 33–34. For the constitution itself, see Mads T. Andenæs and Ingeborg Wilberg, *The Constitution of Norway: A Commentary* (Oslo: Universitetsforlaget, 1987).

4. Opsahl, "The Changing System."

5. Ibid., p. 30.

6. Eivind Smith, *Høyesterett og Folkestyret* (Oslo: Universitetsforlaget, 1993).

7. The issue was more complex than presented here because the discussion was also over which paragraphs were relevant for the Storting when adopting membership in the EU, but that is not the point here. See, for example, Thomas C. Wyller, *Skal folket bestemme? Folkeavstemning som politisk prosess* (Oslo: Universitetsforlaget, 1992).

8. This means that the parties' number of votes (at the constituency level) first is divided by 1.4 before the largest party is given the first seat. Then the parties' votes are divided by 3, 5, 7, etc., as a party list is given additional seats.

9. Henry Valen, "The Recruitment of Parliamentary Nominees in Norway," *Scandinavian Political Studies* 1 (1966): 121–166; Ottar Hellevik, *Stortinget: En sosial elite?* (Oslo: Pax Forlag, 1969); Hanne Marthe Narud and Henry Valen, "Does Background Matter?" in Peter Esaiasson and Knut Heidar, eds., *Beyond Congress and Westminster: The Nordic Experience* (Columbus: Ohio State University Press, 2000).

10. Narud and Valen, "Does Background Matter?"

11. Ibid; 63 percent of MPs had spent at least some years at college/university levels, compared to 24 percent of voters.

12. Narud and Valen, "Does Background Matter?"; Johan P. Olsen, *Organized Democracy, Political Institutions in a Welfare State: The Case of Norway* (Oslo: Universitetsforlaget, 1983).

13. Only if the two chambers do not agree (which almost never happens) is the proposed law discussed in the Storting as a whole.

14. The king has little influence outside some general moral influence; the monarchy has in the past played an important role in emergency situations, such as during World War II.

15. For a presentation and discussion, see Gudmund Hernes and Kristine Nergaard, *Oss I Mellom* (Oslo: FAFO, 1989), especially chapters 5, 6, and 7.

16. Committee assignments are decided in negotiations among the parties.

17. Harald Espeli, *Lobbyvirksomhet på Stortinget* (Oslo: Tano, 1999).

18. See the next chapter for the creation and the importance of party programs in Norwegian politics.

19. Torben Jensen, "Party Cohesion and Cooperation Across Party Lines in Nordic Parliamentary Parties," in Esaiasson and Heidar, eds., *Beyond Congress and Westminster: The Nordic Experience.* The Rice Index of party cohesion is obtained by dividing the number of votes cast by the majority of each party on a roll call by the total number of party MPs who voted and converting to a scale from 0 to 100 (by subtracting 50 from the percentage and multiplying by 2), the starting point being the assumption that a fifty-fifty split in a party signifies zero cohesion.

20. When the issue is covered by the party program, the MP who has explicitly stated his or her disagreement on a particular issue before the election may dissent from the party line in parliament.

21. Hilmar Rommetvedt, "Stortinget: Fra konsensus til konflikt," *Norsk Statsvitenskapelig Tidsskrift* 4 (1988):5–22.

22. This disregards the MPs' fairly ineffectual right to table so-called "private bills."

23. Note the historian Jens Arup Seip's expression that the Storting was in exile from Elverum (when the government fled the country in 1940) until Kings Bay (when the government fell on a "no confidence" motion in 1963; see his book *Fra embedsmannsstat til ettpartistat og andre essays* (Oslo: Universitetsforlaget, 1963).

24. Knut Heidar et al., "Nordic Parliamentary Design: Five Most Similar Systems?" in Esaiasson and Heidar, eds., *Beyond Congress and Westminster: The Nordic Experience.*

25. From 3 years 8 months before 1971 to 2 years 1 month after 1971. See Knut Heidar, "Norway: Party Competition and System Change," in Peter Mair and Gordon Smith, eds., *Understanding Party System Change in Western Europe* (London: Frank Cass, 1990).

26. The state secretary is the political deputy of the minister but cannot meet on his or her behalf in parliament.

27. Olsen, *Organized Democracy*, p. 81.

28. Hege Skjeie, *Vanens makt. Styringstradisjoner i Arbeiderpartiet* (Oslo: Ad Notam, 1999).

29. Hege Skjeie "The Uneven Advance of Norwegian Women," *New Left Review* 187 (1991):79–102.

30. Olsen, *Organized Democracy*, pp. 93–94.

31. Kjell A. Eliassen, "Rekrutteringen til Stortinget og regjeringen, 1945–1985," in Trond Nordby, ed., *Stortinget og regjeringen, 1945–1985.* Institusjoner – Rekruttering (Oslo: Kunnskapsforlaget, 1985).

32. Statskonsult, *Statråden som departementsleder*, report, 1997; and "Minister eller byråkrat," *Aftenposten,* 11 November 1997 (morgennummer), p. 31.

33. "Minister eller byråkrat," *Aftenposten,* 11 November 1997.

34. For example, the requirement that the minister of church affairs needs to be a church member.

35. Tom Christensen and Morten Egeberg, "Sentraladministrasjonen: En oversikt over trekk ved departementer og direktorater," in Tom Christensen and Morten Egeberg, eds., *Forvaltningskunnskap* (Oslo: Tano, 1997).

36. Ibid.

37. Ibid., p. 89. Estimates of the number of directorates depends on how they are defined.

38. See Helge O. Larsen, "Kommunene som forvaltnings- og selvstyreorgan," in Tom Christensen and Morten Egeberg, eds., *Forvaltningskunnskap* (Oslo: Tano, 1997), p. 220.

39. The number of employees increased by 32 percent in only the six years between 1986 and 1992; see Larsen, "Kommunene som forvaltnings- og selvstyreorgan," p. 242. The figure includes teachers in primary schools.

40. See Ottar Hellevik and Tor Bjørklund, "Velgerne og kvinnerepresentasjon," in Nina C. Raaum, ed., *Kjønn og politikk* (Oslo: Tano, 1995).

41. See Larsen, "Kommunene som forvaltnings- og selvstyreorgan."

42. Trond Fevolden, "Fylkeskommunen – fra hjelpeorgan til selvstendig forvaltningsnivå," in Tom Christensen and Morten Egeberg, eds., *Forvaltningskunnskap* (Oslo: Tano, 1997), p. 269.

43. This was a convention of the International Labor Organization (ILO) under the United Nations.

44. Morten Egeberg, "The Fourth Level of Government: On the Standardization of Public Policy Within International Regions," *Scandinavian Political Studies* 3 (1980):235–248.

45. Morten Egeberg and Jarle Trondal, "Innenriksforvaltningens og den offentlige politikens internasjonalisering," in Tom Christensen and Morten Egeberg, eds., *Forvaltningskunnskap* (Oslo: Tano, 1997), p. 339.

46. Johs. Andenæs, *Statsforvaltningen i Norge*, 8th ed. (Oslo:Tano, 1998), p. 245.

47. Egeberg and Trondal, "Innenriksforvaltningens og den offentlige politikens internasjonalisering," p. 340.

48. Rolf Tamnes, *Oljealder, 1965–1995*, vol. 6 of *Norsk utenrikspolitiske historie* (Oslo: Universitetsforlaget, 1997), p. 233.

49. Fredrik Sejersted, "The Norwegian Parliament and European Integration: Reflections from Medium-Speed Europe," in E. Smith, ed., *National Parliaments as Cornerstones of European Integration* (London: Kluwer Law International, 1996), p. 133.

50. Ibid.; and Torstein Eckhoff and Eivind Smith, *Forvaltningsrett*, 6th ed., (Oslo: Tano, 1997), pp. 653–654.

51. Eckhoff and Smith, *Forvaltningsrett*, pp. 131–132.

52. Ibid., pp. 656–659.

53. See Dag Harald Claes and Bent Sofus Tranøy, eds., *Utenfor, annerledes og suveren? Norge under EØS-avtalen* (Oslo: Fagbokforlaget, 1999).

4

Political Forces and Political Participation

The survival of democratic pluralism may depend as much on provisions for effective channels of opposition and protest within the private associations and the corporate bodies as on the chances for a regular alternation of governments at the top.

—*Stein Rokkan*

The political parties are the traditional instruments of mobilization and citizen influence in Norwegian politics. Operating in the "numerical channel" of electoral politics—where the number of votes count—the parties present candidates for elections and issue programs for public policies. The parties originated as products of civil society but have increasingly been acknowledged and supported by the state. In the constitution the parties are today mentioned in two paragraphs, although in fairly immaterial ways, dealing with the election of representatives to parliament.[1] The parties are central, however, in the Election Act, and the parties receive substantial public subsidies.

There are other actors that seek to support or oppose the parties at the input side of the political system. Private interest organizations work in support of everything from the protection of the environment to the protection of chemical industries. These actors attempt to influence the departments through the "corporate channel"—where general social importance and material resources count—and lobby the politicians in government and in the representative assemblies.

The third set of actors working to influence public decisionmaking are the political action committees (PACs). Although these are not always easy to separate from parties or organizations, they direct their activities toward the "media channel," trying to raise debate about an issue. Their strategy is to put political pressure on politicians and bureaucrats. Organizationally, they are by and large also less stable. The PAC's major weapon is the ability to swing mass opinion—which of course is not foreign to party activists or to the secretariats of the interest organizations.

In this chapter I first present the general political profile of Norwegian political parties. Second, I turn to the way these parties select their candidates for political office and, third, the way they interact, in particular when fighting for a position in government. In the fourth part I turn to alternative ways of influencing public policies—through the private interest organizations and the PACs. Fifth, I look at the voters and the ways and degrees to which ordinary citizens take part in political activities. In the last part I turn to the two national referenda on the question of Norwegian membership in the European Communities, later the European Union. These campaigns are both extraordinary compared to "routine" politics and bring out the ways politics is handled when taken outside the ordinary institutional context of Norwegian politics.

The Political Parties

Since the introduction of parliamentarism in 1884, political parties have been the main actors in Norwegian politics. Parties have organized political activists and supporters through formal membership organizations. They have trained politicians and structured the mass vote as well as the vote in representative assemblies. Politics in Norway is by and large *party* politics—individual politicians either rise through the parties or with the help of parties. Politicians depend almost entirely on their party for future political careers. They must in general support the policies of the party to which they belong, although they, of course, may advocate changes in those policies inside the party if they so wish. National politicians changing party affiliation are extremely rare.

In Chapter 2 we discussed the main political cleavages in Norwegian politics. Most parties are political coalitions in the sense that they encompass more than one of these cleavages. The left-right cleavage alone presents a much too simple picture to do justice to Norwegian party politics. The Labor Party, for example, is generally to the left in matters involving the economic role of the state in society. But Labor has also been on the restrictive side in the issue of liberalizing public policies on the sale of alcohol and pursued an active policy of economic transfers to the districts. Most parties, however, stand out more distinctly on one or two of these cleavages. The left-right cleavage is still the most important one in defining the major battleground of Norwegian politics—both in competing for voters and in positioning the party for governmental power. In broad terms, the Labor and the Socialist Left parties have been to the left; the Center, the Christian, and the Liberal parties have been in the middle; and the Conservative and the Progress parties have been on the right. The electoral support of these parties and their presence in parliament is shown for selected years in Tables 4.1 and 4.2, and their government experience is shown in Table 4.3.

TABLE 4.1 Party share of the vote at parliamentarian elections (%), selected years 1945–1997

Party	1945	1953	1961	1969	1973	1981	1985	1989	1993	1997
Red Electoral Alliance[1]	-	-	-	-	0.4	0.7	0.6	0.8	1.1	1.7
Communist Party	11.9	5.1	2.9	1.0	-	0.3	0.2	-	-	0.1
Socialist Left Party[2]	-	-	2.4	3.5	11.2	4.9	5.5	10.1	7.9	6.0
Labor	41.0	46.7	46.8	46.5	35.3	37.2	40.8	34.3	36.9	35.0
Liberals	13.8	10.0	8.8	9.4	3.5	3.9	3.1	3.2	3.6	4.5
Liberal Peoples Party[3]	-	-	-	-	3.4	0.5	0.5	-	-	-
Center Party[4]	8.0	9.1	9.4	10.5	11.0	6.7	6.6	6.5	16.7	7.9
Christian People's Party	7.9	10.5	9.6	9.4	12.3	9.4	8.3	8.5	7.9	13.7
Conservative	17.0	18.6	20.0	19.6	17.4	31.7	30.4	22.2	17.0	14.3
Progress Party[5]	-	-	-	-	5.0	4.5	3.7	13.0	6.3	15.3
Others	0.3	0.0	0.2	0.1	0.5	0.1	0.4	1.4	2.6	1.5
Turnout	76.4	79.3	79.1	83.8	80.2	83.2	84.0	83.2	75.8	78.0

[1] In 1989 the "County lists for Environment and Solidarity".
[2] Socialist People's Party until 1973. In 1973 Socialist Electoral Alliance including. among others. the Communist Party.
[3] Called "The New People's Party" until 1980. Reunited with the Liberals in 1988.
[4] Farmers' Party until 1959.
[5] "Anders Langes Party" until 1977.
SOURCE: Knut Heidar and Einar Berntzen Vesteuropeisk politikk (Oslo: Universitetsforlaget, 1998) p. 53, and *Historical Statistics 1994* (Oslo: Statistics Norway. 1995)

TABLE 4.2 Party share of Storting representatives (%), selected years 1945–1997

Party	1945	1953	1961	1969	1973	1981	1985	1989	1993	1997
Communist Party	7.3	2.0	0.0	0.0	-	0.0	0.0	-	-	0.0
Socialist Left Party	-	-	1.3	0.0	10.3	2.6	3.8	10.3	7.9	5.5
Labor	50.7	51.3	49.3	49.3	40.0	42.6	45.2	38.2	40.6	39.4
Liberals	13.3	10.0	9.3	8.7	1.3	1.3	0.0	0.0	0.6	3.6
Liberal Peoples Party	-	-	-	-	0.6	0.0	0.0	-	-	-
Center Party	6.7	9.3	10.7	13.3	13.5	7.1	7.6	6.7	19.4	6.7
Christian People's Party	5.3	9.3	10.0	9.3	12.9	9.7	10.2	8.5	7.9	15.2
Conservative	16.7	18.0	19.3	19.3	18.7	34.2	31.8	22.4	17.0	13.9
Progress Party	-	-	-	-	2.6	2.6	1.3	13.3	6.0	15.2
Others	0.0	0.0	0.0	0.0	0.0	0.0	0.0	0.6	0.6	0.6
Number of representatives in Stortinget	150	150	150	150	155	155	157	165	165	165

SOURCE: Knut Heidar and Einar Berntzen, Vesteuropeisk politikk (Oslo: Universitetsforlaget, 1998) p. 55.

TABLE 4.3   Governments and party composition 1969–2000

Year	1969	1971	1972	1973	1976	1977
Month	Sept.	Mars	Oct.	Oct.	Jan.	Sept.
Prime Minister	Borten	Bratteli	Korvald	Bratteli	Nordli	Nordli
PM's party	C	Lab.	Chr.	Lab.	Lab.	Lab.
Left–right position[a]	C-R	L	C	L	L	L
Conservative	6	-	-	-	-	-
Christian People's Party	3	-	4	-	-	-
Center Party	3	-	6	-	-	-
Liberals	3	-	5	-	-	-
Labor	-	15	-	15	16	16
Number of ministers	15	15	15	15	16	16
Gov't share of MPs in parliament (%)	50	49	26	40	40	49

Year	1981	1981	1983	1985	1986	1989
Month	Feb.	Oct.	June	Oct.	May	Oct.
Prime Minister	Brundtland	Willoch	Willoch	Willoch	Brundtland	Syse
PM's party	Lab.	Cons.	Cons.	Cons.	Lab	Cons.
Left-right position	L	R	C-R	C-R	L	C-R
Conservative	-	17	11	10	-	9
Christian	-	-	4	4	-	5
Center	-	-	3	4	-	5
Liberals	-	-	-	-	-	-
Labor	17	-	-	-	18	-
Number of ministers	17	17	18	18	18	19
Gov't share of MPs in parliament (%)	49	34	51	49	45	37

Year	1990	1993	1996	1997	2000
Month	Nov.	Oct.	Oct.	Oct.	Mar.
Prime Minister	Brundtland	Brundtland	Jagland	Bondevik	Stoltenberg
PM's party	Lab.	Lab.	Lab.	Christ.	Lab.
Left-right position	L	L	L	C	L
Conservative	-	-	-	-	-
Christian	-	-	-	9	-
Center	-	-	-	6	-
Liberals	-	-	-	4	-
Labor	19	19	19	-	19
Number of ministers	19	19	19	19	19
Gov't share of MPs in parliament (%)	38	41	41	25	39

1. L = left, C = center, R = right.
SOURCE: Knut Heidar and Einar Berntzen, Vesteuropeisk politikk, Oslo: Universitetsforlaget, 1998, p. 55.

Labor

The Labor Party (Arbeiderpartiet) is today a mildly "left of center" party and has been the largest political party in Norway since 1927. Trade union activists founded it more than a century ago in 1887 with links to the international labor movement, particularly in Germany and Denmark. In 1890, the party elected a Danish émigré as party leader. Labor won its first Storting representatives in 1903, and a parliamentary breakthrough came after the question of national independence had been settled in 1905. Labor at the time combined political demands for practical improvements for the workers with a socialist ideology.

The rapid industrialization before World War I, the turbulence created by the war itself, and the Russian Revolution, in particular, radicalized both workers and party members. The schism in the international socialist movement led to a party split in Norway. A close majority at the congress decided that the party would follow the Komintern, the Moscow International, in 1919. The revolutionary interlude was short, however, and Labor left the communist movement four years later. In 1927, they reunited with the reformist social democrats, and the party formed its first, rather short-lived government in 1928. In 1935, Labor entered government a second time, and it was to last for thirty years, interrupted by five years of executive exile in London during World War II.

Labor has never entered a coalition government in peacetime. But because of its size it has remained the main governmental alternative in Norwegian politics since 1945. In the fifty years following 1945, Labor spent thirty-seven in office. During the 1950s and 1960s, the Labor Party pursued a reformist course—at least when compared to its more radical Komintern past—building a modern, industrial society. The party built the new welfare state on the foundation of a mixed economy. Private capital, including foreign investment, was crucial in building the new economy, but the policy was for the state to control commanding positions in major industries like iron and steel production. The party leader for most of this period was Einar Gerhardsen, who was chairman for twenty years and prime minister for about seventeen between 1945 and 1965. He also became—particularly in retrospect—a "father of the nation," a rock-solid captain who led the Norwegian nation safely through the rough waters of the cold war and into increasing prosperity.

The 1970s were turbulent years for Labor. The European issue split the party, and new issues like the environment added to the old left-right and cold war divisions within the party. There was also a shift of generations that weakened the party. Labor was traditionally a "mass party" with a high membership and a robust—the left-wing opposition would say "Leninist"—party culture. In 1981, Gro Harlam Brundtland took over both as party leader and as prime minister. She stayed on as a party leader until 1992 and held the position of prime minister on and off for ten years until 1996.

During the 1980s, Labor changed both organizationally and politically. Through a "modernization" drive, the party aimed at becoming more open and less dependent on closed "processes." The party was also more open to criticism of its own welfare state project (for example, its unintended effects). Public solutions to problems in society were not automatically considered best: Child nurseries needed private supplements not only for reasons of low capacity but also for improving services through competition. In the 1990s, the European Union issue returned to divide the party in the run-up to the new referendum in 1994. Within Labor, however, the issue was now handled much less controversially vis-à-vis the party minority fighting against membership.

The Conservative Party

The conservative "Right" party (Høyre) was founded as the instrument of the old upper class as represented by state officials and the merchant bourgeoisie. Their primary goals were to uphold the rule of law and to fight the political populist democracy of the Liberal Party. These state officials were thrown out of government in 1884 when parliamentarism was practiced in full for the first time. The Conservative Party returned to government office repeatedly between 1889 and 1928 but then had to wait until the 1960s before its next appearance (again, excepting the wartime coalition 1940–1945). Of the thirteen years the Conservative Party has been in government since 1961, eleven have been in coalition with the center parties.

The Conservative Party has been the party of the well-to-do, and in terms of their voters' social profile, it still is. Ideologically, it has a dual heritage from the paternalistic old state officials' culture, stressing the responsibilities of the state, and from the urban bourgeoisie, advocating a liberal market philosophy, individual responsibility, and limited state interference. The party was a fierce critic of the postwar "Labor Party State" with its state industry and increased taxes, which crippled private initiative. And the Conservatives did not appreciate Labor's emphasis on equality and redistribution through taxation.

The Conservative Party formed a one-party minority government from 1981 to 1983, which was at the time of the so-called "right wave" in Norwegian politics. Høyre increased its support from 17 percent in the 1973 election to 32 percent in 1981. In the years of "Thatcherism" and "Reaganomics," the ideological climate was favorable, and many voters were tired of red tape and the "nanny" tendencies of the "social democratic" state. Also, the party's organization opened up for more input from the districts, and the party's profile approached more of a "people's party." After the Conservatives left government in 1986, voter support dwindled, and in the 1993 election, it was back to 17 percent.

During these years, the party experienced a political squeeze between the increased competition from the "modernized" Labor on its left and the populist Progress Party on its right. The old "bourgeois bloc" crumbled in the 1990s, and with it went the old leadership role of the Conservative Party. The issue of EU membership gave the Conservatives few opportunities to present a distinct political profile to the electorate. If the party wanted Norway to join—and it very much did—it had to play second fiddle to the Labor Party. Changing the party leadership four times between 1985 and 1994 did not help either.

The Parties of the Center

The Norwegian Liberal Party (Venstre, "the Left") was founded as the party that succeeded in seizing power from the conservative right in the 1884 confrontation. Later the Liberal Party alternated with the Conservatives in government for more than forty years. The Liberal politicians were frequently in government, until Labor finally broke the "bourgeois" hegemony in 1935.[2] The Liberal Party mobilized the social and cultural forces in opposition to the "official's state"—in the peripheries to the south and the west, in the lay church movement, among the teetotalers, and among the users of New Norwegian. These groups made up a political coalition under the umbrella of a liberal ideology. The ideologues, however, were mostly to be found in the urban centers around the capital.

There were internal tensions between the different segments of this coalition opposing the officials' state, and some subsequently formed parties of their own. First, parts of the agrarian segment broke out to form the Farmers' Party in 1920.[3] In the early 1930s, the Christian People's Party was created by dissatisfied "lay-church" segments. The overall history of the Liberal Party after 1945 is one of electoral decline, and in 1972 the EU membership issue split the party. This contributed to making its parliamentary existence a matter of life or death in the 1980s and 1990s—in spite of a later party reunion. Although the Liberals in the first decades after 1945 captured around 10 percent of the vote, the party's highest count after 1970 occurred in the Storting elections of 1997 with a 4.5 percent vote. The Liberal Party was without representation in parliament for two periods from 1985 to 1993. During these years, the Liberals could not quite decide whether their party's "social-liberal" ideology was sufficiently liberal to give it a place in the bourgeois group of center-right parties or sufficiently social to make it a natural ally of the new Labor Party emerging in the 1980s. Having returned to its liberal heritage in the 1990s, the party again entered parliament and became a coalition party in the government of center parties formed after the 1997 election.

The Center Party (Senterpartiet) was named the Farmers' Party until 1959. Up until then, it literally was a party of farmers for farmers and their families. During the 1960s, the party's policies broadened to make a party in defense of rural and general "district" interests, electorally expanding into the periphery sectors of fisheries and small-scale industry. Nevertheless, as the farming population declined, the party's share of the vote went down, from about 14 percent in the interwar period to 8–10 percent after the war, and further declined to a low point in 1989 with 6.5 percent of the vote.

With the debates on EU membership in the early 1970s and 1990s, support for the party surged. In the view of many people voting against EU membership, the Center Party directed its "no" campaign with skill and leadership. At the 1993 election, the party polled 17 percent of the vote and became the second largest party in parliament. The Center Party continued to present itself as the party defending the interests of the districts, but at this election it also put much emphasis on the need to deepen national democracy (which was threatened by the EU and the bureaucrats in Brussels) and to defend the welfare state. The party vigorously claimed that the old left-right divide by now had become obsolete and distanced itself from one of its coalition partners, the Conservative Party. In 1990, the Center Party broke with the center-right coalition—led by a conservative prime minister—over the policies of EU rapprochement. Later the party claimed victory both in the 1994 EU referendum and when the three parties of the center (the Christians, the Center Party, and the Liberals) formed a coalition government in 1997. This "center government," they claimed, was a truly independent alternative, independent of the old left-right rivalries. In spite of these successes, however, the party lost most of its new-won votes at the 1997 election.

The Christian People's Party (Kristelig Folkeparti) was founded in 1933 and at first ran for election in only the West Coast counties. It became a national party after 1945. Originally, it was the party of the lay Christian movement; later it represented the broader, although decreasing, Christian segments in the Norwegian society. The party targeted the struggle against secular trends in a changing, modernizing society and, in particular, defended the place of religion and the Lutheran state church within the school system. When the abortion issue entered the agenda in the late 1960s, the Christian People's Party turned vigorously against a proposal to permit abortion on demand within the first twelve weeks of pregnancy. Such a law was adopted in 1978 after a long and bitter struggle. Labor had proposed a new abortion law in their 1969 program. Although all the other center-right parties had accepted it, the Christian People's Party refused to sit in the new conservative government in 1981: They would not be part of a government that administered an unacceptable abortion law. Two years later, however, they decided to join the government coalition in spite of the law, hastened by the Center Party, who had grown impatient with their close ally.

The Christian People's Party polled between 8 and 12 percent of the vote throughout most of the postwar period. At the 1997 election, however, they broke a downward trend by getting close to 14 percent—its best result ever—and the party became the second largest in the Storting (shared with the Progress Party). The party also won the prime minister in the new government, Kjell Magne Bondevik, a longtime MP and former party leader. The party leadership has tried to make the party more broadly based in terms of support and policies. Mr. Bondevik has made no secret of his wish to transform the party into the more Christian-democratic type, that is, more like the center-right parties on the European mainland—possibly more to the center than to the right, such as the Christian Democratic Appeal in the Netherlands.

Left and Right and Some Smaller Parties

The Socialist Left Party (Sosialistisk Venstreparti) was created in 1975 by a "left-of-Labor" merger. These parties had just successfully fought Norwegian membership in the European Communities at the 1972 referendum. The bulk of members and voters came from the former Socialist People's Party. This party had been created in 1961 to fight against the threat that nuclear arms might be placed on Norwegian territory and also against the "right-wing drift" of the Labor government. Although new forces joined the Socialist Left Party in 1975—from the old Communist Party and so-called "independent socialists"—the new party basically turned out to be a continuation of the old Socialist People's Party. Ideologically, the party was proclaimed a "third way" party[4]—that is, neither communist nor social democratic—and the party gained momentum from the leftward trends manifested particularly by the young (student) generation of the late 1960s.

During the 1970s and 1980s, the party made environmental protection part of its platform, transforming ideologically from a 1960s "new left" party toward a more "green" party in the 1980s. Organizationally, the party did not, however, adopt the extreme mode of grassroots decision-making and the political action strategy found, for example, in the German Greens. It still considers itself a socialist party advocating an active state in the development of the Norwegian society. Originating from an anti-cold-war platform in the 1960s and 1970s, however, the party has during the 1990s increasingly found itself in search of new policies.

The Progress Party (Fremskrittspartiet) entered Norwegian politics in 1973 on a low-tax, anti-state platform—inspired by a similar Danish populist revolt at the time. In 1978, the party elected Carl I. Hagen as its chairman, and he still serves in this position in 2000. During the 1980s, Hagen proved himself to be a very skillful media performer. At elections, the party profited from a broad-based voter resentment against politics and politicians, and the party played on popular sentiments against taxes, bureaucracy, and preferential treatment of groups like immigrants and welfare clients. Depending on the electoral issues in focus, the party has had a mixed fortune, with 13 percent of the vote in 1989 and 15 percent in 1997 as its best results. Because of Mr. Hagen's one-man performance on behalf of the party, its fate is very dependent on his ability to keep the party in the media and to hold its various segments together. In the early 1990s, the parliamentarian group split over the relative importance of classical liberalism and populist causes in party policies. But Mr. Hagen and the Progress Party kept the voters. In the autumn of 2000 the Progress Party surged in the opinion polls, making it the largest party in the country with close to 35 percent support. The reasons were resentment against the "traditional" parties and their unwillingness to use more of the "oil money" for the sick and the elderly—as well as not lowering the price on gasoline.

The old Communist Party (Norges Kommunistiske Parti), on the far left in Norwegian politics, was created when the Labor Party split in 1923. This was an old-style communist party with strong links to the Soviet regime. Its all-time high came just after World War II with 12 percent of the vote, but it soon dwindled due to the climate of cold war and internal feuding. Since 1961, the Communist Party has not won representation in the Storting. In the 1993 election, another far-left representative from the tiny Marxist-Leninist party Red Electoral Alliance (Rød Valgallianse) was elected from the capital. His election was, however, mostly a personal tribute, since the candidate had been active in uncovering a financial scandal within the municipal authorities.

Twice in the postwar period special county lists have managed to get their candidates elected to parliament. It happened the first time in 1989, when a People's Action Movement favoring the northernmost county, Finmark, succeeded. The second time was in 1997, when a whaling skipper, resenting the restriction on whaling and seal hunting, organized the Coastal Party in the Nordland county and managed to get elected to the Storting.

Candidate Selection and Party Change

A major task of Norwegian political parties is to select candidates to run for election. For parliamentary elections, most parties follow the standards set out in the Act of Candidate Nominations of 1920, which now is a part of the Election Act. With the Norwegian proportional election system, candidates do not run as individuals but as party candidates on a party list. The voters, as such, are not consulted at any stage in the making of the party list; formal selection takes place within the party organizations. The procedures required by the law are optional for the parties, but most do follow them as this allows them public financial support and adds political legitimacy.

In the parties, nominations take place at the constituency level, that is, the county, in general parliamentary elections. Each party conducts a completely separate nomination process, and only party members are eligible for a place on the party list. Since 1974, the nomination meetings have been open to the public and, in practice, to the press.[5] A few months before the meeting, a party committee is appointed, and this committee first consults the local party branches about potential candidates. This is the stage of certifying candidates. The actual candidate selection begins when the committee presents a proposal to the local parties in which the candidates have been listed in order of priority. The local branches then present their comments on the committee's priorities. The debate is not confined to the organization alone. Party activists and others often turn to the media, making the debate fairly broad-based. Nominations do not exclusively take place in the smoke-filled back rooms with only the party elite present. However, only a small percentage of the voters are involved. Altogether about 5 percent of the voters take part in the party nominations.[6] On election day, the voters will in practice not be able to select individual candidates; they can only accept or reject the party list. But voter reactions are nevertheless anticipated and used in the party debate for or against prospective candidates. In the end, a county nomination meeting with elected representatives from the various party branches decides the final list.

In putting together the list, several candidate characteristics are considered. Incumbency is clearly important, but not decisive. If the acting representative does not enjoy the confidence of his or her county party, then he or she cannot be certain of renomination. The county parties also try to balance the ticket between representatives of relevant groups in order to inspire voters' confidence. They must consider a number of criteria: the different geographical parts of the county, gender, affiliation to special organizations like trade unions or religious groups, as well as occupation and age. Lastly, the ticket also has to be balanced in view of the various political tendencies within the party. Individual professional abilities and media skills are, of course, also important factors. Although these criteria to some degree are important in all parties, their relative value may vary.

Decline of Parties?

Are political parties in decline in Norway? Several divergent trends in party development make the answer to this question multifaceted. Overall membership is in decline. Labor had over 200,000 members registered in 1950, including a large number of collectively affiliated trade union members. In 1997, the collective membership was about to be abolished, and the party had registered 68,000 members in their computerized database. The party lost more than 100,000 members between 1986 and 1996. The other party with a fairly large membership, the Conservative Party, reached its peak in membership much later. In 1982, they registered 176,000 members, which was a little more than Labor had at the time. Since the late 1980s, however, membership decline in the Conservative Party has been particularly rapid, from 171,000 members in 1987 to 71,000 in 1997. Also the Center and Christian parties have experienced declining membership during the past decade, but not of the magnitude found in the Labor and Conservative parties. In spite of this development, political legitimacy within most parties still rests with the organization. Legitimate policies and leadership derives from the local and regional party units, and the final authority rests with the decisions made at the yearly or biannual party congresses. At these congresses the county delegates decide the political programs and elect the party leadership.

Have the party organizations run out of steam? Membership has declined, and studies indicate that in the early 1990s only one member in five was active within the party.[7] The parties have for some time complained that it is difficult to get the ordinary members to turn out for political meetings and that a few enthusiasts mostly run local organizations. The parties uses many resources to recruit personnel for public offices, particularly at the local level, and less effort goes into generating political study groups and discussions. A majority of the party members rarely or never take part in internal political debates.[8] The flip side to this change is that at the central level, Norwegian parties today are probably better equipped and more professionally staffed than at any time before. The public subsidy given to parties, which took effect in the early 1970s, gave them a financial basis to employ party members and sympathizers with organizational and media qualifications. The public subsidy is roughly proportional to the number of votes the parties get at parliamentary elections and makes up between 40 and 50 percent of the central party budgets.[9] These two developments—the decline of membership involvement and the rise of professionalism—have changed the character of the parties rather than setting them on a course of general "decline." In varying degrees, the parties have moved in the direction of becoming more professional political agencies.

The Party System and the Government Alternatives

The Norwegian party system in the twentieth century has been *a multi-party system*. In the half-century that has passed since 1945, there have never been fewer than five political parties present in the Storting, and in two terms there were MPs from eight parties represented. Labor has throughout this half-century been the dominant party and has also been the most frequent party in government. The multiparty system has been biased in the sense that Labor often has been about twice as large as the second largest party in the Storting—until 1993 the Conservative Party. Labor has been sufficiently strong not to need to cooperate with other parties in a coalition government.

The first Labor government to last more than a few weeks (in 1935) had the parliamentary support of the Farmers' Party. But from 1945 to 1961 Labor enjoyed a majority on its own. As mentioned earlier, the leader of the party's parliamentary group put the situation rather bluntly during a debate in the late 1950s: No change of government can take place, he argued, unless the party itself wanted a change. Or as the opposition saw it at the time, parliamentarism was suspended. This was the period when the Labor regime met a rather weak and diffuse opposition. The major opposition parties could not agree on a unified, alternative platform. The parties of the center—the Liberals, the Center Party, and the Christians—were suspicious of the Conservative Party, which they considered too right-wing. Gradually, however, the Conservatives relaxed their policies or indicated a willingness to compromise on the issues most important to the center.

As part of a deliberate strategy to build an alternative bloc of coalitionable parties, the Conservatives, under the leadership of John Lyng, a lawyer, managed to form a government in 1963. The issue triggering the short-lived Lyng government was the Labor government's handling of a public report investigating a mining accident in a state-owned company. Labor was in the end ousted because the new left-wing Socialist People's Party decided to vote against the government as a protest against its "arrogance of power." The new government lasted three weeks, but it was the harbinger of the later and more long-lived "bourgeois" coalition government of 1965–1971. From the early 1960s to 1971—when that coalition broke down—there was a fairly clear-cut two-bloc competition for power in Norwegian politics.

This two-bloc system was suspended when the European Communities (EC) membership issue was put to a referendum in 1972. The debate brought into the open the policy areas where the coalition parties had the most divergent policies. After the voters said no to EC membership, the three parties of the center—the Center Party, the Christians, and parts of the Liberal Party—were put in charge of negotiating a free trade agreement. Five years later, however, at the Storting election of 1977, the "two-bloc" alternative was back in business. When the Conservatives formed their minority government on their own in 1981, it was not the EC issue that kept the parties of the center away but the Christian People's Party's restrictive views on women's right to abortion. Between 1977 and 1990, when the last center-right coalition broke down, the two-bloc system was again operating.

The "no-to-EC" center coalition government of 1972 was, however, a harbinger of later events. Following the breakdown of the center-right coalition in 1990—again over an issue related to the EC, now the EU—the Center Party in particular argued that the "old" two-bloc division of Norwegian politics along the left-right dimension was no longer a valid description of the political realities. The Center Party in particular argued that the center coalition was a third alternative,·confronting both Labor and the Conservatives in questions of local democracy, green policies, and support for rural districts against the urban centers.

The minority coalition government formed by the three parties of the center after the 1997 election was based on a premise of "bloc neutrality." Its aim was to stay independent of the left and right parties in parliament. No doubt the debate over the European question and the EU referendum in 1994 again contributed to the downfall of the traditional center-right coalition alternative. It must be added, though, that the strong position of the populist right—in the shape of the Progress Party—contributed to making this multidimensional party landscape of the 1990s much more complex than in the old days. This increased complexity, combined with a more fluid, media-driven public debate, made political debate over issues less central, while the strategic games of the party spin doctors gained increased attention.

The Storting arena has at any rate become much more interesting to the media than it used to be. This is also because more of the decisionmaking process has been moved from the government to the parliament in recent years, particularly after the minority center government gained office in 1997. It culminated in the parliamentary debate in March of 2000 over the building of new gas-fired power plants, which led to the downfall of the government and the return to power of the Labor Party. The political flux, however, still takes place within the fairly narrowly defined frames of Norwegian consensus politics: for the EEA, for NATO, for a universalistic welfare state, and for a high-employment economy.

Channels of Influence and the Media Arena

Metaphors like "channels" and "arenas" are frequently used to describe the institutional settings and important meeting places in Norwegian politics. Stein Rokkan—in an article giving direction to much later research—argued in 1966 that Norwegian politics was a "two-tier system of decisionmaking" with an electoral, "numerical" channel of influence and an organizational, "corporate" channel of influence.[10] The crucial economic decisions, he argued, were rarely taken by the parties or in parliament, but over the bargaining table where public authorities met directly with the trade union leaders, the farmers, the fishermen, and the Employers Association.[11] That proposition was and still is debatable. Later research indicates that it is more likely that the major decisions affecting the state budgets, for example, are worked out with the Ministry of Finance, the government, and the parliament as central actors.[12] No doubt the main organizations in the private economic sector present significant input, but the claim—if interpreted in the strong sense—that the major economic decisions are made at the negotiating table in the "corporate channel" has not been substantiated by later research. The "law of anticipated reactions," however, informs us that these organizations may well have "blocking power" that other actors are forced to consider.

The weaker interpretation, however, that the organizations influence public decisionmaking has been corroborated. Research has confirmed the strong impact of organizations in Norwegian politics. Although Rokkan labeled it the corporate channel, this did not imply that the polity was "corporate" in the old sense, with organizations ordered hierarchically and exercising an organizational monopoly within their sector. To borrow some later terms, it was societal corporatism, not state corporatism.[13] Rokkan was talking about the organizations within a free, pluralist private sector, which connected with public authorities in order to make an impact on public policies. This partly takes place through negotiations over prices in regulated and protected industries like agriculture, fisheries, and health services. Partly, it is also done through public hearings over new regulations and laws covering the issues of interest to the organizations. Finally, these organizations are represented in a wide range of public commissions.

During the Labor regime that commenced after 1945, when the country was being rebuilt after the war, practical needs came together with the reigning "statist" social democratic ideology to create close ties within the corporate channel. The trade union movement and other important organizations—meaning organizations able to halt economic reconstruction—were all considered partners in a "new society" project. The employers, however, and the political right, in general, were by and large (at least in principle) opposed to intimate relations. Labor's new corporatism merged with Keynesian economics and old Soviet-inspired visions of a planned economy to create an intense public debate in the late 1940s and early 1950s. The debate led to Labor shelving its most ambitious plans (see Chapter 6). Nevertheless, during the early postwar period, the social democratic trade union movement was represented not only in an increasing number of corporate bodies but also in committees and boards within the general policy field. The unions were interested not only in wages but also educational and consumer policies. Today the central trade union association is represented in about one-fourth of all corporate state bodies at the national level.

The corporate channel, as such, has grown in depth and breadth during the twentieth century. The old view that private organizations were "interested parties" and thereby disqualified from taking part in public decisionmaking gradually gave way to the view that democracy meant that organizations affected by public policies had special rights in the process. The public authorities came to consider private organizations both useful and legitimate partners. With the development of an industrial society, the number of national organizations grew rapidly. In the early 1990s, roughly 2,400 national organizations claimed 17 million members (in a country with 4 million inhabitants).[14] They employed about 14,000 employees in their secretariats—a formidable army of lobbyists in a small country like Norway where about 3,500 people work in the central civil service. More than half the population is a member of at least one national organization, and about half of these organizations operate within the field of work and industry. And there are more such organizations at the regional and local levels.

Triggered by World War II and the need to coordinate and improvise in difficult times, the number of public committees at the national level increased steadily throughout the century. The organizations also became increasingly engaged. In the mid-1930s, the organizations were represented in about one-third of the permanent committees. This share rose to about one-half in the 1980s. Do they influence public policies? Surveys with the personnel involved—the organizational secretaries, their elected leaders, and the departmental bureaucrats—have found that the organizations in basic industries like trade unions and employers associations were considered particularly important in the decisionmaking process. During the 1980s and 1990s, however, the formal decisionmakers in the government and parliament again strengthened their position vis-à-vis the organizations, according to these surveys. This reflects the growing political sentiment of the early 1980s advocating pro-market policies and a clearer division between markets and politics. Political debate was then much influenced by international trends in the wake of Thatcherism and Reaganomics. The conservative/center-right governments of 1981–1986 attempted, for example, to cut down the number of private-public corporate bodies. The degree to which there has been a "de-corporation" of Norwegian politics during the latter decades, however, is an open question. For one thing, the discontinued corporate bodies were not generally among the most important ones.[15]

Political Action Committees

Organizational spokespersons often talk directly with public authorities through the corporate channel. Sometimes the organizations find acceptable solutions in a committee, through a public hearing. But sometimes there are not any institutionalized points of contact where discussions can take place, or there might just not be any organization around to contact and mobilize—at least not an organization with the "right" point of view. A group of concerned people may then more or less spontaneously organize a political campaign. The "action channel" is often both a supplement and an alternative to the numerical and the corporate channels as ways to influence public decisions.

Political actions have publicity as their main weapon. Public debate may bring home to the politicians that a particular policy position is widely and/or strongly held and that the next election might be affected. Media coverage puts pressure on both politicians and bureaucrats. Political actions are organized attempts to influence a particular issue, and their instruments may be petitions, boycotts, blockades, protest marches, "street theater," media appearances, and so forth.[16] Historically, they reflect the issues of the day as well as the main political cleavages. Political actions in Norway during the 1950s were marked by both the cultural conservatives' and the middle class's protests against the Labor regime, the new social democratic order. In 1947, close to 500,000 people signed a petition against the handout of contraceptives to the Norwegian military personnel posted in Germany. Four years later, there was a large protest against the use of a radical new language policy in the schools. More than 400,000 petitioned against the attempt to make a closer unity of the two official languages, the New Norwegian and the bokmål Norwegian. Parents were encouraged to "correct" the official schoolbooks used by their children. The largest petition came in 1965 against a proposed reduction in the hours scheduled to teach religion in primary schools.

During the 1960s, international issues like the threat of nuclear war and the Vietnam War triggered protest actions, and in the 1970s environmental issues became the central focus for political action committees. The demonstrations in 1979–1980 against the construction of a hydroelectric plant in Alta, a Sami community in North Norway, were rather unusual. This conflict not only was about environmental protection but also raised the issue of ethnic Sami rights in the area. Local people joined forces with demonstrators from other parts of Norway, among them students and academics, to block developers from entering the construction site. The police had to ship in reinforcements under enormous publicity, and there was an intense debate in the national media. Some members of the Sami population went on a hunger strike in front of parliament, and later a group of Sami women staged a "sit-in" at the prime minister's office. The issues of minority rights, environmental protection, and civil disobedience were all brought into the public debate.

In the 1970s there were also local actions over traffic, transportation, and city planning. The referendum on membership in the European Community in 1972 led to the organization of several PACs—for and against. Just as in the 1994 referendum, these were formidable, partly publicly financed political machines. In principle, they were fighting only one issue—EC/EU membership; but in practice this was an issue affecting most other policy areas, making the campaigns multi-issued. I describe the referendum campaigns in detail below.

Increasingly, political actions became a legitimate way of expressing political demands, as both the electoral system and the corporate structure were considered mechanisms that were too coarse-meshed to meet the democratic needs in all areas of public decisionmaking. Of course, objections were raised over the potentially disproportionate influence of angry minorities, but according to surveys in 1975 about half the voters had at least once taken part in a political action group.[17] Later studies show that the proportion having signed at least one PAC petition was 56 percent in 1981 and 61 percent in 1990.[18] However, research also shows that although these actions are widespread, this is not a pure and proper grassroots channel. The activists—just as in the other channels—are more likely to come from the higher socioeconomic status groups, and they are more active in political parties and interest organizations than the average voter. Action politics to some extent is "routine" politics with other means.

There are often diffuse lines among traditional politics through the parties, the search for influence through established interest organizations, and working in single-issue PACs. An example from the early 1950s debacle over the school language shows this: Formally, the interest organization representing the bokmål Norwegian language and the "Parents Action" group were separate organizations. But it was important to make them appear separate, because the first acted as a formal pressure group vis-à-vis the state and had to stay within the limits of acceptable conduct. In reality, however, the two were in close cooperation.[19] A more recent example is the environmental action group Bellona, founded in the 1980s to fight pollution. Originally, it specialized in staging spectacular protests against polluting industry by climbing chimneys and digging up toxic waste. During the 1990s, however, the group gradually developed contacts with industry and with the political administrative establishment; today Bellona is more like a professional consultant to the authorities (recently they have dealt with Russian authorities over the enormous problems of waste disposal and pollution in Northwest Russia). However, they still occasionally appear chained to construction machines staging a protest action at a building site.

The Media

The media have increasingly come to play a central part in the political process. By opening up the process of nomination to the public in the 1970s, the media also became a more central arena in internal party politics. The "medialization" of politics started long before, however, and the introduction of national television in the early 1960s proved crucial.[20] This brought the politicians as well as politics "home" to people to a degree newspapers and radio could not achieve. The highly dramatic change of government after the no-confidence vote in parliament in 1963—when no one knew in advance how the two decisive votes from the Socialist People's Party would fall—was probably the breakthrough for political television in Norway. During the 1960s, however, the one and only public channel transmitting to Norwegian viewers was not the active journalistic force we know today. The public channel televised debates but did not pursue themes and issues on the basis of journalistic criteria of relevance or importance to the viewers/voters.

The investigative and analytic type of journalism was pioneered in the newspapers.[21] There are about two hundred different newspapers published in Norway, and these appear from four to seven times a week. Their joint circulation is close to three million copies. This is among the highest in the world per capita. Norwegians were and still are large consumers of newspapers. The paper journalists have for a long time been actively pursuing and checking the news. The party neutrality required of public broadcasting has not restricted them. On the other hand, about half the newspapers in 1960 had a party political attachment; they were owned by or editorially linked to a political party. The journalists in the party political press fought the good party cause with the means available.

During the 1960s, however, two new tendencies became apparent in political news reportage. First, there was a trend toward not only reporting news but also commenting on it in more analytical, nonpartisan terms—telling the reader what the parties "really" were up to. The second tendency coincided with (and was in part caused by) the new analytical journalism, namely, the decline of the party press. More papers declared themselves independent of party affiliation, and the journalists claimed professional status, declining to be mere party supporters and agitators. This was especially notable in the Labor press, which traditionally had considered "its" papers part of the party propaganda apparatus.

The change became evident to everyone when in 1981 the Labor prime minister had to leave office over a mixture of medical and political problems. It was the party's own press agency that first broke the news—an act of "disloyalty" unheard of in the past. The journalist and party comrade retorted to his shocked employers that the agency quite simply wanted to break the news first. That was the job of journalists. This trend of independence is also apparent in the rising tendency for journalists to advance their careers by moving from one paper to another—regardless of their political affiliation.

Politicians in Norway—like in most other countries—do not appreciate the new inquisitive press. The tabloids' focus on the juicy, irrelevant details and the tendentious massage given to the facts is—cross-party—considered a problem in modern democratic politics. In a mid-1990s survey of MPs in the five Nordic countries, close to three-fourths listed increased influence of journalists as a serious concern for the political system in the future.[22] The greatest threat according to these politicians, however, came from populism and short-term solutions. Presumably, they saw the media as part of the problem. Political advertising is prohibited in Norway. Nevertheless, through a loophole the Progress Party in the 1997 election campaign managed to run several ads on one of the two private television channels. It may be difficult, however, to ban foreign television stations from sending such commercials in the future. But—as of the late 1990s—there is little pressure on parties and candidates to put on and to finance political advertising as in the United States.

The Norwegian Voter

In the first election after universal suffrage in 1913, 44 percent of the *total* population voted. During the 1980s, this percentage reached the seventies. The Norwegian electorate was mobilized gradually as suffrage was extended to younger age groups and as an increasing share of the eligible voters actually went to the polls. The peak in parliamentary turnout rates was in 1965 when 85 percent of the electorate voted. The highest turnout in more recent times, however, came at the EU referendum in 1994 when 89 percent voted. At the local, municipal elections, turnout has regularly been roughly ten points lower than at national parliamentary elections. A significant drop at parliamentary elections came in 1993 when just over 75 percent voted. This rose again at the next Storting election in 1997, but only by 3 percentage points. At the local elections two years earlier, in 1995, a mere 64 percent had voted, the lowest turnout since the 1920s. In 1999 the turnout declined even further to 60 percent.

Although comparatively still fairly high, the downward trend in voter turnout is generally interpreted in the light of increased voter volatility and the lack of confidence in politicians. Traditionally, two factors have been emphasized when explaining changes in level of turnout: the extent to which there is a clear-cut competition for governmental power and whether voters experience political "cross-pressure." It was the clear-cut contest for power between the two blocs—Labor and the bourgeois coalition parties—that mobilized a record turnout in 1965. But in times when the European issue cuts across traditional party allegiances—like in the early 1970s and the mid-1990s—turnout has been low. A major reason has been conflicting voter interests, with the Labor voters particularly affected. At the elite level, the party was strongly in favor of EU membership in 1972,[23] but many traditional Labor voters were against, and some responded to this "cross-pressure" by not voting at the Storting election a year later. In the record low turnout in 1993, both factors seem to have played a part: There was a lack of government alternatives, and there were significant cross-pressures among the voters.[24]

Comparing Participation in the United States and in Norway

Voting is definitely more widespread in Norway than in the United States. The turnout at U.S. congressional elections has generally been in the 50 percent range. Another well-established difference is that party membership, and activities associated with it, are more widespread in Norway.[25] The available data are not conclusive when it comes to supporting the thesis that other types of political participation are more widespread in the United States. This may well be the case, however, inasmuch as contact activities and petition-signing are reported in higher proportions in the United States. Where internal developments in levels of political participation are concerned, we may note a certain symmetry: Conventional forms of political behavior are either stagnant or declining in both countries, whereas the unconventional forms are on the rise.

In both countries there is little doubt that individual political participation generally increases with higher education, income, and social status, but only up to a point, and for certain types of activities. Social inequality is most pronounced in regard to unconventional political activism, like signing petitions and joining demonstrations. Furthermore, the top social layers are not as active within conventional channels of participation as one might expect. Age is another micro-factor operative here: The middle-aged are more active than the young and the very old. However, if our purpose is to explain the large difference in voter turnout between the United States and Norway, these micro-relationships will not take us very far.

The main comparative potential for explaining the difference rests with the contextual macro-factors. These are the institutional, political,

and social structures affecting individual decisions on whether to participate. There is clearly some truth in the statement that the rate of political
participation in a country shows us how its political institutions operate.
The system of voter registration, for example, is doubtless crucial in explaining the low U.S. voter turnout, just as mandatory voting explains
much of the high turnout in other countries. However, this is not "the
whole truth." Rates of political participation also reflect the way *politics*
works within the institutional system—for example, whether it is candi-
date-centered or party-centered, how organizations and technology work
to affect political mobilization, and which issues are politicized in election campaigns.

Voting levels in Norway are higher than in the United States partly because Norwegian citizens are automatically registered as voters. Political
participation in Norway also reflects the strong—albeit somewhat weakened—position of political parties. Modern technology, like television
and modern campaign techniques, may also account for the recent decline in traditional party-focused conventional politics, as well as for the
rise of unconventional, direct-action politics. Next to the registration system, however, the literature gives ample reason to believe that it is *the issues that are politicized* in a country that have an impact on political participation. The reason is that these issues interact with the operative
micro-factors. As Rokkan and Campbell demonstrated more than thirty
years ago, lower social class means a lower likelihood that the individual
in question will participate in politics; *however,* this likelihood is increased when class becomes an important issue subject to political mobilization.[26] As it is worded in the participation literature, class means the
most when class is absent from politics. And since Norwegian politics is
still more focused on, and organized around, class issues than is politics
in the United States, this circumstance will, *ceteris paribus,* yield a higher
level of voter turnout in Norway than in the U.S. That is why the origins
of participatory biases cannot be found in institutions alone, nor in the
technology that sustains them. These biases also reflect the particular issues that dominate the political struggle—issues that originate with the
cultural, economic, and social circumstances of the particular country.

The Political Sociology of Voting

Turning to the question of how voters behave, the political sociology of
the Rokkan-Valen cleavage perspective has traditionally found strong
support. The so-called countercultures on the west and southwest coast
of Norway, with their ingredients of lay Christian movements, teetotalism, and New Norwegian language advocates, has traditionally produced strong support, first, for the Liberal Party and, later, for the Chris-

tian People's Party. In North Norway, Labor got an early foothold when the combination of a polarized class conflict and peripheral protest created a favorable setting. Regional differences, however, have been on the decline in recent decades. The so-called wave from the right—the metaphor used to describe the steep rise in support for the Conservative Party during the early 1980s—rolled over the South, the West, and the North, and this to some degree harmonized the regional voter profiles.

The analytical cutting edge of the cleavage approach is also helpful when we turn to the individual behavior of the Norwegian voters. Social factors, as identified by occupation and class, explain a fair amount of the voting, although their predictive force has declined since the 1960s.[27] The relationship between left voting and social structure has weakened in Norway—as in most Western countries. Underlying values and ideological structures are clearly still important. According to studies of the 1993 and the 1997 elections, four ideological dimensions guided the voters' choice of party: views on immigration, the role of the state in the economy, environmental issues, and traditional moral issues.[28] The role of the state and moral issues clearly belong to the old, traditional cleavages in Norwegian politics, whereas the issues of immigration and the environment are more recent.

The social profiles of party voters have consequently become more blurred since the 1960s. Labor is still the party with the largest share of working-class voters. But whereas working-class persons made up 64 percent of the party's voters in 1965, they were down to 29 percent in 1993, and the Progress Party and the Center Party were tailing Labor with 26 percent workers in their electorates.[29] Similarly, along the urban-rural dimension, party distinctiveness has declined. The Center Party still enlists the farmers among its core voters, but their share has dramatically decreased from about 70 percent of the party's voters in 1965 to about 20 percent in 1993.[30] Among the Conservative voters, the proportion classified as employers and independents was almost halved during the same period—from about one-quarter of the party voters in the mid-1960s.

The most central dimensions operative in the electorate during the 1990s included two new issue clusters: immigration and the environment. Immigration has been an "on-and-off" issue in Norwegian election campaigns during the 1980s and 1990s. Particularly in 1989 and in most elections during the 1990s, the issue has been especially important to the Progress Party, which favored more restrictive immigration practices. In 1997, a survey showed that two-thirds of the voters who listed this issue as the most important one voted for the Progress Party.[31] Environmental issues are "new" only when compared to the old, historic cleavages discussed in Chapter 2. Since the first oil crisis in 1973–1974, these questions have been on the political agenda—although the extent to which they have been central in the campaigns has varied. Both in 1977 and in 1989, the environment was the second most important issue in the campaign, according to surveys.[32]

In terms of the materialist-postmaterialist value dimension, there were decisively more materialists among the Norwegian voters. As measured by standard survey-questions, studies in the 1980s found around 35–40 percent "materialists" and 7–9 percent "postmaterialists." The materialists are also more numerous in Norway than in the other Nordic countries.[33] Among the voters, those of the Socialist Left Party were in particular found to be of the postmaterialist inclination. Other potential new structural cleavages—like gender, generation, and occupational sector (public versus private)—no doubt give rise to important political differences, but their stability and robustness are a matter of debate within the literature.[34] A closer scrutiny of these factors have shown that women over the past decades have become noticeably more left-wing, that younger voters have become more postmaterialist, and that public-sector employees have become more inclined to vote for the Socialist Left Party.

A central theme in the "cleavage literature" has been that the "modernization" of the Norwegian society has reduced the analytical utility of the cleavage approach. The cleavage concept implies that important and enduring conflicts over time have become institutionalized and stabilized in the party system. The match between the structural and ideological cleavages and the parties system has been declining. Class, center-periphery, urban-rural, and the countercultures—these cleavages do not carry the same predictive power today that they used to. The cleavage model explains less, both in terms of the voters' choice and the differences between the party programs. This is the case because the potential new cleavages—like materialism-postmaterialism—have not added sufficient explanatory power to make it possible to speak about a "realignment" process. To describe the changes as "dealignment," that is, the breaking down of the cleavage structure, seems more appropriate.

Modernization leads to more social and geographical mobility. It also means a more rapidly changing economy and occupational structure. In Norway the changes led to more public employees, broader and longer education, and a decline of the organizational grip "the movements" have over their traditional "congregations." Together with the new media, this has created more freedom for individual choices. Voters now more frequently make up their own minds—on the bases of a reasoned argument or on liking or disliking a party leader—rather than on the bases of social and organizational "reflexes." They do not automatically follow the party signal.

Nevertheless, the fact that cleavages have lost some of their predictive power does not mean that they are no longer useful. The countercultural basis of the Christian People's Party, the rural-peripheral protest of the Center Party, and the balancing act involving class and postmaterialism in the Socialist Left Party provide a basis for understanding both the kind of electoral support these parties have and the policies they promote.[35] On the other hand, one cannot seriously doubt that the issues and the personalities count more today than they used to. The impact of issue politics was evident for the Socialist Left Party in 1989, when environmental questions figured prominently on the election agenda. And the importance of personalities showed up in the "Bondevik factor"[36] for the Christian People's Party in the 1997 election.

What must also be added to understand Norwegian voting behavior in the 1990s is that since the 1960s, voters have become less stable and more volatile. The importance of the election campaigns has increased. In the 1965 election, more than eight in ten stuck to their old party. In 1993 and in 1997, only four out of ten voted for the same party as four years previously.[37] The total volatility, that is, people either changing their party or moving in or out of the electorate, was over 40 percent in both elections of the 1990s. During the 1970s, less than one-third made a different choice. In addition, the level of party identification—possibly a stabilizing element in the voters' transfer movements—has decreased since the mid-1980s. Surveys reveal that the percentage identifying with a particular party declined from 71 percent in 1985 to 57 percent in 1993. One must be cautious in jumping to conclusions, however, since this figure was also rather low around 1970.[38] Nevertheless, more voters now make their choice quite late in the electoral campaign—adding strength to the volatility argument. In the 1960s, only 13 percent said they had made up their minds during the campaign or just before election day. This figure increased to above 20 percent during the 1970s and in the 1990s to 50 percent.[39] Finally, the impact of personalities is, of course, notoriously difficult to measure. But the intense personal debate between the Labor leader Gro Harlem Brundtland and the Conservative Kåre Willoch in the early 1980s made the personal component an important aspect of the party profiles as presented to the voters. The Progress Party, in particular, was affected, as their leader since the late 1970s, Carl I. Hagen, was a forceful vote-catcher on television.

Women in Politics

Qualified voting for women was introduced in 1901 at local elections and at national elections in 1907. General suffrage for all, twenty-five years or older, came in 1913. Female suffrage was introduced early compared to other countries in Europe. Only Finland was earlier, in 1906. It took almost fifty years, however, before women, in practice, took part in national elections to the same degree as men.[40]

Women's presence in representative assemblies was slow to develop. The female share of representatives did not exceed 10 percent before 1970—both in municipal councils and in the parliament.[41] The change was marked, however, after 1970. At the 1971 municipal elections, the share of female local representatives increased from about 9 to 15 percent, and at the Storting election in 1973, the percentage rose from 9 to 16 percent.

What happened? Raaum describes the 1970s as a new phase of women's mobilization in Norway.[42] Earlier developments had been leading up to the roughly equal rates of electoral participation reached in the 1960s. In her view, the steep rise in the number of active female politicians during the 1970s followed as an effect of the postwar welfare state. This introduced a new relationship between women and the state. Others point also to the importance of the rise of the new women's movement in the early 1970s—in Norway as well as abroad.[43] Additional factors no doubt also played a part, such as the increased level of higher education among women, participation in the labor market, and the public campaigns organized by the state in cooperation with the political parties to get more women into public offices.

During the 1970s, the new women's movement succeeded in placing the issue of women's rights—politically, socially, and legally—on the agenda. The feminist cause was, of course, fought in many other countries, such as in the United States and in the neighboring Nordic countries, where young, educated women entered the public realm as activists "to make the private political."[44] The debate over women's right to free abortion was particularly intense—also in Norway. These women—by and large found to the left on the political spectrum—at first did not work through the established parties, and they had little support within the traditional political institutions. They generated public debate, however, which made the parties themselves and their women's branches, in particular, more sensitive to the new "women's issues," and some parties made them part of their own programs. "Free abortion" was actually proposed from the floor at the Labor Party's 1969 congress, and its adoption into the party program took the party elite completely by surprise. Moreover, they did not like it, as they feared the voters' reaction.

Gradually, most parties increased their efforts to recruit more women into elected positions. In the mid-1970s, two parties, the Liberals and the Socialist Left Party, adopted new quota rules for the leading bodies of the party organization. These bodies had now to include at least 40 percent of each sex. In 1981 the Labor Party women succeeded in establishing a similar rule. As by far the largest political party, Labor's decision had significant effects, and today only the Conservatives and the Progress Party are without this rule.

In practice, Labor made the 40 percent rule applicable also to its internal committees, to the parliamentary group, and to the government. This meant that the party lists for all elections had to have alternate places for men and women. Its implementation was not without problems. The county parties were in charge of the Storting nominations, and in 1985 one county party placed two men on top. Labor's central committee reacted sharply but did not intervene, as that would have interfered with the decentralized process. It was not repeated, however.

During the 1980s, the overall representation of women in the Storting increased from 26 percent in 1981 to 36 percent in 1989. The record so far was reached at the 1993 election, when close to 40 percent of those elected were women. In local elections, the share of women representatives also increased to reach 32 percent in 1995. However, the fact that the voters were effectively allowed to influence the selection of persons at local elections—but not to the Storting—in part explains the lower level of women elected to municipal councils.[45] This does not necessarily reflect an outright discrimination on the part of the voters against female candidates. More likely other factors like the candidate's experience in party office or his or her general position in the local community favored male candidates.[46]

The changing position of women among Norwegian political elites became very visible in the so-called women's government of Gro Harlem Brundtland in 1986. This Labor minority, one-party government included almost 50 percent women. All governments since 1986 have had more than 40 percent women apart from one—the center-right Syse government of 1989, which was just below that level. Today only the Progress Party has never had a women as leader of the party organization. This high level of female integration into the Norwegian political elites is not, however, matched by a similar development in the corporate channel. Both in the large organizations in the labor market and in the ministries, the advance of women started later. In 1970, about 10 percent of members on national state boards and committees were women. This increased to 30 percent in 1980 and to 40 percent in the 1990s.[47]

Efforts have been made to institutionalize the policies of gender equality. Both the Equal Status Act of 1978 and the Equal Status "Ombud" try to do that. The Ombud is a public office partly independent of the government created to review complaints based on the Equal Status Act and to initiate new policies to fight discrimination against women. The potential for Scandinavian welfare states to create a more "woman-friendly state" is a central element in debates about political representation and equal gender status.[48]

There are still differences between the sexes among Norwegian voters. Women traditionally voted disproportionately for the Conservative Party and the Christian People's Party. This changed for the first time at the 1985 election, as more women came to support the leftist parties.[49] The changes along the left-right scale are not very big, but they probably reflect significant structural changes in the Norwegian society. Women have increasingly entered the labor market—particularly the public sector—and have sought higher education in much greater numbers than at any time before. Their higher level of religious attachment still pulls them away from the leftist parties, but they also favor solidarity and collectivist solutions to a higher degree than men, which explains their overall left-ward trend.[50] The largest gender differences are found among the young, where there is a rather strong polarization. Men disproportionally support the Progress Party, and women support the leftist parties, particularly the Socialist Left Party. Nevertheless, it would be an exaggeration to claim the existence of a political cleavage line based on gender. Women have become effectively integrated into the traditional parties based on the old cleavages. There is no viable party based on gender in Norway like the Icelandic Women's Alliance.

Referenda Politics

The two referenda in 1972 and 1994 on Norwegian membership in the European Union (in 1972 the European Communities) brought a broad range of political actors into the political arena in a "nonroutine" way. These are the only post–World War II, national referenda held in Norway.[51] During the two intense and turbulent campaigns, the political forces of Norwegian politics evolved relatively freely. Proponents of membership lost on both occasions, although narrowly. The side opposed to EU membership won with 53.5 percent in 1972 and with 52.2 percent in 1994.

In 1972 the membership issue had been on the agenda for about ten years. The first Norwegian application was sent to Brussels in 1962 but was halted when de Gaulle issued his veto against Britain. The main arguments in favor of membership in 1972 were the economy and national security. Traditionally, Norway had followed Britain in international economic cooperation (see Chapter 5). In security matters, the Norwegian NATO membership was crucial. The political establishment, however, saw membership in the European Community as instrumental in making a future war unthinkable among Germany, France, and Britain. During World War II, they had learned the lesson that Norway would have trouble staying out of a war that started on the continent. Membership would also be an additional safeguard during the cold war, a further integration into the Western sphere of interest.

The opponents argued that NATO's security guaranties were sufficient and that the likely economic and political effects on the whole would be negative. Economic integration would present severe challenges to agriculture and the fishing industries, posing a serious threat to the long-term viability of many district communities. Finally, being "ruled from Brussels" was not cherished and was seen as undermining the egalitarian democratic tradition found in Norway. As we shall see, the 1972 confrontation, to a remarkable degree, turned into a fight between "the establishment" and "the grassroots."

Although the context had changed significantly, the 1994 referendum was fought with much the same arguments as twenty-two years before. The EC had become the European Union and the trend toward an "ever closer Union" was firmly established. The cold war was over, and the Norwegian economy had changed dramatically due to the impact of North Sea oil and increased "internationalization." The focus in the debate had also changed since 1972, particularly from the advocates of membership. The European Economic Area (EEA) agreement with the EU from 1992 was in place and gave Norwegian industry access to EU markets. Political arguments were more central in 1994, stressing the creation of a new European order in times when the nation-state had proved "too small" for the big decisions necessary under the impact of internationalization. This created a need for a European-level authority to regulate the economy and the threats to the environment: Neither money nor pollution paid much respect to national borders. Swedish and Finnish membership were also likely outcomes, and with Denmark, this would make a strong bloc favoring the Nordic model within the EU. To the no-side the threat to agricultural and fishing interests was still central. And the lack of democracy in the EU institutions was seen as an even stronger reason to say no in 1994 than in 1972.

The parties had voted in parliament to hold an advisory referendum. This left the possibility that a yes victory could later be stopped in parliament by a minority veto, which applied in such matters.[52] Both referenda mobilized parties, interest organizations, and ad hoc movements (PACs). The parliamentary parties had argued that the EU issue was unique, out of line with routine politics, and that the people should have the opportunity to decide for themselves—outside the party political context. This argument reflected the fact that most parties were split on the issue. Only the Conservatives, the Center Party, and the Socialist Left Party stayed more or less united in both campaigns. Labor had on both occasions a strong minority opposing membership, and in 1972 the party tried unsuccessfully to impose a party order. After a serious loss of votes in the parliamentary election following the 1972 referendum, however, a new party generation decided to be more broad-minded in 1994. This also reflected new party sentiments about what party democracy was all about.

The major organizations confronting each other in the two campaigns and working to coordinate activities on both sides were the broad yes- and no-movements. The two sides had very different resources. The yes-side had the most resources in terms of money, organizational backing, and media support, particularly in 1972. The no-side was certainly not without similar backing—particularly from the agrarian interest organizations—but their major weapon was grassroots mobilization. As it turned out, the traditional institutional biases did not work as expected. Precisely because the debate was taken out of the traditional institutional framework, money and "establishment" support did not move the voters to the extent necessary. The deliberating public arenas in, for example, television and radio proved more important than parliamentarian majorities, executive branch dominance, and newspaper control.

The patterns of voting in 1972 and in 1994 were remarkably similar. The no-side won everywhere, apart from the populous counties around the capital. In terms of voter profile, it looked as if time had almost stood still between 1972 and 1994.[53] The peripheral areas simply did not see it in their interests to join the EU. Membership was also considered more as a democratic threat than as a "supplementary democracy" as advocated by the proponents. The political impact of the two referenda on Norwegian politics was large. In the 1970s the issue broke the center-right coalition government and created a minority coalition of center parties opposed to membership. Furthermore, the Liberal Party split and since then has not been able to regain its former strength. The new Socialist Left Party was created with the old Socialist People's Party at its core, but supplemented by dissenters from Labor and the Communists. Most importantly, the 1972 referendum triggered the voter independence—visible also in other countries at the time—that became central to the party political arena in subsequent years.

In the 1990s, the EU issue broke—again—the center-right coalition in 1990 and provided the background for the minority coalition of center parties forming a government after the 1997 election. No party split occurred this time, but the debate boosted the support of the Center Party in the 1993 election. That momentum was absent in the 1997 election, however. Nevertheless, politically the Center Party had marked out a different course than after the 1972 referendum, putting up a front against the Conservative Party and refusing to consider the old-type center-right coalition. The irony, however, is that the minority coalition of center parties created after the 1997 election came to cooperate rather closely with both the Conservatives and the Progress Party in parliament as the Labor Party refused.

Conclusion

Norway is a party democracy. Political parties play a pivotal role in offering the voters political alternatives at elections, in recruiting the state's political personnel, and in controlling the commanding heights of executive power. But Rokkan was right: There is more to Norwegian politics. The interest organizations in the corporate channel clearly are central to the policymaking process. The trade unions and the employers have powers not easily forgotten when the politicians make decisions affecting the economy. Their interests extend far beyond the pure economy. But the process includes more than the two channels. As Rokkan also described, the Labor government fell in a dramatic parliamentarian debate in the early 1960s that was brought home to Norwegian voters by the new medium of television.[54] The new media channel changed the parties, the traditional political institutions, and the decisionmaking process in ways that first became clear to all when "the establishment" lost against "the people" in the first referendum on EU membership.

These changes led to a system where routine politics inside Norwegian political institutions mix with the occasional spontaneous political action and the careful orchestration of media campaigns directed by political parties, interest organizations, and political action committees alike. The process is monitored by frequent opinion polls to let the public and the politicians know who leads the race and how the process might be affected through the politics of agenda controls. The electors are brought in at regular intervals to select a new decisionmaking team. This team works within the context of government proposals, party programs, organizational interests, and the "people's voice."

Notes

1. §59 and §63. See Knut Heidar, "Should the Parties Be Incorporated in the Written Constitution?" in Carsten Smith et al., eds., *The Role of the Constitution in a Changing Society: Joint Polish-Norwegian Conference, Oslo, 14–16 May 1991* (Oslo: Norwegian Academy of Science and Letters, 1991), pp. 299–315.

2. In the Norwegian political vocabulary, "bourgeois" has no derogatory associations. The Conservatives, in particular, considered themselves and their coalition partners from the 1960s onward as proponents of "bourgeois policies."

3. The story is somewhat simplified in covering only still existing parties; also the "offspring" generally had a more complex background than simply emerging from the Liberal Party.

4. "Third way" here is used in the sense of the cold war era of the 1950s and 1960s, not the British "third way" of the Blair government of the 1990s.

5. Hanne Marthe Narud, "Nominasjoner og pressen," in Knut Heidar and Lars Svåsand, eds., *Partiene i en brytningstid* (Bergen: Alma Mater, 1994).

6. Ibid.; and Henry Valen, "Norway: Decentralization and Group Representation," in Michael Gallagher and Michael Marsh, eds., *Candidate Selection in Comparative Perspective: The Secret Garden of Politics* (London: Sage, 1988). This figure is from a 1985 survey reported in Valen, "Norway," p. 214. It is probably somewhat lower today.

7. Knut Heidar, "The Polymorphic Nature of Party Membership," *European Journal of Political Research* 25 (1994):61–86. See also Heidar and Svåsand, eds., *Partiene i en brytningstid*.

8. Heidar, "The Polymorphic Nature of Party Membership."

9. Lars Svåsand, "Partienes finansieringsmønster," in Knut Heidar and Lars Svåsand, eds., *Partiene i en brytningstid* (Bergen: Alma Mater, 1994).

10. Stein Rokkan, "Norway: Numerical Democracy and Corporate Pluralism," in Robert A. Dahl, ed., *Political Oppositions in Western Democracies* (New Haven: Yale University Press, 1966).

11. Ibid., p. 197.

12. Einar Lie, *Ambisjon og tradisjon. Finansdepartementet, 1945–1965* (Oslo: Universitetsforlaget, 1995).

13. P. C. Scmitter, "Still the Century of Corporatism," in P. C. Schmitter and G. Lehmbruch, eds., *Trends Towards Corporate Intermediation* (London: Sage, 1979).

14. For a summary presentation and further references for the figures, see Tom Christensen and Morten Egeberg, "Noen trekk ved forholdet mellom organisasjonene og den offentlige forvaltningen," in Tom Christensen and Morten Egeberg, eds., *Forvaltningskunnskap* (Oslo: Tano, 1997); and Anne Lise Fimreite, "Samspillet mellom privat og offentlig sektor," in Anne Lise Fimreite, ed., *Forskerblikk på Norge* (Oslo: Tano, 1997).

15. See Fimreite, "Samspillet mellom privat og offentlig sektor," and Christensen and Egeberg, "Noen trekk ved forholdet mellom organisasjonene."

16. The political action committee in Norway differs from the PAC of the United States, which is a group formed for the purpose of raising and contributing money to the campaigns of candidates likely to advance the group's interests.

17. Johan P. Olsen and Harald Sætren, *Aksjoner og demokrati* (Oslo: Universitetsforlaget, 1980), p. 46.

18. The European Values Survey and Eurobarometer data, reported in Richard Topf, "Beyond Electoral Participation," in Hans-Dieter Klingemann and Dieter Fuchs, eds., *Citizens and the State*, vol. 1, *Belief in Government* (Oxford: Oxford University Press, 1995), p. 86.

19. Tor Bjørklund, "Aksjon, demokrati, protest," in Ingerid Semmingsen et al., eds., *Underveis — mot nye tider*, vol. 8 of *Norges Kulturhistorie* (Oslo: Aschehoug, 1983), p. 196.

20. Hans Fredrik Dahl, "Massemedia," in Dag Bjørnland, Hans Fredrik Dahl, and Peter Sjøholt, eds., *Vareflom og massemedia*, vol. 3 of *Det Moderne Norge* (Oslo: Gyldendal, 1982).

21. Ture Schwebs and Helge Østbye, *Media i samfunnet*, 3rd ed. (Oslo: Samlaget, 1995).

22. Hanne Marthe Narud and Henry Valen, "Mass and Elite Attitudes Toward Future Problems in the Nordic Countries," in Peter Essaiason and Knut Heidar,

eds., *Beyond Congress and Westminster: The Nordic Experience* (Columbus: Ohio State University Press, 2000).

23. Correct terminology at the time was the European Community (EC), not the European Union (EU).

24. Bernt Aardal and Henry Valen, *Konflikt og opinion* (Oslo: NKS-forlaget, 1995), chapter 3.

25. For an overview of the literature, see Knut Heidar, "Civil Society and the Mobilization of Bias: Comparing Political Participation in the U.S. and in Norway," Working Paper 5/1999, Department of Political Science, University of Oslo.

26. Stein Rokkan and Angus Campbell, "Citizen Participation in Political Life: Norway and the United States of America," *International Social Science Journal* 12 (1):69–99.

27. Henry Valen, "Norway," in Mark N. Franklin, Thomas T.Mackie, Henry Valen et al., *Electoral Change: Responses to Evolving Social and Attitudinal Structures in Western Countries* (Cambridge: Cambridge University Press, 1992).

28. Aardal and Valen, *Konflikt og opinion*, p. 102; and Bernt Aardal with Henry Valen, Hanne Marthe Narud, and Frode Berglund, *Velgerne i 90-årene* (Oslo: NKS-forlaget, 1999), ch. 3.

29. Jostein Ryssevik, *I samfunnet 3* (Oslo: Universitetsforlaget, 1994), p. 100.

30. That figure is somewhat inflated by the strong showing of the Center Party in that election due to the impact of the European Union membership issue.

31. Election day poll from the MMI institute published in *Dagbladet*, 16 September 1997, p. 18.

32. Bernt Aardal, *Energi og miljø*, report 93:15 (Oslo: Institute for Social Research, 1993), p. 211.

33. Oddbjørn Knutsen, "The Priorities of Materialists' and Post-Materialists' Values in the Nordic Countries: A Five Country Comparison," *Scandinavian Political Studies* 12 (1989):221–244.

34. Stein Kuhnle and Ola Listhaug, "Makropolitiske komparasjoner, partier og politisk atferd: Linjer, status og utfordringer i norsk statsvitenskap," *Norsk Statsvitenskapelig Tidsskrift* 13 (1997):215–254.

35. There is, of course, a thin line between the "cleavage issues" and other issues. Taxation and public bureaucracy are obviously left-right cleavage issues. But whether green issues actually have turned into cleavage issues is matter of debate.

36. In the 1997 campaign, Mr. Kjell Magne Bondevik, who was parliamentary leader of the Christian People's Party, scored very high in the polls asking about preferences for prime minister; see, for example, *Aftenposten*, 29 June 1997, p. 4. The extent to which personalities are catalysts of issue voting or reasons for voter choice in their own right, however, is open to debate.

37. Henry Valen, "Partiforskyvninger ved stortingsvalget i 1965," in Henry Valen and Willy Martinussen, *Velgerne og politiske frontlinjer* (Oslo: Gyldendal, 1972), p. 265; and *Ukens Statistikk*, no. 6 (Oslo: Statistics Norway, 1998).

38. Bernt O. Aardal and Henry Valen, "The Stortings Elections of 1989 and 1993: Norwegian Politics in Perspective," in Kaare Strøm and Lars Svåsand, eds., *Challenges to Political Parties* (Ann Arbor: University of Michigan Press, 1997), p. 70.

39. Ola Listhaug, *Citizens, Parties, and Norwegian Electoral Politics, 1957–1985* (Trondheim: Tapir, 1989), p. 115, and Aardal et al., *Velgerne i 90-årene*, p. 16.

40. Nina C. Raaum, "Introduksjon – kjønn og politikk," in Nina C. Raaum, ed., *Kjønn og politikk* (Oslo: Tano, 1995), pp. 14–15.

41. In 1995, the figure for European parliaments was 13 percent. See Lena Wängnerud, *Politikans andra sida*, Göteborg Studies in Politics 53 (Göteborg: Göteborgs universitet, 1998), p. 18.

42. Then there was less than 5 percentage points difference between the sexes in participation at the Storting elections, see Raaum, ed., *Kjønn og politikk*.

43. Anne-Hilde Nage, "Politiseringen av kjønn: Et historisk perspektiv," in Nina C. Raaum, ed., *Kjønn og politikk* (Oslo: Tano, 1995), p. 70

44. Drude Dahlerup and Brita Gulli, "Kvindeorganisationerne i Norden: Afmagt eller modmagt?" in Elina Haavio-Mannila et al., eds., *Det uferdige demokratiet* (Oslo: Nordisk ministerråd, 1983).

45. Ottar Hellevik and Tor Bjørklund, "Velgerne og kvinnerepresentasjon," in Nina C. Raaum, ed., *Kjønn og politikk* (Oslo: Tano, 1995).

46. Ibid., p. 123.

47. Nina C. Raaum, "Politisk representasjon," in Nina C. Raaum, ed., *Kjønn og politikk* (Oslo: Tano, 1995), pp. 104–105.

48. Helga Hernes, *Welfare State and Woman Power: Essays in State Feminism* (Oslo: Norwegian University Press, 1987).

49. Ola Listhaug, Art Miller, and Henry Valen, "The Gender Gap in Norwegian Voting Behaviour," *Scandinavian Political Studies* 8 (1985):187–206.

50. Ola Listhaug, Beate Huseby, and Richard Matland, "Valgatferd blant kvinner og menn: 1957–1993," in Nina C. Raaum, ed., *Kjønn og politikk* (Oslo: Tano, 1995).

51. In Norwegian history there have been altogether six referenda, two in 1905 in seceding from Sweden and establishing a new monarchy, and then two on the issue of prohibition—in 1919 (for) and in 1926 (against).

52. Especially in 1994, this option became part of the referendum debate itself. One issue was whether the minority needed one-third or one-fourth of the votes to block membership. A more heated debate emerged over the political and moral rights of the minority to block a potential majority of the voters in the referendum.

53. See Anders Todal Jenssen, Ola Listhaug, and Per Arnt Pettersen, "Betydningen av gamle og nye skillelinjer," in Anders Todal Jenssen and Henry Valen, eds., *Bryssel midt imot. Folkeavstemningen om EU* (Oslo: Ad Notam, 1995); and Tor Bjørklund, *Om folkeavstemninger. Norge og Norden, 1905—1994* (Oslo: Universitetsforlaget, 1997), chapter 6.

54. See Rokkan, "Norway: Numerical Democracy and Corporate Pluralism"; and Stein Rokkan, *Stat, Nasjon, Klasse* (Oslo: Universitetsforlaget, 1987), p. 99.

5

Political Economy

If we had been free to do so, I think the government and the Labor Party under the present circumstances would have favored regulating imports. Now 75 percent of the imports are on the free list.

—*Prime Minister Einar Gerhardsen*

At the turn of the twenty-first century, Norway is one of the richest countries in the world as measured by GNP per capita. In terms of purchasing parity estimates, Norway in 1995 scored 117 points out of 100, the average for the OECD area as a whole. This was the highest among the Nordic countries and trailed only behind the United States (137) and Switzerland (128).[1] At the same time, income distribution in comparative terms is fairly equal, although inequality increased somewhat during the 1990s. Actually the four Nordic countries head the statistics measuring equality of income—with the United States close to the bottom.[2] This abundance of milk and honey made available to most people is, however, a relatively new phenomenon. During the nineteenth century, Norwegian society was somewhat equal, but it was at the same time among the poorest nations in Western Europe. From Norwegian ports, shipload after shipload of "economic refugees" went across the ocean—all in search of a better future in North America.

Norway's economy is small by international standards. It is fairly open and exposed to developments on world markets. Norwegian governments have not been free to pursue the policies they most wanted due to external constraints. This is evident in the opening epigraph with the prime minister speaking to the parliament in 1955.[3] Traditionally there has been strong state involvement in the economy. Today the "safety net" for Norwegians in old age, in sickness, or in the job market is strong and secure, and it is institutionalized through an active welfare state (see

Chapter 6). Petro-products dominate in statistics on production and exports, and industry in general is heavily based on raw materials. There are structural tensions between the different sectors in the economy, particularly as they relate to the conflict between the urban centers and the outlying districts. A broad-based political commitment underpins core policies such as keeping unemployment low and maintaining a "fair" geographical distribution of wealth. Political involvement in economic activities and in smoothing the relationship between the main groups in industry has traditionally been large. The "negotiated economy" is one label used to characterize a system that is neither a "market" nor a "state" economy.[4] Since the 1980s, however, the dominating trend has been toward less state involvement and more market influence in economic and industrial policies. This has occurred in spite of the fact that market forces—as we shall see below—brought the major banks under public ownership in the late 1980s. Economic liberalization was further reinforced by the European Economic Area (EEA) agreement from 1994, which made Norway part of the EU's single market.

In this chapter we shall look at the political context of the economy, the basic natural conditions, and the integration into world markets. Two themes are stressed: openness to international markets and strong state involvement. The two conditions have produced a strong corporate structure for negotiation between private and public interests, a structure that has come under pressure during the past few decades. By focusing on the emerging petroleum industry, the state "district policies," and the policies on unemployment and wage negotiations, we will look more closely into these processes. Lastly, we will consider the likely effects of the EEA agreement, an arrangement that integrates Norway into the EU single market.

A Small and Open Economy

The Norwegian economy is comparatively small. It depends heavily on a few raw materials and is very sensitive to changes in international markets. In the mid-1990s, the GNP of Norway was less than 2 percent of that of the United States and roughly one-tenth of Great Britain's. Historically, economic development has followed the standard European pattern: The primary sector has been shrinking throughout the century both in terms of the number of people occupied and in terms of market value. Simultaneously the wealth created first in industry and later in services has increased. During the post–World War II period, services became the largest sector, and more than half the economically active population today is occupied in the (public and private) service sector.[5] In the 1990s, roughly one in three employed persons worked in industry, one in ten in transportation, and one in twenty in agriculture and fishing. Periods of economic growth and stagnation have by and large followed the European and international trends: A strong growth up until World War I, then a rough ride through crises, and transformation in the interwar years. From 1945 to 1971, Norway—like so many other West European countries—experienced strong and continuous economic growth. The past three decades of the century have also seen steady growth, but at a slower pace.

The traditional industries of Norway were based on the extraction and low-grade processing of raw materials as well as on Norwegian maritime traditions. This meant mining, wood products, paper, pulp, fisheries, shipping, and shipbuilding. Early in the twentieth century, large electrometallurgical and chemical factories were built close to hydroelectrical power plants constructed near large waterfalls. These industries were greatly expanded after World War II. Shipping was another traditional industry and a key sector in the Norwegian economy. It continued to play an important role after 1945, when crucial foreign currency was earned abroad and invested at home. During the 1970s, the offshore oil industry became increasingly important, not only as the major provider of state revenues, but also by giving rise to onshore bases for supplies and by keeping mechanical industry along the coast occupied. Production on the rich oil fields discovered along the Norwegian coast led not only to a higher GNP growth during the 1980s and 1990s than in most other comparable countries, but also to an even stronger dependency on international markets. The high-cost oil sector also triggered a transformation in the onshore economy through the high wages earned in the offshore industry. Employment increased in the service sector—both private and public—and this threatened the viability of traditional export industries.

Crucial sectors of the Norwegian economy have traditionally been open to fierce competition from international markets. Small countries with small home markets have generally a larger share of their economic activities tied to external markets. Significant parts of Norwegian manufacturing industries have been export driven. The Netherlands and Norway are both examples of West European countries with an extremely high degree of dependency and openness. Looking at the export of commodities only, its share of GNP in Norway rose from 18 percent in 1950 to 26 percent in 1986.[6] In 1990 the value of all Norwegian exports in commodities and services, oil products included, was as much as 44 percent of GNP.

Exports were traditionally limited to a few commodities and services, increasing the vulnerability of the economy to international market fluctuations. Shipping is, of course, the traditional example. In the decades after 1945, this sector accounted for 20–30 percent of all new yearly investments, and in size, the Norwegian registered fleet was only behind Great Britain and Japan. Up until the mid-1970s, the income from shipping made up between 35 and 45 percent of all income from exports.[7] When world shipping declined in the 1970s, this affected employment in shipyards, shipping firms, and supply activities. A Keynesian countercyclical fiscal policy was instituted in the period from 1973 to 1977 in an attempt to stem the forces of the international markets, but this led instead to increased inflation and a record trade deficit.

During the 1980s, the liberalization of the internal credit market and falling oil prices caused economic turmoil. Declining oil revenues weakened the state finances, and in the spring of 1986, a 10 percent devaluation of the Norwegian krone was announced just after the new Labor government had taken office. Since the breakdown of the Bretton Woods system (see Chapter 7) in the early 1970s, it had been increasingly difficult to implement a national monetary policy. After 1986, stable prices and the currency exchange rate became more central to fiscal policies, to some extent at the expense of the (traditionally extremely low) unemployment figures.[8] Increased credit-based internal consumption in combination with a tighter fiscal policy led to an economic recession in 1988–1993, which was the strongest setback for the Norwegian economy since World War II.[9] This caused bankruptcies and led to the insolvency of the country's two largest banks.

A Strong State to Be "Rolled Back"

In the mid-nineteenth century, the public sector was mainly taking care of internal and external security, communications like roads and rail services, education, and the state church. During the twentieth century, the state was gradually given increased responsibilities. The share of GNP in the public budget increased from about one-quarter in 1950 to more than half in 1990 (see Table 5.1). Also the share going to public consumption increased during this period, but at a much lower level, about 20 percent in 1990. The reason is that much of the registered public GNP was transfers like pensions and welfare provisions. Throughout the post–World War II period, public services increased gradually to include broad welfare state services. Between the early 1960s and the mid-1990s, the public sector employment increased from 11 to 27 percent of total employment, and most of this growth took place at the local, municipal level.[10] Taxes have been at a comparatively high level, 42 percent of GNP in 1995 compared with 36 percent in Great Britain and 28 percent in the United States.[11]

During the interwar years, the state took on a broader responsibility in both the economic and the social arenas. In the primary sector of the

TABLE 5.1   Growth in the power of the state 1900–1995 (% of GNP)

	1900	1920	1935	1950	1970	1980	1990	1995
Total public expenditures	9.9	12.8	18.1	27.6	37.9	48.3	51.3	49.3
Taxes	7.5	7.5	16.4	27.0	39.3	42.7	41.8	41.5
Public consumption	6.4	7.5	10.1	11.2	16.6	18.8	20.9	21.1

source: Knut Heidar and Einar Berntzen, Vesteuropeisk politikk, 3rd ed., (Oslo: Universitetsforlaget, 1998) p. 51. The table is based on different sources, which makes the time series not strictly comparable. The 1980, 1990, and 1995 figures are supplemented with data from Historical Statistics 1960–1995 (Paris: OECD, 1997) pp. 70 and 75, and Statistisk Årbok 1998 (Statistics Norway), p. 468.

economy, new regulations of the internal markets of agricultural products and fish were followed by policies that strengthened the power of producer organizations. Internal markets in all sectors were protected from international competition by high tariffs. After 1945 Norway became part of a new international regime—the so-called Bretton Woods system, which came to include the World Bank, the International Monetary Fund (IMF), the Organization of European Economic Cooperation (OEEC, later OECD), and the General Agreement on Trade and Tariffs (GATT). This regime gradually opened up internal manufacturing markets. At the same time the social democratic government in Norway started to build state industries in key sectors like energy, coal, steel, and aluminum. In the early 1950s, however, this policy came to a halt. Instead of using this direct intervention, the government sought to guide economic development through macroeconomic instruments like credit regulations. In the primary sector the interwar policies of protection from international competition and the regulatory powers of the producer organizations were developed further. An elaborate system based on set prices and subsidies was created both to keep up producer income and to reach nationally specified production goals.

The building of the postwar welfare state was based on a broad political consensus. Some welfare-state elements preceded the war, such as several compulsory social insurance and pension plans. After 1945 these welfare rights were broadened considerably as reflected in the figures on public expenditures presented in Table 5.1. A universal child allowance was introduced in 1946, mandatory sickness insurance came in 1956, universal pension rights in 1957, and disability allowance in 1961. In 1966 it was all incorporated into a large new "Social Security" act (Folketrygdloven).[12] The public money supporting these welfare provisions increased as Norway became a richer country, the bulk of the money all the time going to pensions.

Low unemployment and a wide distribution of wealth in social, demographic, and geographic terms have been central goals to all postwar governments of Norway. The political measures advocated to keep unemployment low and wealth distribution broad, however, have been contested. To the social democrats, a large public sector was crucial, almost as a matter of faith, well into the 1970s. In the 1980s, that faith—which was all along strongly attacked by liberal and conservative politicians—was challenged also from within the labor movement. The center-right parties differed in their views on public-sector size, but the need for more competition and market exposure of industry was by and large seen as greater on this side.

Both the economic changes after 1973 and the new ideological winds from Thatcher's England and Reagan's United States gave a new twist to the economic debate in the 1980s. The new message was "more markets, less state." The first attempts to handle the international economic downturn of the mid-1970s had included a counter-cyclic policy. This policy was presented as "taking the oil money in advance," based on the projected huge state revenues from the oil fields in the years to come. A range of industry-specific support to aid ailing sectors materialized. In addition, increased transfers to agriculture followed as a result of a new policy to create "income equality" between farmers and industrial workers. The huge subsidies added to the fiscal problems of the state. To ease inflation "wage and price controls" were attempted, but these did not work, and around 1980 a new policy was tried with more general measures that were not aimed at specific industries. Except for the more sector-specific policies of the mid-1970s, the general trend—after the postwar "directionist" policies were scaled down around 1950—has been toward less direct state intervention and more market exposure.

This turn toward the market was particularly pronounced in the 1980s, first through the more liberal policies of the Conservative-led governments (1981–1986), then through increasingly market-oriented Labor governments (1986–1989; 1990–1997).[13] In the latter half of the 1980s, several "flagship" state-owned companies from the early postwar period had to close or regroup. A major example was the closure of an iron and steel plant in North Norway. This had been a postwar prestige project of the Labor government, the "socialism in practice" of its day. Another example was the gradual removal of the public telecommunication company from the state sector, starting with the permission to establish more than one network for cable television in 1987. In the not too distant future, it will most likely be noted on the stock exchange, possibly as early as the autumn of 2000. Preparation for a possible EU membership in the early 1990s and the single market regulations following the membership in the European Economic Area in 1994 enhanced the process. The 1980s was also a decade when many old state monopolies were dissolved—from national broadcasting, including television, to an increased openness toward state support of private nurseries.

Increased market exposure paradoxically also led to increased state ownership. When the credit markets were liberalized in 1984, the new freedom led the banks to issue too many insecure loans. In 1991 the three largest commercial banks in Norway were "taken over" by the state to avoid going bankrupt. This was an old "socialist" policy demand. Many decades ago the Labor Party had advocated it. The intention now, however, was to let the banks operate as commercially viable institutions, although the state had to step in to put them on a sound economic footing. The banking crisis, however, proved not only the old strong state involvement in the Norwegian economy but also the newly found riches of oil revenues. During the 1990s, the strategic position of the state in industrial development increased as the money started pouring into the new "oil fund."

Traditional Industries and the New Petro-Politics

Since the 1970s, there has been a decline in the economic importance of traditional industries and an increasing importance of the petroleum sector. The Norwegian economy has become even more integrated in and vulnerable to the international markets. There has also been a continuous rise in the service sector. Apart from the petroleum business, these are familiar trends within the OECD countries.[14]

During the twenty years from 1975 to 1995, the contribution of manufacturing and mining to the GNP declined from 22 to 13 percent, while its share of total employment declined from 24 to 16 percent.[15] This Norwegian "de-industrialization" was, as elsewhere, partly a product of technological change, making production generally less labor demanding. In part, it was also—as we will see below—a statistical side effect due to the increased importance of petroleum products in statistics dealing with investments, exports, and GDP. In political debate about economic issues, there was a tendency to discuss the "mainland industry" separately from the total economy, which included the offshore petroleum industry. The mainland industry remained an important basis for employment, particularly in the districts where energy-demanding industries—like chemical, metallurgical, and pulp processing—along with shipyards and mechanical industries, traditionally had been the only major workplaces in many local communities. Another industrial development of the 1970s was that production increasingly moved away from high-cost areas in the old urban centers leaving the industrial headquarters behind, particularly in Oslo.[16] In the 1980s de-industrialization—meaning workforce reduction—continued but now affected the whole country. And as discussed above, previously "sheltered" state industries were experiencing downsizing and closures. However, some new industrial development came in the emerging high-tech industries.

Shipping went into a recession in the 1970s and never regained its previous strong position in the Norwegian economy. Its contribution to the GNP declined from roughly 9 to 2 percent from 1975 to 1995. The Middle East war of 1973 triggered the fall, when market rates, in particular for oil tankers, fell dramatically. This was also closely related to the oil embargo and the subsequent decline in world trade. By the mid-1970s, more than one-fourth of total capacity (tankers included) was idle.[17] Shipping and shipbuilding had been economically very important to Norway for more than a hundred years, not least as generators of capital for industrial investments onshore. Now this importance was drastically reduced, partly due to downsizing and restructuring, partly because ship-owners moved their activity abroad to reduce costs. It is very telling that the shipping interests—so important in shaping Norwegian foreign policies for so long—are completely left out of the most recent standard textbook on Norwegian foreign policy.[18] The reason for this "silent death" of shipping in the Norwegian economy and politics is probably that oil emerged as its functional equivalent—both as currency earner and in terms of shaping foreign policy interests.

Agriculture and fisheries continued to play an important role in the economy and in politics in the last quarter of the twentieth century. The primary sector's share of GNP declined from 5.6 to 2.4 percent, and its share of employment was reduced even more—from 15.5 to 6.8 (both 1975–1995). In the heavily subsidized agricultural sector, the new policy adopted by parliament in 1975 sought, as mentioned above, to give the farmer an income equal to that of the industrial worker. This improved the economy for the farmers but only temporarily stemmed the tide in the declining number of farms and the human exodus from the countryside into towns. Fishing was traditionally very important to local communities and to employment along the coast. But it was also a risky business, as the resource base fluctuated and was threatened by overfishing. The herring disappeared on the West Coast and in the North Sea in the 1950s and 1960s. This moved the fleet north and led to similar problems outside North Norway. A central conflict throughout the postwar period has been between the increasingly efficient seagoing trawlers and the local fishermen using smaller boats, who returned daily with their catch. This tension has also been heightened by the geographical fact that the trawler fleet, to a large degree, has been owned and manned from West

Coast communities, whereas the local fishermen have dominated along the coast of North Norway. This has caused policy problems at the national level as well as internally for most political parties. Territorial rights at sea have traditionally been an important aspect of Norwegian foreign policy, and it was hailed as a national victory when an area extending 200 nautical miles into the seas with exclusive national economic rights was declared in 1977 (see Chapter 7). Although manning requirements at sea have declined, the new fish farming (salmon, in particular) plants along the coast still offer many jobs in West Coast communities. Fish farming also supports the export of fish, one of the most important export articles of the mainland industries and the third largest "traditional" export commodity in 1995.[19]

The service sector gradually increased its share of employment. It is one indication that the employment in the public sector almost doubled to 30 percent from 1975 to 1995. However, service-sector jobs underwent significant changes. High growth rates came in work related to health care and the information services. Also financial services increased during this period, although banking had experienced serious problems in the late 1980s and early 1990s, as discussed above.

The banks shared the general trend toward increased "economies of scale," a process involving frequent mergers. That still left the comparatively small Norwegian corporations exposed to foreign companies. The official policy, however, was that financial institutions should remain nationally owned. In industry there was a growing trend toward international mergers; and many companies were bought by foreigners, but in a few cases, it was the other way around. One large Norwegian consultant and engineering firm, Kvaerner Engineering, bought a British company and moved its operative leadership to London. Another traditional engineering company, Aker, was taken over by a Seattle-based Norwegian fishing mogul. A third, the state telecommunication company, entered into a merger deal with its Swedish sister company in 1999, but this broke down after a short while. In addition, foreign investors increased their ownership in Norwegian firms. From 1986 to 1996 their share of stocks traded on the Norwegian stock exchange rose from 21 to 34 percent.[20]

The petroleum industry has become increasingly important and now accounts for the largest share of exports, having increased its share of the total from zero in 1970 to one-third of all commodities (in terms of value) in 1995. However, the industry is more important in financial and foreign policy terms than employment terms; its share of total employment has stayed at roughly 1 percent since the mid-1980s.

The oil business is risky not only in terms of exploration at sea, where high-cost investments may or may not lead to a finding and production of oil or gas, but also in the sense that prices on the international market

fluctuate enormously.[21] This makes the Norwegian economy very vulnerable to the vagaries of the international oil market. The politics of oil
has therefore become central to the Norwegian parliament since the early
1970s. The debates have flourished: How should foreign companies be
dealt with—what terms should they have? How should state control be
exerted—through a state company or through regulation? Where should
the exploration take place, and what risks are acceptable? How much oil
and gas should be produced? How much of the revenue from oil should
be used to support the mainland economy?

The 100-percent-state-owned company, Statoil, was established at the
start along with the large chemical company Norsk Hydro, which was 50-
percent state owned but operated like any private company and was traded
on the stock exchange. In addition, a new fully private company, Saga, was
given preferential treatment when licenses were issued for exploration and
development. This company, however, eventually got into trouble in the
late 1990s and was bought, in part, by Statoil and Norsk Hydro in 1999.

In issuing production licenses, the state had reserved some of the discovered oil as state property. Until 1984, this state oil was handled directly by Statoil, but under the bourgeois government a new organization, the State Direct Economic Involvement was created and legally
separated from Statoil, although it was still administered by Statoil. The
reason for this move was to prevent the Statoil company from becoming
"unduly" powerful in the Norwegian economy. In 2000 there was an intense debate within the ruling Labor Party about whether to sell part of
Statoil to private interests and, if so, whether to include some part of the
assets belonging to the State Direct Economic Involvement.

The reserves of oil and, in particular, gas that have been found during the
past thirty years of exploration on the Norwegian continental shelf are
enormous. As the largest producer of oil and gas in Europe, Norway faces
new challenges in foreign policy issues, particularly in relation to the EU
and its member states. Actually, Norway was very much involved in bringing the producer perspective into the EU directive; Norway was an interim
member of the EU before the referendum in 1994, just as the EU was
preparing its directive on state licenses for oil and gas production.[22] Petro-
politics is also central to the Norwegian mainland economy, as the industry
requires onshore supply activities—the building of oil rigs, repairs, and so
forth. Where to land oil and gas and where to place the supply centers for
new activities are indeed crucial "pork barrel" issues in Norwegian politics.

Regional and "District" Politics

The center-periphery conflict in Norwegian politics emerges from the
different cultural and economic interests found in different regions. The

most important dimension of this conflict is the urban-rural cleavage that in part arises from the conflicting consumer and producer interests in the agricultural market. This cleavage is also central to debates about numerous other sectors: conditions for small-scale industry, transport and communications policies, the energy market and the "enclave" production in the company towns based on cheap energy, the educational sector, the military infrastructure, and policies affecting public administration jobs in general.

Norwegian agriculture is conducted on a small scale and is based on family farms. The system of alodial rights gives the oldest child—since 1974, regardless of sex—the right to take over the farm when the parents retire. To sell the farm on the market requires a public license, and that is given only if the new owner will live on the farm. The natural conditions for farming vary much around the country, from the wheat-producing areas around the Oslofjord, parts of the Southwest, and Mid-Norway to the marginal areas for farming in the valleys along the West Coast and in North Norway, where livestock is the main source of income.

Farming is tightly regulated with a system of production quotas. This makes it possible for farmers to survive in marginal areas. A complex system of price regulations and subsidies are devised to promote self-sufficiency in agrarian products and to keep jobs in the districts. The economic conditions are negotiated yearly between the major producer organizations and the state. Estimates of total public subsidies vary. According to the OECD, they amount to 20 billion NOK, which means that only 25 percent of production costs are covered by market sale.[23]

The status, the goals, and the price of agriculture have been recurring themes in Norwegian politics. In 1974, a farmers' rebellion took place on an island off the North West Coast, Hitra, when the farmers refused to pay tax as a protest against tough economic conditions. It was a widely publicized political action, which came in the aftermath of the referendum on EU membership in 1972. The EU referendum debate had mobilized the countryside and the political left in the successful "no-to-membership" alliance. The "Hitra rebellion" led to the 1975 parliamentary decision to gradually increase the income of farmers until it reached the level of an average industrial worker. The aim was to create parity between the agricultural and the industrial sectors in terms of income. Increased subsidies caused the income in agriculture to rise for some years. Toward the end of the 1980s, however, the parity goal was abandoned, and during the 1990s, the market was given an increasingly important place in determining production and prices. Also international pressure to ease the import restrictions on agricultural products was felt by Norwegian farmers. However, agriculture was not included in the EEA agreement on bringing Norway into the single market. The World Trade

Organization (WTO) treaty on agriculture of 1995, on the other hand, signaled a long-term change toward increased international competition. A
major conflict in the Norwegian policies toward agriculture—never quite
resolved and still very much present—is whether the main policy aim is
to achieve a high production in order to be reasonably self-sufficient in
food production or to keep up district employment and a high number of
productive farms.

To maintain the number of people living in the districts—or, more real-
istically, to stem the tide moving to the cities and the main urban centers—new jobs needed to be created in industry and services in small
places and rural districts. Some of the major state industries built just after
the war, like the huge iron and steel plant in North Norway, were located
to provide work in such areas. Based on a program to rebuild North Norway after the war, the state in the early 1960s set up a general "District
Fund" in order to help establish viable industries in the districts.

Support for district-based jobs was much more extensive than the
money channeled though the various public agencies and investment
banks created to aid economic activities. In the 1970s, there was increased
support to specific sectors. Agriculture was, of course, the largest recipient in terms of public money, but industry (such as shipbuilding), mining, and fisheries also received money. During the 1980s, the state gradually scaled down direct involvement in industry, and the flow of public
money to industry was reduced.

International agreements made public subsidies to particular industries problematic, such as when the OECD countries (Norway included)
agreed to end public support of the shipbuilding industry. The EEA
agreement in the 1990s also made it difficult to uphold traditional forms
of support. For example, in 1999 the general low employment tax for industry in North Norway was found to be incompatible with the rules of
the single market. The government had to look for new devices, like a
transport subsidy, to reduce the disadvantages of peripheral location.

The term "district politics" is extremely multifaceted and reflects the
diverse conditions found in the different Norwegian regions. But it also
reflects the strong political representation of district constituencies and
interests in the Norwegian political system. The examples are legion:
Since the 1970s, the fight for new jobs strongly affected decisions on the
location of new supply bases for the oil industry. Roads and transportation have always been important. The extension of the railway to the city
of Tromsø in North Norway was—despite its unrealistic economic basis—for many years an important political issue, although it was never
built. Building roads not only helped industry and improved social conditions but also created jobs in the districts. Military bases were solid
sources of income for many local communities, sometimes the only

source of income. Increasingly, public services and educational centers provided the main economic base for many local communities.

It is important to stress, however, that "district politics" was not only motivated by its direct economic benefits. Its main aim was to maintain viable local communities. This also meant giving youth the option to attain higher education without moving to the central areas. With this aim in mind, the university in Tromsø was founded in the late 1960s and a new system of district colleges was created from the 1970s onward. But although several of these policies succeeded, the trend of people to moving to the cities and to the central areas continued. Without these policies to counter the "market forces," however, migration would most likely have been much stronger. It invariably gives insight into the workings and structure of Norwegian politics, however, to ask whether the outcome of a particular public policy will affect the *geographical* distribution of resources. If the answer is yes, one can be fairly certain that this will be reflected in the political debate about the issue.

Unemployment

Since 1945, Norwegian governments—also the bourgeois governments—have pursued a policy of "full employment." The background for this broad political consensus was the still fresh memory of mass unemployment in the 1930s. Although there were obviously different conceptions of what policies it would take to keep unemployment low, any talk about the "need" for higher unemployment (for example, to counter inflation) was found almost morally offensive in public debate. Actually, in 1954 an amendment to the Norwegian constitution made it a public responsibility to create the conditions necessary so that every citizen who wanted to could find a job. This amendment was a statement of intent, so no citizen could sue the state if unemployed, but nevertheless it was a strong political signal that the state would do its utmost to keep unemployment low.

And it did so successfully until the late 1980s—although one could debate whether this was caused by public policies or by general economic circumstances. Comparatively, however, it is a fact that the Norwegian level of unemployment has been extremely low. Between 1945 and the late 1980s, it varied roughly between 1.5 and 3 percent. In 1980, unemployment was 1.7 percent of the workforce.[24] A few years later, the figures started to rise, however, and in 1993 it reached an all-time high of 6 percent. If one added those in search of a permanent job but engaged temporarily in some public work or reeducation scheme, the figure was over 8 percent.

Unemployment was fairly evenly distributed across the country and was not, as it had been previously, higher in the peripheral districts.

Young people were particularly affected, and men more so than women. After 1973, Norwegian unemployment remained comparatively low in spite of the slack in world markets. The average unemployment from 1970 to 1995 was 3.0 percent, while the European OECD countries had an average of 7.0 percent.[25] And during the second half of the 1990s, unemployment gradually declined from the high point in 1993, of 6 percent, down to 3 percent in 1999.

Since the 1970s, policies to alleviate unemployment have become more complex, involving a mixture of macroeconomic and microeconomic measures. A number of resources have been used to try to keep unemployment down. The countercyclical policies of the mid-1970s did not work well in this respect. Pouring money into ailing state industries proved too costly and were probably counterproductive in the long run. Much emphasis was instead put on public schemes to prepare the workforce for a changing labor market by teaching new skills and putting more resources into higher education. The situation in the late 1970s was due not only to the post-oil-shock turbulence in the international markets and the increased internationalization of the Norwegian economy but also to the fact the labor force grew substantially. From 1972 to 1996, the share of the population who were economically active (ages 16–74) increased from 61 to 71 percent.[26] Women, in particular, entered the labor force in greater numbers than before. The work frequency for women between twenty-five and fifty-four years of age increased from 52 to 82 percent in this period.

The Corporate Sector and Wage Negotiations

Norway has a high level of union membership. Countries such as the United States, Japan, and Germany have union membership rates of between 15 and 30 percent, whereas Norway has a union membership of 55 percent of the workforce.[27] This level of unionization has remained fairly stable during the past two decades in contrast to, for example, Great Britain, France, and Austria, where unionization has declined substantially. On the other hand, this figure is not so high in a Nordic context; Sweden has 80 percent union membership. Close to half of all the unionized members today are women, reflecting the growth of women in the workforce and the surge in highly unionized public-sector jobs.

Unions in Norway are organized in three main groups. The largest is the Norwegian Federation of Trade Unions (LO), traditionally a social democratic movement and closely affiliated with the Labor Party. In addition, there are the smaller Federation of Vocational Unions (YS) and the Federation of Norwegian Professional Associations (AF). The latter, however, went through a period of division in the late 1990s and is today somewhat reduced in size. The LO, with close to 800,000 members, is more than twice as large as the other two federations taken together. However, one-fourth of the LO members are not occupationally active (students or retired), and the LO's share of all unionized workers has decreased from 83 percent in 1956 to 54 percent in 1997.[28] The LO is a federation of close to thirty trade unions, the largest being the union of municipal workers, organizing 165,000 workers in the local government sector. Traditionally, the private-sector unions were by far the strongest inside the LO. Today the LO has about 60 percent of its members in the private sector in contrast to the other two federations, where two-thirds of the membership is publicly employed.[29] The two smaller federations both also organize unions that oppose the close political cooperation between the LO and the Labor Party. In the case of the AF, this includes most higher education professions. The changing labor market and the challenge of keeping employees in the unions have led to discussions about a closer cooperation between the trade union federations. In spite of changing alliances and division, however, the basic picture is one of fierce competition over new members, particularly in the expanding service sector. Some unions remain outside all three federations; in 1997—before the AF split up—these unions organized 11 percent of all union members.

Employers in Norway are also organized in a few major federations. The main organization for private employers is the Norwegian Employers Association (NHO) which is the central actor in the wage negotiations on the employer's side. Its member companies employ about 400,000 workers. But there are also large associations that are not part of the NHO, such as the Federation of Norwegian Commercial and Service Enterprises, which covers about 85,000 workers. In the public sector, the state and the Association of Local Authorities (KS) have about the same number of employees, about 250,000 in the state sector and 300,000 at the local level.[30]

Wage Negotiations

The Norwegian labor market is highly organized. Strikes are comparatively infrequent, and usually few workdays are lost in industrial conflicts. The system of wage negotiations is tightly regulated and institutionalized, and in comparison to other countries, it is marked by a high level of centralization and state involvement, often labeled "tripartite" or "corporatist."[31] The historical record speaks about fairly orderly affairs, particularly since the signing of the "Basic Agreement" between the employers (NHO) and the trade unions (LO) in 1935. Today a complex system of laws, regulations, and agencies are in place to guide the parties through wage negotiations.

The Basic Agreement regulates procedural rules and defines the rights of shop stewards. It deals with the employers' right to organize work and their duty to inform and consult. The agreement is renegotiated every four years and often supplements minimum standards set by law. The framework for wage negotiations is guided by collective labor law and by neutral state institutions for arbitration and compromise, such as the National Mediator and the National Wage Board. The National Mediator arbitrates between the parties when negotiations are stalled. The National Wage Board decides cases referred to it by a special law for compulsory settlement. The system for wage settlement was gradually institutionalized in the decades following World War II. In the 1960s, the corporate elements were organized through the Contact Committee, which consists of state, employer, and trade union representatives. This was supplemented in 1967 by the Technical Reporting Committee. In the Contact Committee, central actors from the union, the employer, and the government have informal discussions about upcoming wage negotiations and the economic prospects; then the Reporting Committee presents their agreement on mutually accepted and relevant facts.[32]

During the 1950s, bargaining took place under strict central control at the level of nationwide industries. A new model designed to produce "responsible" wage growth characterized the 1960s. According to this model, wage increases ought to reflect growth in world market prices and increased productivity in the export industry. In these industry-level negotiations, it was usually the iron and metal workers union that started out, and the agreement reached in this sector provided in broad terms the guidelines for negotiations in other sectors. Several conditions made this model possible. First, the iron and metal workers union had a strong position inside the trade union movement as a whole. Second, the model was based on a broad acceptance that to keep the Norwegian economy healthy, the export industry needed to establish the general guidelines on wages.

The high point in state involvement in the wage settlements came with the so-called combined settlements of 1975 and 1977. This was an effort to rein in the economic turbulence following the oil price shock and the decline in international markets. In practice, it meant that the state entered the negotiations between employers and trade unions in centralized bargains where the state contribution was tax relief, increased child allowances, and subsidies for particular necessities. The aim was to reduce the "need" for wage increases and thereby to increase industrial competitiveness and reduce inflation. It is estimated that the state footed between 40 and 60 percent of the bill for these settlements.

The combined settlements gave people more money—whatever the source—to spend. Inflation was not curbed. An attempt was made by the

Labor government to freeze both prices and wages in 1978. By 1981, how-ever, it was clear that this would not work and might even contribute to slowing down much-needed structural changes in industry. In addition, the liberal trends of the 1980s and the Conservative-led government (1981–1986) signaled less centralization and state involvement. The wage negotiations of 1982 and 1984 were again at the industrial level, although bargaining was recentralized in 1987. The 1987 negotiations led to an un-precedented zero-increase agreement nationally, but at the local plant, wage drift prevailed. In 1988 and 1989, there was again an attempt at a mandatory pay freeze (not prices this time).

The rising unemployment in the early 1980s and around 1990 worried trade unionists and politicians. The wage negotiations of the early 1990s provided moderate increases and combined strict central control with some decentralization. A state commission in 1992 proposed a five-year "solidarity pact" for 1993–1997. The purpose was to improve competi-tiveness with other countries and to reduce unemployment. The trade unions (LO) promised wage restraint, and the government promised an active labor market policy and that welfare schemes like the sick pay sys-tem would be upheld. These wage negotiations have been described as a "renationalized corporatist approach,"[33] and they came to be taken as proof that even in an increasingly internationalized economy and within the terms of the EEA agreement, small countries like Norway may tackle international pressures through the flexibility and compromises of their social partners. However, the solidarity pact also created internal ten-sions, in that the other union federations and the political parties on the right felt that it gave the LO too much power.

Industrial Democracy

Workplace participation and cooperation in productivity issues go all the way back to the early post–World War II period. During the 1960s, the Basic Agreement between the LO and the NHO was supplemented by a new scheme for cooperation between workers and employers. This re-quired employers to inform and consult the trade unions regarding the economic situation of the firm and its future plans. In 1973 the new Joint Stock Company Act introduced representation of the workers at the board and assembly levels. The employees were given the right to elect one-third of the representatives to the board in companies with more than fifty employees. In the Environmental Act of 1977, the workers' right to cooperate in decisions regarding production and safety was ex-tended. At the symbolic level, a new amendment to the constitution in 1980 stated that law should set the regulations for employee co-determi-nation at the workplace. None of this challenged the owner's ultimate right to determine investment, production, and the organization of labor. But it gradually developed organizational devices for cooperation and consultation both at the plant level and in the enterprise as a whole. In spite of recurring, although low-level conflicts between labor and capital, these arrangements have fostered a strong "we-are-all-in-the-same-boat" sentiment. This has been felt at the political level when worker-management delegations have traveled to the capital to ask for improved industry support.

The European Economic Area (EEA) Agreement

The EEA agreement was negotiated between the European Union and the EFTA (European Free Trade Association) countries while most EFTA countries, including Norway, at the same time negotiated for EU membership. One year after the EEA agreement came into effect in 1994, its EFTA pillar comprised only Norway, Iceland, and Liechtenstein. Switzerland had opted out earlier after a referendum, and Austria, Sweden, and Finland had in the meantime joined the EU as members.

The EEA is part of the new international regimes (WTO, GATT, World Bank, IMF, Kyoto Agreement, etc.) with an increasingly strong impact on Norwegian internal economic policies and international trade (see Chapter 7). In principle these are all intergovernmental agreements, but the EEA agreement is particularly institutionally biased in favor of the EU. Norwegian sovereignty is, in principle, intact. Norway has a veto option regarding new single market regulations, but to make use of the veto is very difficult. Any veto against an EU regulation of the internal market will undermine the existence of a unified single market in the EU-EFTA region.[34] The EU may retaliate by suspending some parts of the EEA agreement and thereby damage Norwegian exports. It is therefore expected that the EU regulations will take precedence and be accepted by Norwegian authorities. One example of this mentioned earlier is the regional variation in employment taxes, which have been found to be illegal by the control agency overseeing the agreement. These tax reductions were devised to create employment in the industrially weak, northern regions. The Norwegian government has been asked to change this into a system of transport subsidies, which is allowed inside the EU, and will most likely do so. On the other hand, the EEA countries are allowed to monitor the EU's internal decisionmaking process on new internal market regulations and to present its potential queries before the EU Commission finalizes its proposals.

The EEA agreement should give Norwegian companies free access to the single market. In practice, however, experiences have been mixed, as some companies report that the agreement is not well known inside the

EU market. But there are also examples that Norwegian industries have been successful in insisting on their rights.[35]

Several areas are exempt from the agreement. Oil and gas is a special sector; the Norwegian government argues that the EU Treaty of Rome gives the member states sovereignty over natural resources. Agriculture and fisheries are explicitly not covered by the EEA agreement. It was politically impossible for Norwegian authorities to include agriculture, and the EU responded by also exempting fish, one of Norway's main export articles to the EU. The export of salmon—where Norway is a leading producer with the EU countries as its main market—was later hurt when the EU claimed that Norway was selling below market prices. The EU subsequently introduced minimum prices and threatened Norway with extra import duties in 1997. Large fish-farming companies inside the EU argue that the Norwegian fish-farming industry receives large subsidies from the state.

Conclusion

In the second half of the twentieth century, the Norwegian economy changed enormously. Most noticeable from a historical perspective was clearly the growth in GNP per capita. At the same time, central elements of both the economy and the way the economy and politics interacted remained the same. During this half-century, agriculture and fisheries continued to decline. The population growth occurred mainly in the urban centers. The pattern with industrial "enclaves" in many districts persisted, with chemical and metallurgical industries based on high energy-consuming processes. Old industries like pulp, engineering, and construction remained important on a restructured basis. Shipbuilding was in part scaled down and in part reshaped—in particular to meet the needs of the new oil and gas sector. Fish farming became a new growth industry in coastal districts, and the service sector grew everywhere. For many peripheral local communities, public services, health care, and education became the major source of employment. Finally, the decline of shipping after 1973 and the formidable rise in the economic importance of the petroleum industry, both to the Norwegian economy in general and to state finances in particular were crucial economic events. The postwar policy of building state-owned industry was ended, and with the exception of the state's oil company, Statoil, the direct public engagement in industry declined through closures and sales. Nevertheless, the Norwegian state remained a large owner and investor within the economic field. Increasingly, the policy for companies with a state majority stake was that they should be managed according to commercial criteria alone. When the state had to take over the largest banks in the early 1990s to prevent them from going bankrupt, the explicit policy was not to interfere in their daily activities and to return ownership to private investors in due course. The general trend of the 1980s and 1990s was, in other words, more markets, less state.

This change was in line with political sentiments. The international context changed enormously, and liberalization of internal markets followed from a closer integration into the new "international regime." In the 1990s the EU's single market and the EEA agreement made Norway part of that market. This both gave Norwegian industry access to new markets and exposed Norway to stronger domestic competition. The policy of maintaining low unemployment has been persistent and broad based, although it was more difficult to pursue during the 1980s and 1990s, in part as a consequence of increased internationalization of the economy. Other international agreements, such as those presented by the WTO and the Kyoto Agreement on the emission of greenhouse gasses, currently affect, and will increasingly affect, domestic economic policies.

The constants are as evident as the changes, however. The Norwegian economy is small by international comparison, and the state is still a strong force in the economy. Public policies are mostly directed at the macro-level, as market withdrawal has been a dominant trend in terms of direct state involvement for about two decades. The Norwegian economy continues to be very vulnerable to changes in international markets, especially in the oil and gas industry. The large organizations in the labor market cooperate closely with the state, and to some extent, it is still a "negotiated economy." Finally, the political cleavages between right and left, and center and periphery are still entrenched in the economic structure. Wealth is, in comparative terms, quite equally distributed along both the social and the geographical dimensions. Although this is under pressure in the 1990s, it is a fairly stable element in the political economy of Norway.

Notes

1. See *Statistisk Årbok 1997* (Oslo: Statistics Norway, 1997), p. 447.

2. Luxembourg Income Study, Working Paper no. 137, quoted in "Langtidsprogrammet 1998–2001," special attachment, *Stortingsmelding*, no. 4 (1996–1997), (Oslo: Finans- og tolldepartementet, 1997), p. 231.

3. Quoted in Geir Lundestad, "Hovedtendenser in norsk politikk, 1945–1965," in Trond Bergh and Helge Ø. Pharo, eds., *Vekst og velstand* (Oslo: Universitetsforlaget, 1977), p. 465.

4. Gudmund Hernes, "Mot en institusjonell økonomi," in G. Hernes, ed., *Forhandlingsøkonomi og blandingsadministrasjon* (Oslo: Universitetsforlaget, 1978).

5. The figure was 55 percent in 1990; see *Historical Statistics, 1994* (Oslo: Statistics Norway, 1995).

6. Angus Maddison, *The World Economy in the 20th Century* (Paris: OECD, 1989), p. 143, quoted in Øyvind Østerud, *Globaliseringen og nasjonalstaten* (Oslo: Ad Notam, 1999), p. 21.

7. Fritz Hodne, *Norges økonomiske historie, 1915–1970* (Oslo: Alma, 1981), p. 579.

8. Jonathan W. Moses and Bent Sofus Tranøy, "Norge i den nye verdensøkonomien," in Torbjørn L. Knutsen, Gunnar Sørbø, Svein Gjerdåker, eds., *Norges Utenrikspolitikk*, 2nd ed. (Oslo: Cappelen Akademisk Forlag, 1997), pp. 132–137.

9. "Langtidsprogrammet 1998–2001," p. 51.

10. Registered in terms of working hours; see "Langtidsprogrammet 1998–2001," p. 33. The figures do not include employees in state-owned industry.

11. *Statistisk Årbok 1998* (Oslo: Statistics Norway), p. 468.

12. Stein Kuhnle and Liv Solheim, *Velferdsstaten*, 2nd ed. (Oslo: Tano, 1994), chs. 2–3.

13. For the changes in the Labor Party, see Knut Heidar, "The Norwegian Labour Party: 'En attendant L'Europe,'" in Richard Gillespie and William E. Paterson, *Rethinking Social Democracy in Western Europe* (London: Frank Cass, 1993).

14. See, for example, Helge Hveem, *Internasjonalisering og Politikk* (Oslo: Tano 1994), chapter 2.

15. "Langtidsprogrammet 1998–2001," Table 3.8 and 3.9, pp. 75–76.

16. For a description of this development, see Edgeir Benum, *Overflod og fremtidsfrykt, 1970-* , vol. 12, of *Aschehougs Norges Historie* (Oslo: Aschehoug, 1998), pp. 62ff.

17. Statistics Norway, *Historical Statistics 1994* (Oslo: Statistics Norway, 1995), p. 490.

18. Torbjørn L. Knutsen, Gunnar Sørbø, Svein Gjerdåker, eds., *Norges Utenrikspolitikk* (Oslo: Cappelen, 1997).

19. Jennifer Leigh Bailey, "Norsk fiskeripolitikk," in Torbjørn L. Knutsen, Gunnar Sørbø, Svein Gjerdåker, eds., *Norges Utenrikspolitikk* (Oslo: Cappelen, 1997), p. 145.

20. See "Langtidsprogrammet 1998–2001," Table 7.2, p. 160.

21. Dag Harald Claes, "Norsk olje- og gasspolitikk," in Torbjørn L. Knutsen, Gunnar Sørbø, Svein Gjerdåker, eds., *Norges Utenrikspolitikk* (Oslo: Cappelen, 1997), pp. 164–182.

22. Lars Mjøset, "Norge og Den europeiske union," in Torbjørn L. Knutsen, Gunnar Sørbø, Svein Gjerdåker, eds., *Norges Utenrikspolitikk* (Oslo: Cappelen, 1997), p. 317.

23. Steinar Vagstad, "Næringspolitikk," in Anne Lise Fimreite, ed., *Forskerblikk på Norge* (Oslo: Tano, 1997), p. 174.

24. Statistics Norway, *Historical Statistics 1994*, p. 249.

25. Asbjørn Rødseth, "Why Has Unemployment Been So Low in Norway?" in Erik Dølvik and Arild H. Steen, eds., *Making Solidarity Work?* (Oslo: Scandinavian University Press, 1997), p. 157.

26. "Langtidsprogrammet 1998–2001," p. 131.

27. For the facts here, see Anders Kjellberg, "Fagorganisering i Norge og Sverige i et internasjonalt perspektiv," in *Årbok for Arbeiderbevegelsens Arkiv og Bibliotek* (Oslo: Arbeiderbevegelsens Arkiv og Bibliotek, 1999), pp. 57–84.

28. Ibid., p. 68.

29. Jon Erik Dølvik et al., "Norwegian Labour Market Institutions and Regulations," in Erik Dølvik and Arild H. Steen, eds., *Making Solidarity Work?* (Oslo: Scandinavian University Press, 1997), p. 83.

30. Ibid,. p. 82.

31. See several contributions in Erik Dølvik and Arild H. Steen, eds., *Making Solidarity Work?* (Oslo: Scandinavian University Press, 1997).

32. See Dølvik et al., "Norwegian Labour Market Institutions and Regulations," p. 87.

33. Ibid., p. 93.

34. EFTA minus Switzerland, which is not a member of the EEA.

35. Lars Mjøset, "Norge og Den europeiske unionen," in Torbjørn L. Knutsen, Gunnar Sørbø, Svein Gjerdåker, eds., *Norges Utenrikspolitikk* (Oslo: Cappelen, 1997), p. 317.

6

Public Policies

The Norwegian state is a "strong state." Close to half the GNP is channeled through public budgets, and close to one in three employees works in the public sector. The state influences society through three main instruments: creating norms in the form of laws and regulations; using money to shape activities both when extracted as tax and when used in transfers and payments; and finally by spreading advice in the form of knowledge and behavioral preferences through education and public campaigns. Laws and money are clearly the most important policy means, but quite often all three are combined to achieve a goal. It is illegal for restaurants not to set aside smoke-free areas, the tax on cigarettes is high, and there are frequent public campaigns against smoking.

In the previous chapter I focused on economic policies, and in the next I will deal with foreign affairs. Of the policy areas that could be discussed in this chapter I have chosen to focus on three: the policies of the welfare state, the public efforts to protect the environment, and gender equality measures. These are all policy areas with a lot of public attention as well as political controversy. Still they reflect the consensual view that the state ought to be involved in and take responsibility for "society," even in matters that would be considered "private" in some other countries. All three make use of laws, money, and advice, but in different mixes. The policy areas are also different in scope and timing. Welfare policies have occupied a central position in Norwegian public debate during the entire twentieth century. Public policies on green issues and gender have more recently become major policy areas and—so far—with a considerably lighter impact on public budgets.

In Chapter 3 we presented the basic structure of Norwegian public administrative with its three levels: the state, the county, and the municipality. The national political institutions have the general responsibility for all policy areas, and parliament decides what policies should be handled at what level. In education, for example, the primary schools are the responsibility of the municipality, while the counties handle the secondary schools—curriculum exempted in both cases. The ministry of education sets broad national standards regarding educational standards. Public welfare services are offered at all levels. The general laws and rules are a matter for government, parliament, and the civil service; the counties are responsible for psychiatric and child care institutions, while the municipalities manage social aid. Gender equality and environmental questions are to some extent dealt with at the lower levels, although both are mainly the responsibility of the central authorities.

The Welfare State

Two major elements distinguish the social policies of the Scandinavian countries from the rest of Europe: They are generally universalistic, in the sense that they cover all citizens qualifying for support, and they are fairly generous. The first distinguishes them from the German tradition; the second from the British.

Historically, the social insurance laws enacted in the 1880s by Bismarck in imperial Germany placed social policy on the European political agenda. In Germany, Bismarck saw this not only as a support to the needy but also as insurance against the emerging revolutionary socialist parties that threatened the very foundations of the state. Social policy initiatives taken at about the same time in Sweden were part of this trend, and the Swedish-Norwegian king proposed to the Norwegian government to study the German laws in order to come up with something similar.[1] In Norway, there existed a "poor law," providing the bare necessities to people unable to take care of themselves. From the 1890s onward, the early foundations of what later became the "welfare state" were put in place. An accident insurance law was enacted in 1894. This made it compulsory for all employers to pay—as a part of their production costs—the premium to a state insurance company on behalf of their workers. In 1909, a health insurance plan was adopted. This was compulsory for all workers below a certain income level. The insurance was fairly progressive for its time—effecting a transfer to the poor—as it also covered the workers' families.

The economy made further reforms difficult in the 1920s and early 1930s. The second half of the 1930, however, was an active period for social policies spurred by the incoming Labor government of 1935. Pension reform was first. There had been several attempts at a state pension plan earlier, but these had failed due to the economy. In 1936 the first public pension was introduced, covering citizens above seventy years of age provided they qualified on the basis of need. This was financed by a general tax on taxpayers and companies. The last of the major reforms before the war was an unemployment insurance plan. Some private plans had operated earlier, mostly organized by the trade unions with some public support. In 1938, parliament established compulsory unemployment insurance for workers in industry.

The Postwar Welfare State

Most of the prewar elements of the social policies—accident, sickness, pensions, and unemployment insurance—had emerged out of the political battles between the left and right parties in Norwegian politics. The Labor Party in particular advocated universal and publicly financed plans, often supported by the Liberals, whereas the Conservative Party held back and generally preferred private solutions. The postwar political climate was different in that now there was a general consensus about building a welfare state that covered all citizens with benefits as generous as the economy could provide. Much of the inspiration for the postwar changes came from Swedish social democratic practice and from British politics in the wake of the Beveridge report of 1942.[2] During the war, neutral Swedes had been able to continue their efforts at building a welfare state, closely watched by exiled Norwegian politicians and trade unionists who had fled from German occupation.

The wartime experience is crucial in order to understand the postwar consensus on welfare issues. For the major parties, the welfare state goals were shared, although the economic base was a restricting factor in determining the speed of implementation. Class confrontation had softened considerably, and this gave rise to an expansionist phase in building the welfare state. Universal child allowance from the second child was adopted in 1946; compulsory health insurance for all wage earners came in 1953 and for the whole population in 1957. One year later, there was established a universal insurance plan for occupational casualties, and in 1961 a universal plan for the disabled. In 1959 the state set up insurance covering all wage earners against unemployment. The principle of universality was firmly established in the 1950s. The insurance systems should cover everybody: Rich and poor alike should have child allowances, and both rich and poor should have insurance against illness. The social democratic point of view was that no one should be socially stigmatized for receiving public support in difficult times, and all should pay—the rich more than the poor.

This step-by-step creation of a broad public safety net was gradually extended to cover more people and a wider scope of human mishaps. Over time it became a conglomerate of different plans. In the 1960s, therefore, the big issue in social policy debates was whether one could create one big plan to cover it all, incorporating pensions, programs for the disabled, the widow/widower benefit, child allowances, and so forth. The political debate before the Storting election in 1965 was very focused on this new reform. But it is illustrative of the broad consensus on social policies that the party confrontations did not deal with the content—that is, the principle of universality, the premium payments, the scope of arrangements, or the redistribution from rich to poor. Instead the debate was over who could most efficiently implement the reform. The Labor Party argued that a new government, based on a center-right coalition, could not possibly get the reform in place in time, but would need more time for preparation. They were proven wrong, however. The "bourgeois bloc" won the election and the new Folketrygd, or People's Insurance Plan, was adopted by parliament in 1966 and put into effect in 1967.

Four contributors financed these public insurance schemes: the insured, the employers, the state, and the municipalities. Until the mid-1960s, the insured themselves were the main source of finance, but from then on employers had to foot the largest part of the bill.[3] The employers' share increased from about one-quarter to about one-half in the years from 1960 to 1980. The state contributed roughly one-fifth until the mid-1970s, and the share of the municipalities was declining from one-tenth to virtually nothing in the late 1970s. The number of people benefiting from the various social policies increased—as the provisions widened in scope and with changing demography. In 1950, 5 percent of the population received pensions (age or disability); in 1980 that figure was 19 percent.[4] Similarly, 14 percent qualified for child allowance in 1959, but 25 percent qualified in 1980.

From Consensus to Questions

The legacy of a broad consensus among major political parties on welfare state issues has also marked the past three decades. Since the early 1970s, however, questions have been raised concerning whether the plans are too generous and whether the economy will be able to sustain them in the long run. These questions have been particularly pronounced in the periods of economic stagnation that partly coincided with the ideological influx of Tatcherism and Reaganism during the 1980s. In particular, the Progress Party has on several occasions politicized what they claimed was misuse of welfare rights and pointed to the questionable ethics of supporting those with "self-inflicted" mishaps that qualified for social benefits. There has also been much discussion on the health waiting lists—on inefficiencies in public health care and why an oil-rich country like Norway cannot afford better health services.

The years from 1945 to 1980 represent in retrospect the founding and also the most expansionist years of the Norwegian welfare state. This was also the case in many other countries, but the difference was that in Norway the costs continued to rise *after* 1980. The 1970s were—despite the international economic problems of the early 1970s—not a period of significant welfare cuts in Norway. The welfare state continued to expand under a relatively favorable state economy. The late 1970s were marked by the state taking the oil money "in advance," and politicians did not have to face the fiscal restrictions so problematic in many other countries. Actually, when looking at social aid, the figures show that both the number of clients and the total costs rose steeply from 1970 to 1995.[5]

A 1969 law made hospital finance part of the general welfare plan. This triggered a steep rise in costs, and doubled the number of people working in hospitals during the 1970s. The law also made all treatment free of charge, provided that it qualified according to certain criteria. The plan also included treatment in the few private hospitals in operation. In 1973 full pension rights were made optional from sixty-seven years of age. All wage earners above sixty were given an extra, fifth week of vacation in 1976, and in 1978 the sick leave plan was expanded to give full wage compensation from day one—paid by the employer. A new law from 1977 covering the work environment set strict rules for protection of workers' health.

The questions associated with such a wide-ranging and expensive welfare state became more pronounced in the public debate from the early 1980s onward. The cost of health and social services had risen to about 20 percent of the GNP around 1980 compared to 5 percent in 1950.[6] Concern was widespread in the political parties, and the OECD report "The Welfare State in Crises" issued in 1981 signaled a new climate where individuals were expected to take a larger economic responsibility for their own lives.[7] This was reflected in party rhetoric when, for example, the Conservative Party promoted the term "welfare society" as an alternative to the social democratic "welfare state."

· Two themes became central in this political debate: how to finance increasing costs, and how to deal with potential misuse. It was agreed that something had to be done about the long-term rise in costs. A major problem was that in the future there would probably be too few people in the active workforce to carry the costs of the approaching "pensioner's wave." The demographic trend predicted a much higher proportion of pensioners after 2010 when the postwar baby-boomers reached their

pension age. On a randomly chosen day in 1994, 30 percent of the Norwegian people received some kind of social insurance for their liveli-
hood.[8] This was up from 21 percent in 1980.

Several adjustments were made during the 1980s in an effort to counter
this trend. The levels of future rights were scaled down, and politicians
resisted renewed demands to lower the pension age. In addition, somewhat stricter rules for disability pensions were introduced in order to
counter a steep rise in numbers. And since the early 1980s, recipients of
medical prescriptions have had to share the cost of those prescriptions,
which had earlier been free. It is interesting to note, however, that the
changes made to the insurance system during these years were made in
such a way as to minimize cutbacks in women's benefits (see also the
next section).[9]

Toward the late 1980s, some public welfare programs came under increasing attack, and the critics alleged that abuse was widespread and
that some arrangements were morally wrong. This gave rise to heated
debates. In particular, the leader of the populist Progress Party was active
in complaining about people that misused welfare and attacked provisions encouraging what, in his view, was questionable behavior. In one
newspaper interview, he denounced the lazy, the disrespectful, the irre-
sponsible, and the frivolous women.[10] Simultaneously he advocated improved services for the elderly and for people in "real" need. Politicians
from other parties, including Labor, were also open to discussions about
a reconsideration of welfare arrangements. Still, the general consensus on
the welfare state did not subside among the public at large. Surveys consistently showed a broad support for the welfare state. From the mid-
1960s, these had shown that at least 65 percent of citizens wanted to keep
or to develop further public welfare arrangements.[11] At the same time,
many people were skeptical about how efficiently the money was being
used. About one-fifth believed that misuse occurred to a large degree.
The low support for housing and social aid, in particular, was most likely
due to mistrust toward the clients in these sectors. Findings from the
1980s supported this rather two-sided view on the welfare state: People
at large wanted both more welfare services and more efficient use of the
money.[12]

This situation may very well present the political parties with major
problems in the future if economic conditions require major cutbacks in
welfare provisions. There will be political pressure favoring extended
public services rather than shrinking them. During the 1990s, the debate
on public welfare has accordingly been focused on how to expand services in health care and care of the elderly. Debate on downsizing the
welfare state has been avoided in oil-rich Norway, although the uncer-
tainty of future pension rights has been touched on from time to time.

Another finding in the welfare state surveys has been that women are the strongest supporters of the welfare state. This proved politically important at the 1994 referendum on membership in the European Union, which was successfully presented as a threat to the welfare state by the side opposing EU membership. The gender difference is not very large, but it is consistent along all welfare dimensions. Women also generally appear more skeptical toward private solutions in the welfare field. One way to explain this is that women had come to depend more on the welfare state, as much of the work women used to do in the family now to a much greater extent was done through public services.[13] Particularly women working outside the home felt more dependent on these services. Women were also more likely than men to find employment within the welfare sector.

During the EU referendum, the future of the welfare state inside the EU was a major theme in the debate.[14] It was by and large agreed that the EU would not demand cuts in Norwegian welfare rights, but the no-to-membership advocates argued that the EU policy of harmonizing taxes would undermine public welfare finances. Under the European Economic Area (EEA) arrangement, Norway is not a party to the Maastricht agreement or to the European Monetary Union, and this allows more freedom in budgetary and tax matters. Being part of the single market, however, requires coordination of the social security rights as workers move from one country to another. EU citizens are entitled to the same social rights when working in Norway as Norwegian employees and vice versa. The level of services varies, and only for paid birth leave does there exist a minimum EU standard. This system of mutual rights is not new to Norwegians, however, as it has been found among the Nordic countries since 1955.

Green Policies

The breakthrough for environmental policies in Norway came during the 1970s.[15] So-called "classical" environmental issues had been on the agenda for almost one hundred years, but only as single issues. The focus had been on nature preservation: specific unique areas, the habitat of rare species or plants, and important recreational areas. Inspired by the English policies favoring landscape protection and the establishment of American national parks (especially Yellowstone in 1872), the first achievement of the classical Norwegian environmentalist advocates was the protection—"for all time"—of a special beech forest close to the southern town of Larvik in 1884. Advocates of these causes were mostly people in the higher social circles and in urban areas—among them professors and scientists. In the 1950s, a new law on nature conservation established a legal basis for setting up national parks, and the Open-Air Recreation Act of 1957 confirmed the old right of access for all to nature areas, even when privately owned. The 1960s were an important time in this classical nature conservation movement; many activists were inspired by Rachel Carson's 1962 book, *Silent Spring*, about the effects of pesticides on the food chain. In this decade, several new national parks were established along with—the less-restricted classification—"protected landscape" areas.

Long-distance pollution hit Norway in the 1960s as a result of the British Clean Air Act of 1956. When new regulations were implemented in Britain, much local air pollution decreased, but these changes led to increased long-distance sulfur dioxide pollution in Southern Norway. This was seen as a major factor behind the fish dying out in the freshwater lakes.

During the 1960s and 1970s, protest movements mobilized against the continued development of hydroelectric power plants. These energy plants had been at the core of the modernization process in Norway, and many waterfalls and rivers were developed to meet the huge demand for new energy in the 1950s and 1960s. In the early 1970s, a protest action was conducted against the development of a hydroelectric plant that would destroy an extraordinary waterfall in Western Norway. Protesters were very successful in engaging the media in its efforts, as national celebrities participated and advocated civil disobedience on prime-time television. Activists blocked the road to the development and had to be forcefully removed by the police, and it became a major media event.

Organizations and Politics

During the 1960s, many new organizations and PACs took up the environmentalist cause, and the political parties also paid increasing attention. This resulted in the establishment of the Department of Environment headed by a senior minister in 1972.[16] The department was given the task to propose and execute policies on pollution control, physical economic planning, nature conservation and open-air recreation, and international environmental cooperation.[17] In the process leading up to the creation of this new department, there were internal disputes among the ministries about the "cross-sector" nature of its tasks. The ecological argument was that environmental issues cut across most departmental sectors and that the new department consequently needed to be of an overarching character. The Ministry of Finance, however, reacted to this competition and eventually (and predictably) won the fight.[18] Routine implementation of the public policies administered by the department was organized in several directorate agencies, of which the most important is the Pollution Control Authority. At the county level, environmental tasks have been organized as administrative sections under the county governor's office (since 1982). There are also administrative offices for environmental issues at the municipal level.

The 1970s witnessed a growing political engagement in environmental issues and a transition toward more ecologically inspired politics. The issues were increasingly seen in a global, rather than a local or national, context. Energy and pollution were the two central environmental issues. Various planning issues deriving from new roads, airports, and refineries were still on the agenda, but it was the old question of hydroelectrical power developments that triggered another and probably the most spectacular environmental single-issue confrontation in postwar Norway. The "Alta issue" in 1979–1981 concerned the Storting decision to build a power plant in North Norway in an area that would affect the traditional Sami reindeer industry. The ethnic dimension made it very touchy, and demonstrators had to be removed by special police forces shipped in from other parts of Norway. In addition, there was also a hunger strike by a Sami group in front of the parliament and an occupation of the prime minister's office. Although the plant was built, it generated a debate about the position and status of ethnic minorities in Norwegian society and politics.[19]

The energy question was also central in debates in the 1970s about extending oil drilling to the rough waters outside Mid-Norway and North Norway. The fishermen were particularly worried about the effects of a potential blowout on the rich fishing fields in these areas. The parliament, however, went ahead with the plans in 1980, in spite of strong local protest. Plans to build nuclear energy plants also worried a lot of people, and this became the basis for several active PACs. There was a heated debate about the need for energy to secure industrial growth versus the danger of nuclear accidents. The Harrisburg accident of 1979 was the decisive factor in burying the plans for nuclear energy in Norway. In 2000 an energy question was for the first time instrumental in bringing down a government. The coalition of center parties fell on the issue of how to deal with the building of new gas-fueled energy plants (see Chapter 8).

Pollution from industry and agriculture was another field for environmental policies. Long-distance pollution from the United Kingdom or Eastern Europe was one worry; another was industrial waste and the increasing water pollution both of freshwater and in the fjords. In 1970 it was discovered that the largest lake in Norway, Mjøsa, was strongly polluted as a result of waste from surrounding industry, households, and agriculture. Rivers and fjords close to traditional large-scale industry and cities were polluted and needed to be cleaned up. Finally, the North Sea Basin was threatened as it received waste from the many surrounding countries—the fisheries, in particular, were at risk. The Pollution Control Authority declared early that its major task was to find and clean up existing waste. Another major challenge was to remove deposited waste from industry no longer in business.

The 1980s and 1990s added new problems, perspectives, and political actors to the environmental field. It was discovered that much had been left undone in the first pollution cleanup campaigns during the 1970s. A new type of investigating PAC entered the media front pages staging spectacular—sometimes illegal—waste hunts. Bellona, an organization created in 1986, was a political action group that did not practice the traditional membership democracy but was directed by professional employees (see also Chapter 4). It was organized as a nonprofit organization financed by donations from industry and private donors. Its employees were skilled personnel, recruited to match the expertise in industry and public agencies, and its activities were strongly media-oriented. Their strategy was to make an impact on decisionmakers through mobilizing strong public opinion. In the mid-1990s, about twenty environmental interest organizations were in operation—including old as well as new types.[20] Increasingly, these organizations have been integrated into the traditional corporatist framework of Norwegian public administration. They are asked to be on public committees, to comment on commissions' recommendations, and so forth. Still, their trademark and power base is the spectacular media campaigns and the civil disobedience actions that are meant to catch the public eye.

In national politics the new issues and political campaigns since the 1970s have made an impact on the voters. Public opinion, however, has not been very stable. People react to the news: Harrisburg, Chernobyl, holes in the ozone layer, algae invasions along the coast, and so on. Both in 1977 and in 1989, the voters rated energy and environmental issues as the second most important campaign issues.[21] From being rated as one of the two most important issues by 37 percent of the voters in 1989, they dropped to 7 percent at the Storting election in 1993. In 1989, the public had been presented the previous summer with the upsetting news of an invasion of seals in North Norway and the algae invasion in the South. Both were taken to indicate that there was a distorted ecological balance. The election of 1997 also showed that environmental issues did not automatically get top scores among the Norwegian electorate: 10 percent found environmental concerns to be the most important campaign issue.[22] In spite of these ups and downs, surveys have found evidence of an emerging green cleavage in the electorate, cutting across the traditional left-right dimension and affecting the voters' electoral choice.[23] The Socialist Left Party and the center parties, particularly the Liberal Party, have consistently been the strongest environmental advocates in

Norwegian politics. Labor has had a more mixed record with a "responsible growth" policy.

Policies

The public policies since the 1970s reflect the transition from classical preservation of nature to policies based more on a broader ecological perspective. Several policy guidelines reflect this change. A central early guideline in environmental public policies was the "polluter pays" principle. This was central to the early pollution cleanup efforts by the Department of the Environment. This has gradually been interpreted to include not only the pollution created by production but also the total pollution created by the product's entire life cycle from production to waste dump.[24] New perspectives emerged in the 1980s triggered by the work of the United Nations World Commission on Environment and Development, headed by the Norwegian Prime Minister Gro Harlem Brundtland. This commission coined the phrase "sustainable development" and inspired a new set of principles to guide policy initiatives. One was the "precautionary principle," meaning that one needed to evaluate all possible ecological consequences of a particular policy before it was implemented. In doing this, one should apply "the notion of critical loads on nature's carrying capacity."[25] The point was to focus on the broad effects of laws and public policies. Pollution control in itself was no longer sufficient. This led to a change of emphasis from administrative regulations—prohibitions or preconditions—to a focus on influencing the incentive structure of behavior affecting the environment. In 1996, the so-called "green tax" commission presented new proposals on how taxes could be shaped in order to achieve a better environment and lower unemployment. It advocated higher taxes on polluting production and lower taxes on work (employment taxes).

Successive Norwegian governments have been very active in working for international agreements to reduce long-distance pollution and the emission of greenhouse gasses. Norway has for a long time been a net importer of pollution originating in the United Kingdom and Eastern Europe. Also the pollution of the North Sea Basin was the result of pollution from many countries. In North Norway, pollution came from the industrial complexes at the Kola Peninsula in Russia. The threats posed by a potential nuclear accident close to the Norwegian border created anxiety. Diplomatic activities and international treaties have been legion—from the Oslo Convention on marine pollution in 1972 to the Kyoto agreement on greenhouse gasses in 1997. In part as a result of the UN "Brundtland Commission," Norway gained the international reputation of being a front-runner in environmental awareness, although the image was somewhat tarnished by the unilateral decision to resume whaling in the early 1990s (see Chapter 7). That decision, however, was vigorously defended on the ecological grounds that the hunt was again sustainable.

The image of front-runner in the environmental field was difficult to sustain. In 1989 the parliament declared a unilateral policy to stabilize the emission of carbon dioxide at the turn of the century—with 1989 as the base year. This decision implied that the government had to regulate in much more detail areas not previously included in the environmental sector: transportation, oil and gas production, and agricultural production. In 1995, however, the government admitted that this aim was not possible to achieve.

Gender Equality

Another political outcome of the 1970s activism was a much more active public policy in support of improved gender equality. The political power of women and the increased centrality of equality issues became prominent during this decade (see Chapter 4). There were parallel developments in the neighboring countries, and these are frequently seen as a special case in comparison with other Western countries.[26] Helga Hernes has argued that the Scandinavian countries have special institutional and cultural characteristics that may account for this. They are less marked by the "separation of private and public, personal and community aspects of life" than most other Western societies. The general characteristic outside of Scandinavia is a rather strict private-public separation, and this is seen as a major obstacle to increased state-directed gender equality.[27] Other researchers have emphasized the work of activist groups in furthering the cause of gender equality in Scandinavia.[28]

The historic evolution of public policy on gender equality has broadly followed the familiar pattern described by T. H. Marshall—starting with general civilian rights, subsequently moving on to political rights, and finally to social rights.[29] Marshall identified the struggle for these rights in Western Europe as belonging to the eighteenth, nineteenth, and twentieth centuries, respectively. This is clearly not the case for women's rights in Norway. In Norwegian history, the most basic civilian rights were achieved in the second half of the nineteenth century and early in the twentieth. In the 1850s, women were given the legal right to inherit on equal terms with their male relatives. Excepted were the alodial rights to take over the farm. This remained the privilege of the oldest son for another 120 years. Until 1990 only male relatives could inherit the crown. As an individual, women were granted full legal rights in the 1880s, although the right to manage industry on equal terms with men was not achieved until 1913. In the 1880s, the university was opened for women, and all secular public positions became open in 1938. Women had, however, to wait until the 1950s to become priests in the Norwegian state church. In practice, of course, there were substantial lags in the entry of women into these positions.

The debate on political rights was presented in Chapter four, and this was definitely a struggle where the victories, by and large, belong to the twentieth century. The first public election open to (some) female voters was the local election of 1901. In 1913, universal voting was established for parliamentary elections. From voting rights followed the right to take office even though this in practice took some time to achieve. The first woman to enter parliament as a full representative did so in 1921. The first female mayor was elected in 1925, and the first minister was appointed in 1945. The first prime minister came with Mrs. Brundtland in 1981, and the first parliamentary president—the Speaker—was elected in 1993.

Social rights provide a minimum of economic safety and the ability to live in accordance with generally accepted social norms. Integration into the educational institutions is important and so are public welfare services. Equal rights to education evolved gradually from the eighteenth century until women were accepted at the university. In terms of social policy, in 1890 the fight against publicly accepted prostitution led to an end to enforced public control. In 1915 the struggle to secure the rights of single mothers and children born out of wedlock succeeded in attaining increased financial support to single mothers. Children born out wedlock were given the right to the father's name and equal rights of inheritance. Local municipalities later adopted special social security arrangements for single mothers, and these were implemented nationwide in the 1960s and 1970s, and in 1980, these rights were also extended to include single fathers. In the early twentieth century, women activists emphasized control over reproduction as the main policy to achieve social equality for women—the slogan had early on been "voluntary motherhood"—and it included the right to abortion. That eventually became law in the late 1970s. The struggle for equal pay and equal pension rights was part of this fight, but it has thus far achieved fewer practical results.

1970s: Lawmaking

The new feminist movement emerging in the late 1960s and early 1970s argued that although many formal, legal rights had been won in the past, some important rights remained—the right to abortion was one—and many of the formal rights lacked effective devices for implementation. Although some of the methods of the new feminists were unorthodox, their rather successful strategy was familiar in the political history of Norway: the use of lawmaking and state power to achieve goals.

In 1972 the public Equal Pay Commission changed into a more general Equality Council and was given the broader task of working for gender equality in all sections of society. The Equality Council is expected to advise the public authorities on matters that are a hindrance to the creation of such equality. In Chapter 4, I discussed the importance of the corporate channel of influence in Norwegian politics. Representation on public boards, committees, and councils at the intersection between the state, organized interests, and technical expertise are central arenas of power. In 1973 new rules were adopted to improve the representation of women in the corporate sector. A change in the alodial law in 1974 gave—as noted above—women the right to inherit the farm if they were the oldest child in the family. This was a controversial break with ancient tradition, strongly entrenched in Norwegian culture. At the municipal level, special equality councils were appointed throughout the country after 1975, and similar councils at the county level followed later. Their task was to give advice and to establish contact between interested groups. In 1977 a new section in the (then) Ministry of Administration and Consumer Affairs was set up that was given the responsibility to coordinate public policies promoting gender equality at the ministerial level. Probably more important to most Norwegians, however, was the new abortion law of 1978. This gave women the right to choose abortion—within the first twelve weeks of pregnancy. From the early 1960s until passage of the 1978 law, the final decision in these matters had been given to councils composed mostly of doctors, who considered the medical and social circumstances of the women seeking an abortion. The 1978 law came after an intense debate where an anti-abortion PAC collected 610,000 signatures against passage of the abortion law.

Next to the abortion law, the new law on gender equality that came in 1978 was probably the most important change in public policy within this field of the decade. Its purpose was to promote equality between the sexes in the labor market, at home, and in society in general. In particular, such equality was to be achieved by "furthering the interests of women." The central focus of the law was to avoid discrimination of women in the labor market. It also established positive efforts to improve the employment opportunities for women, given that qualifications were equal. It made discrimination on the basis of sex illegal in appointments, job advancement, and layoffs. The law was presented to parliament by a Labor Party government after a long fight with the trade union movement. The women's movement wanted more active backing to further women's interests, but the trade unions did not want any more interference with the process of free bargaining. In 1979 the new public position of "ombud for gender equality" was created. She—it has always been a woman—has the responsibility of monitoring the law on gender equality and ensuring that the law is followed.

Implementation and New Debates

The 1980s were busy years for implementing public policies on gender equality. New labor market policies were put in place: Subsidies were given to firms employing women in "nontraditional" jobs; special public support was given to women who started their own firms; and quotas were established for women in several educational programs and in some public service jobs.[30] The policy focus changed slightly during the 1980s, away from labor market policies and toward policies affecting mother and child. To borrow a title summarizing these developments, "reproduction went public."[31]

As more women entered the labor market during the late 1970s and early 1980s, increasing political pressure was put on politicians to improve conditions for working mothers and their families. Maternity leave with full pay was extended to eighteen weeks in 1986, and in 1993 a whole year was granted. Publicly supported nurseries were built to meet the increasing demand, but in spite of high priority and "action plans," the long-term goal of full coverage has not been achieved.

In 1990 a new arrangement gave pension rights to women looking after a relative in need of care on an unpaid basis. The question about pensions introduced a new phase in the public debate on women's rights. The demand was that public pension plans ought to reflect the kind of lives women live, which are characterized by more periodic economic activity than are the lives of men. As a consequence, women, by and large, come out worse in terms of pension rights.

The demands for extended public services to improve the lot of women had generally been supported by the center-left parties. Support for policies giving increased help to women choosing to remain at home came mainly from the center-right parties. The new government of the center parties from 1997 promised a cash support for all children under the age of three. This support roughly matched the per-child public subsidy given to nurseries. The policy was the main campaign issue of the Christian People's Party and was implemented by the new center government with the support of the right-wing parties in parliament. In 1997 this support was provided for children under two years of age who did not attend a nursery that received public subsidies. In 1999 this cash support was extended to children under three years of age. The Labor Party strongly fought this "attack" on public nurseries, but in the autumn of 1999 the party felt more or less compelled to support it on a temporary basis in order to gain influence over the budget in general in parliament. In this case, both the left and right parties advocated a "state feminism"; that is, they supported policies that made the state the central actor in furthering equality between the sexes, although their profiles were very different.[32]

Conclusion

The three public policy areas discussed in this chapter bring out the same message as in the previous chapter about the political economy. The Norwegian state is an active, strong state. The policies are generally based on a broad consensus. There are, of course, party political differences along the traditional left and right divide as to how far the state has a responsibility to act.

The embryonic welfare state policies originate in conservative efforts to fight off the revolutionary workers' movement. Nevertheless, in Norwegian politics their practical implementation was spearheaded first by the liberals and later by the social democrats, although both had some conservative support. The Labor government built the major welfare state arrangements in the postwar years, but with broad political backing. And it was a center-right coalition government that "crowned" the work with the general Social Security Act of 1966. This act brought all the various elements of the welfare state project under one legal heading.

Welfare issues have been popular among the voters. Women, in particular, were strong supporters as "reproduction went public." Potential misuse, however, has been a political issue since the 1980s, particularly with politicians on the populist right. The cash support to families introduced by the center coalition government of 1997 showed the gap between a statist and a family-centered focus on how to support families with young children. This was very much an ideological debate over the best interests of children, families, and women. What united the parties, however, was that they all wanted to use public money.

Green policies have changed from a narrow aesthetic and leisure-focused interest into a broad ecological concern with overarching implications for state and society. The Alta dam project led to a strong confrontation between environmentalists and ethnic activists and police forces in 1980. This was the most spectacular showdown of the old nature protection type and a harbinger of the broader significance of environmental policies for society as a whole. Increasingly, green policies were directed at making structural changes aimed at prevention—the "green tax commission" is a good example—rather than repair and cleanup after environmental damage had occurred. In addition, the international component of environmental policy became very important in Norwegian diplomacy during the 1980s (see Chapter 7). Environmental policy alternatives were also key issues in the EU referendum debate in the early 1990s: The pros argued that only international cooperation could save the environment, whereas the cons viewed EU membership as leading to increased pollution.

Gender equality policies gained a broader significance during the 1970s and led to new laws and new administrative structures. Earlier gender equality advocates had focused on legal equality between the sexes; now the focus was directed more at the end result. The Abortion Act of 1978 and the Gender Equality Act of the same year were the two most important results of the struggle of the new feminist movement in the 1970s. This legislation integrated gender politics into the state, and the movement itself was transformed into a "state feminist" movement. Like the abortion debate of the 1970s, the debate in the late 1990s on cash support to families with young children was anchored in the ideological views of the relationship between the state and society. In both debates the Christian People's Party confronted the liberal and left forces, the first time with Christian values written on their banners, the second with family values as their guiding principle. They lost the first and won the second. Cash support to families with young children was a conscious attempt to redirect the general trend of "reproduction going public" in the 1980s and 1990s.

Notes

1. See Stein Kuhnle, "Historisk oversikt," in Stein Kuhnle and Liv Solheim, *Velferdsstaten – vekst og omstilling,* 2nd ed. (Oslo: Tano, 1994). Most of the factual information presented on the Norwegian welfare state policies and history are found in this book and in Aksel Hatland, Stein Kuhnle, and Tor Inge Romøren, *Den norske velfersstaten,* 2nd ed. (Oslo: Ad Notam Gyldendal, 1996). For a thorough historical analysis, see Anne-Lise Seip, *Sosialhjelpstaten blir til: Norsk sosialpolitikk, 1740–1920,* 2nd ed. (Oslo: Gyldendal, 1994), and Anne-Lise Seip, *Veier til velferdsstaten: Norsk sosialpolitikk, 1920–1975* (Oslo: Gyldendal, 1994).

2. *Social Insurance and Allied Services,* a report prepared by British economist William Henry Beveridge for the British government, proposed a social security system "from the cradle to the grave" for all British citizens.

3. Stein Kuhnle, "Finansiering av velferdsstaten," in Stein Kuhnle and Liv Solheim, *Velferdsstaten – vekst og omstilling,* 2nd ed. (Oslo: Tano, 1994), pp. 66–67.

4. Stein Kuhnle, "Mottakere og goder," in Stein Kuhnle and Liv Solheim, *Velferdsstaten – vekst og omstilling,* 2nd ed. (Oslo: Tano, 1994), p. 72.

5. *Stortingsmelding,* nr. 4 (1996–1997), "Langtidsprogrammet 1998–2001," special attachment, p. 250.

6. See Edgeir Benum, *Overflod og fremtidsfrykt 1970-* , vol. 12 in *Aschehougs Norges Historie* (Oslo: Aschehoug, 1998), p. 93. For the 1950 figure, see Einar Bowitz and Ådne Cappelen, "Velferdsstatens økonomiske grunnlag," in Aksel Hatland, Stein Kuhnle, and Tor Inge Romøren, *Den norske velfersstaten,* 2nd ed. (Oslo: Ad Notam Gyldendal, 1996), p. 49.

7. Stein Kuhnle, "Velferdsstatens politiske grunnlag," in Aksel Hatland, Stein Kuhnle, and Tor Inge Romøren, *Den norske velfersstaten,* 2nd ed. (Oslo: Ad Notam Gyldendal, 1996), p. 32.

8. Aksel Hetland, "Trygdepolitikken ved et veiskille," in Aksel Hatland, Stein Kuhnle, and Tor Inge Romøren, *Den norske velfersstaten,* 2nd ed. (Oslo: Ad Notam Gyldendal, 1996), p. 159.

9. Kuhnle, "Velferdsstatens politiske grunnlag," p. 220.

10. *Dagbladet,* August 8, 1989; see Kuhnle, "Velferdsstatens politiske grunnlag," p. 33.

11. Kuhnle, "Velferdsstatens politiske grunnlag," p. 32. The references for the figures in this part are found in pp. 32–36.

12. Ibid., p. 35.

13. Helga Hernes, *Welfare State and Women Power* (Oslo: Norwegian University Press, 1987).

14. Anders Todal Jensen, Ola Listhaug, and Per Arnt Pettersen, "Betydningen av gamle og nye skiller," in Anders Todal Jensen and Henry Valen, eds., *Brussel midt imot. Folkeavstemningen om EU* (Oslo: Ad Notam, 1995).

15. A brief introduction to environmental policies in Norway is found in Alf-Inge Jansen and Per Kristen Mydske, "Norway: Balancing Environmental Quality and Interest in Oil," in Kenneth Hanf and Alf-Inge Jansen, *Governance and Environment in Western Europe* (Harlow: Longman, 1998).

16. See Alf-Inge Jansen, *Makt og miljø. Om utformingen av natur- og miljøvernpolitikken i Norge* (Oslo: Universitetsforlaget, 1989).

17. Jansen and Mydske, "Norway: Balancing Environmental Quality and Interest in Oil," p. 183.

18. Jansen, *Makt og miljø,* chapter 5.

19. See Chapter 3, "The Sami Assembly."

20. Jansen and Mydske, "Norway: Balancing Environmental Quality and Interest in Oil," p. 187.

21. Bernt Aardal and Henry Valen, *Konflikt og opinion* (Oslo: NKS-forlaget, 1995), p. 183.

22. Bernt Aardal et al., *Velgere i 90-årene* (Oslo: NKS-Forlaget, 1999), p. 21.

23. See Chapter 4, and Jansen and Mydske, "Norway: Balancing Environmental Quality and Interest in Oil," p. 185.

24. "Langtidsprogrammet 1998–2001," p. 103.

25. Jansen and Mydske, "Norway: Balancing Environmental Quality and Interest in Oil," p. 195.

26. See, for example, Lauri Karvonen and Per Selle, *Women in Nordic Politics: Closing the Gap* (Aldershot: Dartmouth, 1995).

27. Helga Hernes, *Welfare State and Woman Power: Essays in State Feminism* (Oslo: University Press, 1987), p. 162.

28. For example, Lena Wängnerud, "Representing Women," in Peter Esaiasd-sen and Knut Heidar, *Beyond Congress and Westminster: The Nordic Experience* (Columbus: Ohio State University Press, 2000).

29. This point is made in A.-H. Nagel, "Politisering av kjønn—et historisk per-spektiv," in N. C. Raaum, ed., *Kjønn og politikk* (Oslo: Tano, 1995), p. 52. The his-torical account given here is based on this work.

30. See Benum, *Overflod og fremtidsfrykt 1970-* , p. 116.

31. Hernes, *Welfare State and Woman Power.*

32. The term is taken from Hernes, *Welfare State and Woman Power.*

7

Foreign Relations

Kleiner Land—was·nun? *("Small country—what now?")*

—*Knut Frydenlund*

The late Foreign Minister Knut Frydenlund's play on words pointed to the changing situation for Norway's foreign policy in the 1980s.[1] The Nordic countries traditionally constituted a "quiet corner" of the European continent. Nevertheless, in the second half of the twentieth century their foreign policies have been shaped by two wars—one hot, the other cold. During World War II (1939–1945), they were all in some way drawn into the maelstrom of war. The following decades of cold war left all of them outside the "iron curtain," although some (Finland, in particular) felt the need to perform more of a balancing act than the other countries. Norway became a founding member of NATO in 1949. Geography, or geopolitics, is the main explanatory factor according to the standard analysis of Norwegian foreign policy. The argument is that the policy of westbound military integration is shaped by Norway's seaward position and by the long distance to the major political, economic, and cultural centers of Europe.[2] The view is—in the formulation of one critic—that "geography is destiny."[3]

Norway's presence at the world scene is at best sporadic, except for the yearly Nobel Peace Prize awards. It is an understatement that the international community makes a greater impact on Norway than Norway does on the international community. Economically and culturally, the Norwegian society tends to respond more than shape, and—just as in the United States—the sophisticated tend to complain that the many not-so-sophisticated doubt whether we really need the rest of the world, the difference being, of course, that Norwegians by and large know they do.

Foreign policy issues have often been discussed in terms of three concentric circles: the Nordic, the European, and the Atlantic. This spatial perspective indicates that the policy preferences and the debating constituencies have varied according to the "circle" in question. The neighboring countries have constituted the immediate, almost local, arena. Since the 1950s, this has been a fairly frictionless, pragmatic field for close cooperation. The European arena increased in importance after the end of the cold war, particularly with the rise of the European Union. European questions used to be about economic policies and culture, and increasingly about legal matters, but during the 1990s and the second referendum on EU membership, these questions turned out to be on policy issues in general. The Atlantic sphere has been the dominant field in security policies since 1949, and the strong dependence on NATO—with a U.S. military guarantee—replaced the old policy that implicitly relied on British support in times of crisis. Today one would need to include "the globe" as a fourth circle.

The end of cold war brought increased complexities to the foreign policy field—particularly as demonstrated by the debate on EU membership in the early 1990s. The increasing impact of world markets has made domestic economic policies more vulnerable. Although it should not be exaggerated, it has become more difficult to govern by the old national policy instruments alone. The wage policy of the 1990s is an example. The solidarity pact (see Chapter 5) aimed at moderate wage increases to get the production costs of Norwegian companies more in line with competitors abroad. The division between foreign and domestic policies has been difficult to uphold.

However, Norwegian external policies have traditionally been more complex than dealing exclusively with national security, where the internal-external dividing line has been most clear. The Norwegian merchant marine depended historically on the freedom of the seas, and a government fell in the 1920s on the issue of importing wine from Portugal in return for the export of fish. Nevertheless, the "high politics" of any state does includes security, especially in a country that was occupied by foreign military troops for five years (1940–1945). But security is a much broader policy field at the turn of the twentieth-first century than it was during the twentieth century.

The Geopolitics of Security

"Never again the 9th of April" was the political slogan signaling a pro-NATO membership stand, close U.S. cooperation, and a strong military. The April 9,1940, was the date of the German attack on Norway. It became a political trauma, much like December 7th with the Japanese attack on Pearl Harbor in 1941. The military resistance following the attack on Norway in 1940 was weak, and the country was occupied in a matter

of a few weeks, the major cities in southern Norway (the capital included) on the very first day of the campaign. The German forces almost
caught the fleeing king and the government. "Never again . . ." was the
slogan of the right-wing politicians, in particular. It had an edge against
what they saw as an unprepared, politically unsuited prewar Labor government. Labor's low-spending approach to defense had been rooted—it
was alleged—in general antiwar and antimilitary attitudes. The postwar
Labor governments, however, were strong supporters of NATO membership. At the same time, they expressed a commitment to international cooperation to protect freedom and peace against the threats of totalitarian
communist expansionism.[4] This western anchor in the security policy
was, however, challenged from both the left and also from inside the Labor Party itself.

In Stein Rokkan's "conceptual map of Europe," which was developed
to explain variations in the structure of twentieth-century mass politics,
Norway was listed as a Protestant country as well as a "seaward periphery" at a far distance from the economically important "city belt" of Europe.[5] Dependence on external seaway supplies had been made very
clear during the Napoleonic wars when England cut off the sea traffic to
Norway (1807–1809). This caused starvation among the poor. During the
union with Sweden (1814–1905), foreign policy affairs were directed from
Stockholm. Friction over the interests of the Norwegian merchant marine
was among the reasons why Norway left the union with Sweden. During
the World War I (1914–1918), Norway remained neutral but with a defi-
nite bias favoring England. None of the warring countries, however, saw
it to their advantage to bring Norway into the war. Neutrality was also
the policy throughout the interwar period. It ended with the German attack in 1940, when the government joined the Allied side. In the late
1930s, the tacit strategy of the government had been—if worst came to
worst—to join the war on the "right side." This they did.

After 1945 the government returned to neutrality, and in the first years
it pursued a policy of "bridge-building" between the major powers, East
and West. This was the traditional "small state" approach so central to
foreign policy formulation during the cold war: bridge-building, cooperation, and fear of isolation.[6] What had changed with World War II, however, was that defending Norwegian territorial integrity, democratic values, and westward trade now required a security guarantee from the
Western powers. The decision to join the NATO alliance in 1949 was nevertheless taken after a searching debate, particularly inside the Labor
Party. This was later portrayed as a fight over Prime Minister Gerhardsen's political soul. This was a break with the past.

Norway had for its short history as an independent nation pursued a
policy of neutrality. As a small nation, its government had persistently

advocated a strengthened international rule of law. Norway had been a strong supporter and a member of the League of Nations and was actively engaged in the organization of the United Nation. The Norwegian minister of foreign affairs, Trygve Lie, was appointed the first general secretary of the United Nations. In the debates in 1949, the alternative to NATO was not old-style neutrality but a Nordic defense union. In the end a solid majority at the Labor Party Congress of 1949—where the prime minister come out in favor of NATO—decided to opt for membership, and this decision was soon afterward corroborated by parliament.

After twenty years—in 1969—the signatories of the NATO pact had the opportunity to leave the alliance if they wanted. The Norwegian parliament decided without much opposition to stay on. Membership had served Norwegian security interests well during the years of high tension. The strong military buildup by the Soviet Union on the Kola Peninsula close to the Norwegian border made withdrawal less likely than ever. During those twenty years of membership, the perception by countries like the United States and the United Kingdom was that Norway had been a loyal and reliable ally.[7] The Norwegian self-perception, on the other hand, was that it had been a "reluctant ally." First of all, the government had set up several restrictions on military operations and deployments in order to avoid giving offense to the Soviet Union. One such restriction was to not allow the deployment of nuclear arms on Norwegian territory in peacetime. Others were to prohibit the establishment of military bases with permanent foreign troops and to prohibit military maneuvers including NATO troops close to the Soviet Union border.

Another factor giving rise to the domestic perception of "reluctance" was the persistent and vocal opposition on security matters in Norwegian politics. This was particularly troublesome to the government because the NATO skeptics were strong inside the governing Labor Party itself. The Socialist People's Party, founded in 1961 in opposition to the foreign policy of the government, contributed to Labor losing a Storting parliamentary majority in that year's election. The party presented itself to the voters as an alternative "third way" between the pro-NATO Labor Party and the pro-Moscow Communist Party.

In spite of the Socialist People's Party and the few Communists, the NATO membership was strongly supported by Norwegian voters during the entire period. Fear of the Soviet Union, particularly after what happened in Hungary in 1956 and in Czechoslovakia in 1968, reinforced this support. NATO membership was also seen as contributing toward a "Nordic balance," where Norway and Denmark were NATO members (Iceland had a security guarantee from the United States), while Sweden was (westward leaning) neutral and Finland was neutral, although bound by a special "treaty of friendship and support" with the Soviet Union.

The End of the Cold War

Norwegian territory had a crucial strategic position in the military confrontation between the Soviet Union and the United States. This was partly a consequence of the large military buildup on the Kola Peninsula, where the Soviet Union also based the submarines that gave that country a second-strike nuclear capability. This capability made the leaders in Moscow a deadly threat to NATO, including the United States. Norwegian territory was important for surveillance and to make Soviet marine access to the North Atlantic more difficult. Hardly any NATO country received—relative to population size—as much economic support to its defense infrastructure as Norway. Before the iron curtain was lifted, and while Ronald Reagan was president in the United States, NATO went through a "second" cold war. According to reports in the media, the Soviet Union quadrupled its military activities at sea outside Norway from 1984 to 1985.[8]

In Norway political debates in the first part of the 1970s were dominated by the referendum on the European Community membership. In 1977, however, a fierce struggle started both against the "neutron bomb" and against the NATO two-track decision to deploy new intermediate nuclear missiles in Europe. This triggered the new peace movement, which got a broad backing from the traditional left, including significant sections in the Labor Party. The party leadership felt it had to accommodate some of the views of the peace movement and adopted some of the old bridge-building rhetoric. A serious conflict with the United States occurred when the Labor Party returned to government in 1986.[9] The Norwegian government noted publicly its skepticism toward the American Strategic Defense Initiative (SDI)—in a footnote to a NATO resolution. Just afterward it was revealed that the Norwegian defense industry had broken NATO export rules by exposing advanced, sensitive technology to some communist countries. The crisis was soon over, however, as major actors in both countries wanted to return to the traditional policy of close cooperation. The end of the cold war and the emerging new debate on Norwegian membership in the EU changed the old left-right struggle over NATO. This had been a continuous political debate in Norway since the founding of NATO. When the cold war ended, the strategic situation soon looked very different. NATO changed, and the EU emerged as a more important actor in the field of security cooperation than it had been before.

A New European Security Order?

After the dissolution of the Soviet Union, the military threat to Norway became less tangible. Clearly "new" Russia still was a formidable military power with a nuclear second-strike capability. During the 1990s, however, the Russian leadership focused more on its southern flank inside the former Soviet Union than on the old cold-war frontiers to the west. In Norway, the Russian danger was seen as the long-term threat of a militarily strong and politically unstable neighbor.[10] During this period, the NATO alliance changed from a strict military alliance to a collective security organization, which became more preoccupied with crisis management—such as in Bosnia and Kosovo—than with containment of communist expansionism.

The new NATO strategy adopted in 1990 implied that the flanks—where Norway was the northern one—were less important. The traditional Norwegian policy had been to build a military defense inside NATO that could contain invaders until allied help arrived, and it was based on the belief that this assistance had to be prepared in peacetime. The policy now came under pressure. The NATO command system was altered so that northern Germany and Denmark—previously under the Northern Command just outside Oslo—now came under the Central European Command, making Norway more vulnerable. Moreover, some of the supplies stored in Norway to equip incoming NATO forces and the infrastructure to bring them in were removed or scaled down. The extension of NATO membership to former East-bloc countries also made the old commitments feel less secure.

In the context of the 1990s, the Norwegian security debate took a new turn. NATO was not considered the sole security anchor—as it used to be. The instruments of security now had to be broader, including active participation in international institutions and organizations that had an impact on Norwegian security.[11] The Organization for Security and Cooperation in Europe (OSCE), with its efforts to improve the human rights situation as well as its work on conflict prevention and crisis management, was such an institution. The new European order with the potentially strong role for the EU became increasingly important in the debate on national security. This was a difficult debate, however, as it inevitably merged with the general debate on Norwegian membership in the EU—both before and after the referendum of 1994.

As a generator of party political conflict, security policies definitely remained in the background for most of the 1990s. Even the Socialist Left Party, whose predecessor, the Socialist People's Party, was founded on resistance against the pro-NATO policies of the Labor governments, took up a more nuanced view of the role of NATO in post-cold-war Europe. One of the most heated debates of the decade, however, came after revelations about serious illegal infringements on citizens' rights during the cold war era. A public commission set up by parliament—not by the government as usual—presented in 1996 a report on the activities of the secret surveillance organizations since the war. The report uncovered a whole series of illegal registrations[12] and rather uncomfortably close ties between these services and leading persons within the labor movement during the 1950s and 1960s. This turned into a battle over the interpretation of cold war history, and the Labor Party, in particular, was attacked in the process. The defenders of the secret service argued that one had to consider the atmosphere of the cold war, and it was revealed that the Communist Party had received large amounts of money from Moscow.[13] The Communist Party, however, had long since become a spent force in Norwegian politics, but to some this made a more relaxed view on the legal status of (necessary) surveillance activities more justified. Others argued that this violation of civil liberties was unacceptable.

Part of the much broader security scenario after 1989 was the changing role of the Western European Union (WEU), a lingering defense organization that included some European members of NATO. In 1989–1990 an attempt was made to revitalize the WEU, and it was made a joint organization of NATO and the EU. Norway became an associate member. After the Maastricht Treaty in 1991, the EU made it part of its emerging "security pillar." This threatened to leave the security interests of Norway on the sideline.

The changes implemented by NATO, together with a weaker U.S. engagement in European defense matters, generated a more Euro-centric security perspective in the domestic security debate in Norway. Until the NATO bombing of Kosovo in the spring of 1999, this debate was largely confined to elite circles—in military, political, journalistic, and research environments. During the operations in Kosovo, however, there was a short but heated debate over Norway's participation in the joint NATO forces, although the opposition did not find much support in parliamentary circles. It was mostly some of the old NATO skeptics who were generating debate. The Socialist Left Party was split on the issue. The official government policy of participation on humanitarian grounds was not affected.

International Regimes: Trade and Rights to the Seabed

Cooperation among states is increasingly organized in multilateral arrangements, often creating new international organizations to implement the agreements. Norwegian governments—defending a small state in the international arena—have generally held the view that Norwegian interests are best served by broad cooperation rather than by a free-for-all system. Sometimes—as with the United Nations—early postwar ambitions superseded what could be achieved. In the economic field, Norway has been part of the Bretton Woods regime,[14] which sets international guidelines for economic relations and trade in the postwar years through the World Bank, the International Monetary Fund, and the General Agreement on Trade and Tariffs (GATT). This U.S.-centered, Western free-trade regime was a catalyst of economic prosperity in Western Europe during the 1950s and 1960s. It did not succeed in achieving free trade in full, but especially compared to the protectionism of the 1930s, international trade was liberalized significantly.

In Chapter 5, it was noted that Norway has an open economy and is highly dependent on foreign trade. Support for the "freedom of the seas" and access to foreign markets was anchored in the historic role played by shipping and foreign capital in the modernization of Norway. This open market approach has, however, been pursued alongside a policy of protectionism that sought control over domestic national resources and key industries, particularly agriculture and fisheries.[15] The prime symbol of this in the industrial sector was the so-called "concession laws," first enacted early in the twentieth century. These laws were directed at foreign companies—although they applied to all companies—and required them to acquire a license before they were allowed to buy sites for power generation, open mines, or otherwise conduct business. This balancing act between openness and protection spans the entire century.

In 1990 the center-right government fell apart over the issue of modifying the current version of the concession laws to accommodate the EU. The EU had asked for modifications in the negotiations for Norway joining the "single market" through the EEA. Norwegian negotiators met their own arguments in the swinging door when—vis-à-vis the EU or WTO—they in one moment pressed for free trade (of fish), while in the next argued for protection of Norwegian agriculture. This was, however, not an unusual "double act" in international negotiations on trade.

The Norwegian economy provided good reasons to pursue both free trade and protectionism. Since the 1950s, foreign trade has amounted to about 40 percent of GNP, which is high even for a small Western state. At the same time, less than 30 percent of economic production (since the mid-1960s) has taken place in sectors exposed to foreign competition, which is a significantly lower figure than average in Western European countries.[16] All political parties wanted to keep the national economic control necessary to develop the Norwegian economy. At the same time, there was vigorous political debate over how much control was necessary, as well as possible, particularly during the liberalization pursued by the governments in the 1980s. This political debate coincided to a high degree with positions taken on Norwegian membership in the EU. Those in favor of EU membership tended to view "excessive" national control as both futile and counterproductive, whereas those against membership found "excessive" liberalization both damaging and naive.

After World War II, the Labor governments had pursued an export-led economic growth combined with a domestically sheltered and politically guided credit policy. This policy was designed to fit within the liberalized (Western) world trade regime. Like many other countries, however, the government simultaneously pursued national control over capital movements.[17] In the early 1970s, the international system changed significantly. The United States left the gold standard in 1971, and currency exchange rates lost their relative stability after the oil shock. These changes signaled a less U.S.-centered international economy. Between 1973 and 1986, Norway devalued its currency a number of times in order to give its export industry a boost and to keep unemployment low.[18] Norway followed international trends during the 1980s by deregulating and removing state controls over the credit market and the currency trade. It also took part in GATT's Uruguay Round, which led to the creation of the World Trade Organization (WTO) in 1995.

Internationalization of finances and production has led Norwegian companies to move part or whole of their production abroad. Cheap labor is the main reason. In public debates this was often met with protests as employees were laid off at home. In the early 1980s, Norwegian ship owners not only sold their ships abroad but invested the capital there as well.[19] Industrial companies followed the trend, and even the relatively young state oil company, Statoil, invested in foreign markets. These investments grew during the 1990s, and Norway has now become a net exporter of capital. Foreign investment in Norway has traditionally been high, and the recent trend of internationalization of Norwegian companies has contributed to a diminished distinction between foreign and domestic politics in Norway. The EEA treaty making Norway part of the EU single market also contributed to the process.

The Impacts of Oil and Gas on Norwegian Policy

During the 1970s and 1980s, the oil and gas production in the North Sea dramatically changed the export profile of Norway. Production of oil and gas products rose from no production in 1970 to accounting for more than one-third of all exports in 1985. The petroleum sector gave the Norwegian state a high degree of freedom in external economic relations. The other side of the coin was that the economy became more vulnerable, as so much depended on the price of gas and oil. Other foreign policy implications also followed. The huge reservoirs of gas made Norway a safer long-term supplier of energy to West European markets than the Soviet Union. This had obvious security implications for the region and made Norway's position more exposed. In addition, the question arose of whether Norway—for political reasons—ought to sell oil on special terms to the other Nordic countries, or in support of Israel. Political pressure was brought to bear both from within and from abroad, particularly from the United States, on the question of supplying Western Europe.

Economically, the domestic expansion in the 1970s was largely financed by the policy of "taking the oil money in advance." The oil industry itself was gradually "domesticated" during the 1970s and early 1980s. The state founded its own oil company, Statoil, in 1972 and gave special favors to two other Norwegian companies. Foreign companies were allowed to explore and develop on the condition that they gradually transfer know-how and licensed rights to Norwegian companies. From the mid-1980s, there was a change of policy in the direction of a stronger market orientation, giving the foreign multinationals a more central place. And in contrast to the first years, licenses for exploration were now more balanced between different nationalities, particularly between American and European companies.[20]

Fisheries and Jurisdiction at Sea

Fishing rights and oil exploration depend on the limits for national jurisdiction. Controlling resources at sea has been a central aim in Norwegian foreign policy since independence in 1905. When coastal states gained exclusive rights in the 1970s to fish and natural resources in the seabed to within 200 miles of the coastline, Norway "at sea" (including the islands) became about five times the size of Norway "onshore." However, this policy of expansion had to be balanced against the shipping interests of Norway. The shipping sector depended on free access to the sea routes along foreign coasts; but, in the end, coastal rights did not include jurisdiction over sea traffic so far from the shore.

Fishing is the economic lifeline of many coastal communities—directly for the fishermen living there, indirectly through fish processing, shipbuilding, and the supply industry. There are not many fishermen left (about 27,000 in 1990), as fishing has become increasingly mechanized and dependent on large sea-going trawlers.[21] Its share of GNP has declined from 2 percent to just above 1 percent in the postwar period. What makes fishing economically significant is that 90 percent of all fish products are exported. Fish farming has increased the importance of this industry, but in this sector fish is an industrial commodity where market entry counts the most, not the limits on resources at sea. The differences between these two industries were important in the debate about EU membership. The government argued that the two sectors had different needs and tried to balance them. It was agreed that Norway would get better access to European markets for fish products, but it had to accept increased EU access to Norwegian fishing waters.[22] In the negotiations with the EU, it was also agreed that Norway should have a dominant influence on the future EU fishing regime in the northern waters. At the referendum, however, voters in the fishery communities did not trust the promises made and rejected membership by a large majority. In their judgment, control over the resource base was in the long run more important than regulated market access.

The 1970s and 1980s brought new problems over market access as international environmental groups staged campaigns against Norwegian fish exports because of Norway's seal hunting and whaling. In 1976 an international campaign against the hunting of seals collected one million signatures.[23] The following year the U.S. Congress expressed resistance to continued hunting, and the EU introduced a ban on imports of seal skins in 1983. The protests were basically similar in regard to Norwegian whaling. In particular, the U.S. policy was a problem as the government threatened a ban on the profitable export of Norwegian salmon. The economic interests were not large, although they were important to some local communities. The Norwegian government considered it unreasonable to discontinue a practice that harvested a surplus in a way that did not threaten the species. The "sustainable development" thesis of Gro Harlem Brundtland's government was the major argument backing a policy that actually threatened Norwegian economic interests abroad.

In the 1960s, the fishing zone had been extended from four miles to twelve miles, and the fishing banks to the south of Norway were divided up among the North Sea countries. At the same time, the increasing fleet of oceangoing trawlers threatened traditional fishing stocks closer to the shores further north. The growing threats to fish stocks and the pressing economic interests in petroleum and metals exploration led to the UN conference on the seas in 1973–1982. Based on discussions during the conference and the fact that the North American countries would extend their rights at sea, the Norwegian government in 1976 decided to declare a 200-mile (nautical) economic zone with exclusive economic rights. This was later adopted as a general principle by the UN conference and accepted by most countries. To Norway it was a particularly welcome agreement, as it did not—as noted above—involve jurisdiction over shipping outside twelve miles.

Security matters were also involved when Norway extended jurisdiction over new territories. In the cold war years, this was a problem, especially in relation to the Soviet Union. Norway has since the 1920s held jurisdiction over the Svalbard Islands (to the north and west of Norway). The Soviet Union had economic interests in coal mining on the islands— although it was suspected by NATO to be potential military bases. The Soviet government did not appreciate the NATO presence in the north and wanted to tie Norwegian economic activities to bilateral arrangements. The initiation of the 200-mile zone prolonged negotiations with the Soviet Union over where to draw the line at sea outside the Norwegian-Soviet land border. In the late 1970s, agreement was reached on an intermediate solution giving both countries joint but separately exercised jurisdiction over parts of the disputed area—as well as some undisputed parts on both sides—the "gray zone" agreement. Twenty years later, the two countries—now with Russia on the other side—have still not reached a permanent agreement. Following the end of the cold war, the Norwegian government initiated increased economic cooperation in the Barents region bordering Norway. This also included Norwegian efforts to control and to initiate a cleanup of the large problems in pollution and ecology caused by industrial and military waste on the Russian side of the border. Extensive nuclear waste and old nuclear energy plants were seen as a major threat to the population in the whole region, particularly after the Chernobyl accident in 1986.

Globalization: Interests and Ideals

In terms of security and trade, Norway is still basically a West European and North Atlantic country. In technological and cultural terms, Norwegians are firmly anchored in what used to be called "the Western world." Among the organizational acronyms still very central to Norwegian foreign policies are Western organizations such as NATO, the EU, and OECD. The UN has, of course, been there all along. Relative newcomers like the OSCE (Organization for Security and Cooperation in Europe), the WTO (World Trade Organization), and an emerging international environmental regime—so far without a recognizable acronym—now show the contours of a post-cold-war and increasingly global world. The popular culture, the PCs and their Microsoft programs, and the fear of international money-handlers are telling signs of the new global world within Norwegian society—just as in most other countries. Even back in the 1970s, it was considered rather funny when a leading politician stated that "Norway is a country in the world," as most people knew that already.[24] Shipping and the missionary expeditions had made Norway global early on. The merchant marine had brought thousands of young boys to foreign countries. They brought their experiences and stories back. The Christian lay movement had knitted sweaters to keep their missionaries in Africa, India, and China for a long time. And a large-scale emigration to North America had made lasting transatlantic ties.

Seeking Out the World

International relations built on shipping and missionaries highlight the dual basis of Norwegian foreign policy: interests and ideals. This historical legacy and the tension between them are parts of Norwegian political consciousness. The importance of shipping in the industrialization of Norway was discussed in Chapter 5. Before the oil crisis in 1973, shipping was crucial: It contributed roughly 10 percent to the GNP and raised one-third of all foreign currency earnings. Norway had one of the largest merchant fleets in the world, and until 1970 about 80 percent of the traffic went between foreign ports.[25] Norwegian economic interests depended on openness in world trade.

Following the organization of the United Nations and the high priority given to its work by successive governments, Norway faced the need to formulate policies on a wide range of international issues: distant wars, de-colonization, famine and poverty, dictatorships, and illiteracy. Parts of Norwegian society had long been engaged in relief and humanitarian work. This was the case not only with the early religious lay movement but also with—more recently—the labor movement. No other country is so active in missionary work relative to its population apart from Ireland.[26] This work started back in the mid-nineteenth century when missionaries first went to India, and later to Madagascar and to southern Africa. In the late 1980s, eighteen organizations supported about 1,400 missionaries in fifty-six countries.[27] The secular part of the missionary work—in schools, hospitals, and so forth—was increasingly financed with public money. Other voluntary organizations such as the Red Cross and the labor movement's Norwegian People's Aid also became part of this voluntary aid complex. This sector enormously increased its (publicly financed) work in the developing world. In the early 1960s, seven organizations received 3 million NOK from the government, whereas in the early 1990s, about five hundred organizations received 1,500 million NOK for the same purpose.[28]

State development aid to poor countries started early in Norway, and today there is a huge program spread over many countries. In the early 1950s, when the Kerala project started in India, Norway was the only country without colonies of its own that was engaged in this kind of activity.[29] The project was aimed at using Norwegian expertise to help the local fishermen increase productivity and to improve the systems for distribution and sales. Another (domestic) concern was to give the Norwegian voters something more positive to think about than the high defense spending. The aid was channeled through the directorate for aid and development. In the early 1980s, the sector was politically upgraded with a ministry of its own. In line with a UN proposal from the early 1960s, it became a political goal to bring aid to the developing world up to 1 percent of GNP. This was achieved in 1982 after prolonged and engaged political debate. Among the parliamentarian parties, only the Progress Party today wants to cut development aid significantly, but among the other parties there are differing views on magnitude, profile, and worthy receivers. In the 1990s, public development aid fell below the 1 percent goal, mainly because the GNP grew with increasing petroleum sales. The aid has traditionally been divided roughly equally between bilateral and multilateral projects, the latter mostly channeled through the UN organizations. As domestic budgets grew, the UN part decreased. In the mid-1990s, 30 percent of the aid money went to the UN system, the Development Bank, and other related organizations.[30]

From the 1960s onward, many Norwegians had temporary engagements as aid workers on state projects in developing countries. It was intended that these projects would eventually trigger self-sustained growth in the receiving countries. During the 1970s, there arose a political debate about the structural problems of the north-south divide. A central argument was that the developing countries were locked in a poverty trap and that this fueled demand for a new economic world order.

In the 1980s, doubt set in about the viability of many local projects. Also a controversy arose over the demands by the World Bank and the International Monetary Fund (IMF) for economic restructuring and liberalization in debt-ridden developing countries. In Norway the optimism of the early decades subsided; development aid became less of a missionary project and more of a standard economic and foreign policy issue. Norwegian industries were increasingly included as partners in development projects.

Since the early 1990s, the promotion of peace, democracy, and human rights has become an integral part of development projects. Improving the position of women in developing countries was made an explicit aim of aid projects in the 1980s. The policy field changed, in other words, from a relatively uncontroversial altruistic project—where aid was given more or less without ties—to the complex relief and intervention policies through which the Norwegian government increasingly pursued broader political objectives. As such, these policies have become more enmeshed in controversy within the domestic political arena.

The policy focus was extended even further during the 1990s, when the relationship between development and the environment became a central theme. The UN Brundtland commission pointed to the destructive impact that poverty could have on the environment within developing countries. The vicious circle of poverty and environmental destruction had to be broken and a process of "sustainable development" put in its place. Development aid was increasingly debated in the combined context of pollution, globalization, and security interests. Norwegian aid programs gradually took this into account. In the mid-1990s, South Africa, the former Yugoslavia, and the Palestinian territories were among the largest receivers of Norwegian aid, reflecting the broader public policy concerns of peace and security. China, on the other hand, also received much help, and this reflected the growing economic interests of Norwegian industry in the Far East.

Peacekeeping and Human Rights

Peace work and human rights are central to the foreign policy of Norwegian government. The work done in Russia in the 1920s by the marine scientist, humanist, and hero of polar expeditions, Fridtjov Nansen, to prevent hunger and help refugees has been an inspiration for much later relief work in Norway. Norway is annually in the international limelight as the country awarding the Nobel Peace Prize; a committee appointed by the Norwegian parliament selects the winner.[31] In 1993 Norway was host to the groundbreaking "Oslo agreement" between the Israelis and the Palestinians.

Norwegian interwar governments strongly supported the League of Nations. In the postwar period, the support was transferred to its successor, the United Nations. The policy was not only pursued out of humanitarian values but also out of the self-interests of a small nation. In international affairs—the argument went—a small country like Norway would benefit from strong international regimes, that is, from the rule of international law, human rights institutions, and effective international organizations. The point was and is to influence and restrict the exercise of unilateral power on the part of the large and powerful nations. Neighboring a huge superpower nation like the Soviet Union/Russia made the support of international organizations and cooperation a security interest. During the cold war, security matters were handled through NATO, and later other organizations—such as the OSCE—came to play an important supplementary role.

In addition to the interests of a small state, there is the strong value dimension of Norwegian foreign policy. Support for democratic regimes and democratization has been a very important element. After World War II, there was a bitter domestic political struggle over whether to trade with Spain under the Franco dictatorship. The Norwegian government gave in to the interests of Norwegian shipping and U.S. pressure on the question of trade, but the government later fought hard to keep Franco's Spain out of NATO. This stand, however, was not really put to a test, as the United States had a bilateral agreement on defense with Spain and did not press the issue of Spanish membership.[32] The coup in Greece in 1967 mobilized Norwegian politicians in favor of the democratic forces inside the country. The government worked actively to exclude the Greek dictatorship from participation in the European Council. After Greece and Portugal became democracies in 1974 and Spain went the same way

in 1975, the Norwegian government pursued a policy of support and sta-
bilization vis-à-vis the new regimes.

When the Berlin Wall fell in 1989, the human rights perspective became
more visible in the foreign policy formulations and actions of the Norwegian government. The "activist" argument was now that Norway, as a
small state with a noncolonial past, a high profile in development aid,
and established human rights traditions, could make an impact and to a
greater extent should let these values guide its bilateral engagements.[33]
Since the mid-1970s, human rights issues have had a strong impact on
the selecting of "main partners" in the development aid programs. Since
the mid-1980s, regular academic reports on the human rights situation in
project countries have guided official policies.[34] For example, human
rights were instrumental in the changing policy toward Sri Lanka in the
late 1980s. An internal war was going on in the country, and its government had a poor human rights record. As a result, Norwegian support
was channeled away from government projects and increasingly toward
voluntary organizations and to the victims of the conflict. During the
1990s, this human rights policy and the support for democratic forces
have had manifest consequences for Norwegian aid to Nicaragua, South
Africa, Namibia, and Ethiopia.

Norway's strong involvement in the UN led to participation in the UN
peacekeeping missions. Norway became an early and regular supporter
of UN missions, including sending military personnel. This was the case
in the Congo in the 1960s, in Lebanon in the late 1970s, and in Kosovo in
the 1990s. At present, Norway gives more money to the UN system than
ever before (even though its share of the total development aid budget decreased). The high level of financial support is not only a result of the
peacekeeping missions but is part of the policy to channel much development aid through multilateral projects. Another tangible aspect of the
peace diplomacy during the 1990s has been a series of peace initiatives directed at more or less distant conflicts. It started most spectacularly with
the Oslo agreement between the Israelis and the Palestinians in 1993.
From the outset, this was a semi-private initiative, but it was also all along
supported by the government and in the end embraced as official policy.
Norway has also been active in peace negotiations in conflicts in countries
as diverse as Guatemala, the former Yugoslavia, Sudan, and Sri Lanka.

Human rights and peace initiatives focus on the potential clash between ideals and material interests in international affairs. Balancing
trade and human rights made relations with China a difficult task for the
Foreign Ministry. After China started its modernization in the late 1970s,
trade with Norway increased. The Norwegian government avoided criticism of the human rights situation in Tibet, as this was considered an in-

ternal Chinese affair. After the Tiananmen massacre in 1989 and, in particular, after the awarding of the Nobel Peace Price to the Dalai Lama the same year, relations became frosty. Normal relations were soon resumed, however, and the government resumed its effort to increase trade and investment. At the same time, Norway engaged in a dialogue about human rights with Beijing. Human rights organizations in Norway reacted sharply against this realpolitik on the part of the government.[35]

Sales of weapons to foreign governments have created similar dilemmas. Norwegian companies could export weapons only after they had received a public license for that specific shipment. License was not given for exports to countries in war or where there was an imminent threat of war. This policy was difficult to handle for the government, as the industry wanted to sell and the definition of "worthy" buyers was politically extremely touchy. The case causing the most trouble, however, involved the U.S. government, not the Norwegian public. This was the sale of new technology capable of producing very silent propellers for submarines. In 1987 it became public that this equipment had ended up in the Soviet Union, and this triggered, as discussed above, severe problems in relation to the United States.

Decisionmaking

Foreign policy making has traditionally been the prerogative of the government in close consultation with the Foreign Relations Committee in parliament.[36] Formally, it is parliament that ratifies treaties with foreign governments. The parliamentary system also means that the government can be toppled if it does not have the confidence—generally or in any particular question—of the parliamentary majority. Inside the government, the foreign minister and his department have traditionally been the central actors along with the prime minister and the minister of defense. In parliament the parliamentary leaders of the pro-NATO parties and a small circle around them have been particularly important. In the cold war era, when security dominated foreign relations, politics, by and large, was more domestically oriented, and the national economy was in some respects less exposed to external markets. There were certainly rivalries among actors both within and between institutions, but these were kept within small circles and mostly behind closed doors. National consensus about foreign policy was strongly pursued, and a small but vocal anti-NATO opposition was kept at a safe distance from policymaking. Even in the inner circles, however, some NATO skeptics could be found—both in parliament and in the prime minister's office.

Increased Complexity

Today foreign policy is made in a more complex context. The external surroundings continuously shift, and the internal forces are more important. In the old days, when alarming new weapons were spotted at the Kola Peninsula in the Soviet Union, discussions were more controlled and signals were directed at Norway's NATO allies. Security issues around the turn of the twenty-first century are handled within the context of what has become the "new NATO." The possibility of a new EU defense dimension also ties these issues up with a "Norway and the EU" debate. Other issues like trade, human rights, and peace initiatives today generate debate primarily within the domestic political arena with a much broader range of interests involved.

Today foreign policy decisionmaking is both more open and less exclusive than it used to be. More political actors, more bureaucrats, and more interest groups are engaged. The media are more active. At the same time—perhaps somewhat paradoxically—the debates are less polarized compared to the cold war period, when the "no-to-NATO" segment fought recurrent and rather predictable battles with the establishment. Mobilization in the public arena has been part of the process since the early postwar period. The protest actions against Franco's Spain in the late 1940s, the anti-nuclear weapons campaign in the late 1950s and early 1960s, and the mobilization against the European Economic Community in 1962 prove that. Nevertheless, the broad public engagement and the breadth of issues covered during the two referenda campaigns on EU membership in the 1970s and 1990s (Chapter 4) testifies to more open and more inclusive decisionmaking.

Three significant changes—in addition to the fall of the Berlin Wall—may account for the changes in foreign policy decisionmaking: the new journalism, the increased number and diversity of foreign policy issues, and the predominance of minority governments since 1971.[37] The media have become more active and more inquisitive and have pursued a more participatory role in the foreign policy field. The foreign minister from 1946 to 1965, Halvard Lange, held confidential press briefings with selected journalists.[38] This would be almost unthinkable today. Most major newspapers during the early postwar period had fairly close ties to particular political parties, and journalists, in general, were much less independent in their capacity to raise new and controversial issues.[39] The aura of foreign policy issues as a special "National interests: Hands off!" arena gradually subsided beginning in the 1970s. As a consequence, foreign policy issues are much more openly reported, and governmental policies are more strongly criticized than was ever the case before.

Simultaneously, there has been a substantial increase in the number of international issues to be handled by the politicians and in the departments. The rise in interstate contact was noted in Chapter 3. Norway was in 1980 party to about 2,000 international treaties and a member of roughly one hundred international organizations. In the 1990s, bureaucrats used about one-third of their time dealing with international issues. This was, in part, a consequence of the work to integrate EU legislation that came with the EEA treaty. Internationalization took its toll on all departments, not only the ministries that traditionally deal with the external world. Voluntary organizations increasingly joined so-called INGOs (International Non-Governmental Organizations) to become part of a "new diplomacy." These organizations were often present at important international conferences to attract attention in the media and to influence delegates. The same organizations also used their influence at the national level to get their points across to bureaucrats and politicians. At the UN Conference on Environment and Development in Rio de Janeiro in 1992, the Norwegian delegation had about one hundred envoys and forty journalists, mostly paid for by the Norwegian state.[40] In the delegation there were representatives from the government, bureaucrats, and parliamentarians alongside the major environmental organizations. "Grandmothers Against Nuclear Weapons" and the Coast-Women League "Cry of Distress" (Kystkvinnelaget Nødrop) were also present. Some of the environmental organizations took the opportunity to attack what they considered the double standards of the Norwegian government in environmental issues. The prime minister registered this with some bitterness.[41] On the other hand, close cooperation with organizations can also be valuable to governments, for example, when giving out development aid and monitoring human rights efforts. However, this cooperation has always been double-edged: Success or failure, involvement or interference—was the government to be praised or be blamed?

Since the 1970s, politicians and parties have become more directly involved in international cooperation. Increasingly, this has become transnational politics rather than interparliamentarian get-togethers. In the latter respect, Norwegian parliamentarians have regularly been delegates to organizations like the UN and to meetings in the Nordic Council. Most parliamentarians do not, however, have any international contacts of this kind, and among those who do, the Nordic and European level of interaction dominates.[42] Among the political parties, the Labor Party has a long tradition of international cooperation with fellow social democrats. At this international party arena, they do not represent Norway but participate as politicians to promote and to learn from other politicians with broadly the same ideological viewpoints. During the 1980s and 1990s, the other Norwegian parties were also increasingly involved in international organizations, especially at the Nordic and the European/EU levels.[43] This brought new political ideas and gave Norwegian politicians an opportunity to influence other governments in a kind of "party diplomacy."

The third factor contributing to this opening up of the foreign policy field is the predominance of minority governments after 1971. Minority governments must take parliament more seriously not only in the interest of a broad national consensus but in order to survive. The center government of 1997–2000 had a weak parliamentary base in terms of numbers and needed to consult broadly before making important decisions. This was the case particularly in controversial areas like the EU and the EEA.[44] Parliamentary weakness also made it easier for organizations, politicians, and journalists to use the media to generate political pressure on the government.

Segmentation and Problems of Coordination

"Foreign policy is not any longer only about the relations between nations, but about nations' and societies' relations to common problems."[45] This was the view of the late foreign minister, Knut Frydenlund, in the early 1970s and reflects the background for subsequent developments. Today foreign policy decisionmaking can be divided into three main areas according to the issues, and these issue areas tend to mobilize somewhat different sets of actors.[46] First, there is the traditional security segment, where some old habits are still present: exclusive, secretive, with external forces as the most important movers. It must be noted, however, that "national security" has taken on a much broader meaning since the end of the cold war. This is perhaps most noticeable in the debates about the "new NATO" and how to tackle the EU initiative to develop a security dimension of its own. Second, there is the economic segment, where internal forces are more central and exclusiveness is less prominent. In this area the distinction between national and international has become less workable than it used to be. The same political and economic actors that debate domestic economic policies also debate their foreign policy aspects. Other actors join in, however, when security interests are involved—such as when debating the sale of gas to Western Europe. In addition, political, humanitarian, and aid organizations join the debate when Norwegian policies on north-south problems in the World Bank and the WTO are discussed. Third, there is the aid and humanitarian segment. Humanitarian and religious aid organizations take part here along with experts on international law and human rights. But, of course, the industry and trade organizations are also active in these debates, favoring trade and sales orders to domestic companies.

During the first decades after World War II, the Foreign Ministry's position as the major actor in the foreign policy field was reinforced by several strong personalities heading the ministry. As foreign policy issues became more integrated into domestic politics from the 1970s onward, the ministry remained central, but the rise of new institutional divisions and new policymaking arenas weakened its position and brought rising problems of coordination. Major issues in foreign policy making had all along been taken care of in departments like Defense and Trade.[47] During the 1970s, the Ministry of the Environment and the Ministry of Petroleum and Energy were founded, and both departments have dealt extensively with issues that are very much a part of Norwegian foreign policy. In 1983 political forces brought about the creation of the Ministry of Development as part of the deal bringing a new majority coalition into government position. During the late 1980s, the departments of Trade and Development were integrated into an enlarged Ministry of Foreign Affairs. This at least brought the problems of coordination under the new "umbrella" of the foreign ministry.[48] In 1997, however, some trade issues were again taken out of the department.

Several public committees addressed the problem of foreign policy coordination. A report on development aid presented in 1995 pointed to the problem that the practical aid work in the developing countries was not sufficiently integrated into the general framework of Norway's foreign policy.[49] During the 1990s, the staff working directly with the foreign minister was strengthened. The aim was to improve policy development and presentation of a more unified foreign policy within which the sector departments could work. A large number of political secretaries and political advisors were also appointed in the enlarged department to meet the increased policy coordination needs. Interdepartmental work was also increasingly coordinated through a series of government committees consisting of ministers and other political personnel. Another instrument was the strengthening of the administrative and political capacity in the prime minister's office. In 1991 this was formalized through an international division in the prime minister's office. This is a small and flexible unit that is used by the prime minister to develop and oversee policies in areas given high priority.

Conclusion

The two constants in Norwegian foreign policy are Norway's geographical location and its size. Today the government worries over the declining interest of the United States in European affairs in general and toward the "northern flank" in particular. Another challenge is the potential development of an EU security dimension that over time may reduce the effectiveness of NATO. These interests reflect geographical location and have a strong security component. Neighboring Russia, a long coastline, and a sparsely populated territory at a long distance from Central Europe are important elements in this scenario based on geography. When it comes to size, Norway is a very small nation on the international scene. A senior adviser to the foreign minister used to argue that when the international going got rough, Norway could crawl under the table, but it could not take up that position on a permanent basis.[50] In other words, Norway responds much more than it acts in the international arena.

To argue that geography and size are "national destiny" is, however, only part of the story. Norwegian foreign policy has other—more or less stable—parameters and has also changed in some respects since the 1970s. Take three examples: The importance of the Atlantic ties has declined, European issues have become increasingly important, and global issues like trade, the environment, and the economy present a steady and increasingly intriguing stream of challenging issues to Norwegian politicians.

Next to the monumental changes brought about by the end of the cold war, changes in the culture, the economy, and the rise of the EU are important factors in explaining developments in Norwegian foreign policy. Cultural factors can be used to explain both stability and change. A strong missionary movement and a tradition of humanitarian aid are part of the national cultural heritage underlying the early and strong involvement with aid to the developing world, the recent peace initiatives, and the movement for a more activist human rights policy. The petroleum economy has brought changes in domestic wealth and more freedom of action in foreign trade relations. The EU is the European institution most central to Norwegian foreign policy today. It is probably also the institution that has contributed the most to transforming foreign policy into domestic politics, triggering the two referenda on membership and the EEA agreement. The increased exposure of foreign policy to domestic political processes—making it both less exclusive and more open—is also the result of internal changes such as the new media and the dominant parliamentary mode of minority government. Not only has national sovereignty become more vulnerable at the turn of the century; this is also the case with foreign policy decisionmaking. Or, to put it more positively, decisionmaking has become more democratic.

Notes

1. Knut Frydenlund, *Lille land—hva nå? Refleksjonmer om Norges utenrikspolitiske situasjon* (Oslo: Universitetsforlaget, 1982). The play of words reflects Hans Fal-

lada's interwar German novel *Kleiner Mann—was nun?* In English, "Small Country—What Now? Reflections on the Foreign Policy Situation of Norway."

2. See, for example, the preface to the six-volume history of Norwegian policy by the leader of the steering committee, Olav Riste, "Forord," in Narve Bjørgo, Øystein Rian, and Alf Kaartvedt, *Selvstendighet og union. Fra middelalderen til 1905,* vol. 1 of *Norsk utenrikspolitikks historie* (Oslo: Universitetsforlaget, 1995).

3. Tor Egil Førland, "En empirisk bauta, et intellektuelt gjesp. Kritisk blikk på Norsk utenrikspolitikks historie, 1–6," *Historisk Tidsskrift* 78 (1999):234.

4. The history of postwar foreign policy is presented in volumes 5 and 6 of the series *Norsk utenrikspolitikks historie.* Knut Einar Eriksen and Helge Øystein Pharo, *Kald krig og internasjonalisering, 1945–1965* (Oslo: Universitetsforlaget, 1997), and Rolf Tamnes, *Oljealder, 1965–1995* (Oslo: Universitetsforlaget, 1997).

5. See ch. 4 in Peter Flora et al., eds., *State Formation, Nation Building, and Mass Politics in Europe: The Theory of Stein Rokkan* (Oxford: Oxford University Press, 1999).

6. Eriksen and Pharo, *Kald krig og internasjonalisering, 1945–1965,* p. 406.

7. Ibid., p. 414. The authors also note a certain worry in the years 1955–1960.

8. Iver B. Neumann and Ståle Ulriksen, "Norsk forsvars- og sikkerhetspolitikk," in Torbjørn L Knutsen, Gunnar Sørbø, and Svein Gjerdåker, eds., *Norges utenrikspolitikk,* 2nd ed. (Oslo: Chr. Michelsens Institutt/Cappelen Akademisk Forlag, 1997), p. 96.

9. Tamnes, *Oljealder, 1965–1995,* p. 95.

10. This view was reflected in the 1992 report presented by the official Defense Commission appointed in 1990; see Neumann and Ulriksen, "Norsk forsvars- og sikkerhetspolitikk," pp. 97ff.

11. Ibid., p. 101.

12. The secret services had compiled registers of people on the basis of legal political activities, which was illegal.

13. Tamnes, *Oljealder, 1965–1995,* p. 141.

14. Named after the place in the United States where an agreement between forty-four nations was reached in 1944 to support an international system of stable exchange currencies.

15. Tamnes, *Oljealder, 1965–1995,* p. 150.

16. Ibid.

17. Jonathan W. Moses and Bent Sofus Tranøy, "Norge i den nye verdensøkonomien," in Torbjørn L Knutsen, Gunnar Sørbø, and Svein Gjerdåker, eds., *Norges utenrikspolitikk,* 2nd ed. (Oslo: Chr. Michelsens Institutt/Cappelen Akademisk Forlag, 1997), p. 126.

18. Ibid., pp. 132–133.

19. Thorbjørn L. Knutsen, "Norsk utenrikspolitikk som forskningsfelt," in Torbjørn L Knutsen, Gunnar Sørbø, and Svein Gjerdåker, eds., *Norges utenrikspolitikk,* 2nd ed. (Oslo: Chr. Michelsens Institutt/Cappelen Akademisk Forlag, 1997), p. 35.

20. Tamnes, *Oljealder, 1965–1995,* p. 195.

21. Jennifer Leigh Bailey, "Norsk fiskeripolitikk," in Torbjørn L Knutsen, Gunnar Sørbø, and Svein Gjerdåker, eds., *Norges utenrikspolitikk,* 2nd ed. (Oslo: Chr. Michelsens Institutt/Cappelen Akademisk Forlag, 1997), p. 145.

22. *Stortingsmelding* 40 (1993–1994). See also ibid.

23. Tamnes, *Oljealder, 1965–1995*, p. 317.

24. Lars Korvald, former prime minister and leader of the Christian People's Party in a parliamentary debate on foreign affairs in 1974.

25. Eriksen and Pharo, *Kald krig og internasjonalisering, 1945–1965*, p. 108.

26. Helge Hveem, Sverre Lodgaard, and Kjell Skjelsbær, *Vår plass i verden*, vol. 7 of *Det Moderne Norge* (Oslo: Gyldendal, 1984), p. 300.

27. Olaf Kortner et al., eds., *Store Norske Leksikon*, vol. 9 (Oslo: Kunnskapsforlaget, 1986–1989), p. 587.

28. Terje Tvedt, "Norsk utenrikspolitikk og de frivillige organisasjonene," in Torbjørn L Knutsen, Gunnar Sørbø, and Svein Gjerdåker, eds., *Norges utenrikspolitikk*, 2nd ed. (Oslo: Chr. Michelsens Institutt/Cappelen Akademisk Forlag, 1997), p. 260.

29. Eriksen and Pharo, *Kald krig og internasjonalisering, 1945–1965*, pp. 173ff.

30. Gunnar M. Sørbø, "Norsk bistandspolitikk," in Torbjørn L Knutsen, Gunnar Sørbø, and Svein Gjerdåker, eds., *Norges utenrikspolitikk*, 2nd ed. (Oslo: Chr. Michelsens Institutt/Cappelen Akademisk Forlag, 1997), p. 245.

31. This is due to the testament of Alfred Nobel, who wanted the Norwegian parliament to hand out this prize. At the time, Norway was still part of the union with Sweden.

32. Eriksen and Pharo, *Kald krig og internasjonalisering, 1945–1965*, pp. 47–49.

33. Jan Egeland, *Impotent Superpower—Potent Small State* (Oslo: Norwegian University Press, 1988).

34. Sørbø, "Norsk bistandspolitikk," p. 250.

35. Tamnes, *Oljealder, 1965–1995*, pp. 373–374.

36. Its full name is the Constitution and Foreign Relations Committee. The leaders of the parliamentary parties and the most senior politicians are usually members of this committee.

37. Olav Fagerlund Knudsen, "Beslutningsprosesser i norsk utenrikspolitikk," in Torbjørn L Knutsen, Gunnar Sørbø, and Svein Gjerdåker, eds., *Norges utenrikspolitikk*, 2nd ed. (Oslo: Chr. Michelsens Institutt/Cappelen Akademisk Forlag, 1997), p. 73.

38. Eriksen and Pharo, *Kald krig og internasjonalisering, 1945–1965*, p. 19.

39. Svennik Høyer, *Pressen mellom teknologi og samfunn* (Oslo: Universitetsforlaget, 1995), ch. 12.

40. Tamnes, *Oljealder, 1965–1995*, p. 345.

41. Gro Harlam Brundtland, *Dramatiske år 1986–1996* (Oslo: Gyldendal, 1998), p. 396.

42. Martin Brothén, "International Networking," in Peter Esaiasson and Knut Heidar, eds., *Beyond Congress and Westminster: The Nordic Experience* (Columbus: Ohio State University Press, 2000), p. 328.

43. See Knut Heidar and Lars Svåsand, eds., *Partier uten grenser?* (Oslo: Tano, 1997).

44. Dag Harald Claes and Bent Sofus Tranøy, eds., *Utenfor, annerledes og suveren?* (Oslo: Fagbokforlaget, 1999).

45. Quoted from a debate in parliament; see Tamnes, *Oljealder, 1965–1995*, p. 449.

46. Knudsen, "Beslutningsprosesser i norsk utenrikspolitikk," p. 72.

47. Their official names have changed over the years. Today, for example, there is a Ministry of Development and Human Rights.

48. Tamnes, *Oljealder, 1965–1995*, p. 463.

49. See Sørbø, "Norsk bistandspolitikk," p. 257.

50. Knut Frydenlund, *Lille land—hva nå? Refleksjonmer om Norges utenrikspolitiske situasjon* (Oslo: Universitetsforlaget, 1982), p. 7.

8

Conclusion

The great Norwegian political scientist Stein Rokkan focused on the interaction between time and space in his work to develop a generalized map of the political systems of Europe.[1] Time was crucial in determining what effects critical historical events—their sequence and how they evolved—had on political developments. The Reformation, the national revolution, the Industrial Revolution, and the Russian Revolution were critical junctures in the evolution of all European national political systems. Space, on the other hand, was crucial in that these historical developments interacted with the territorial distribution of the population and the functional division of labor. It was important how far away the country was from the dynamic market system of the Central European "city belt" and the relative strength of urban and rural economies within a territory. The diverse historical and geographical conditions created a multitude of political trajectories within Europe, but they were still something that could be described and explained on the basis of some critical variables.

Comparative Perspectives

How does Norway differ from other political systems? Although the attention here has been primarily on Norwegian politics, this book has indirectly highlighted comparative similarities and differences. Stein Rokkan described Norway in several ways, depending on focus. When looking at the process of "state- and nation-building," Norway was a Protestant country with a weak impact from the city network and a weak territorial center. In geopolitical terms, Norway was a "seaward periphery." When the focus turned to political cleavages, the important parameters in the evolution of Norwegian politics were the operation of the state church, the state's close attachment to urban interests, and the split in the labor movement in the wake of the Russian Revolution.

Rokkan's comparative approach was historical and theoretical. In this book I have focused attention on Norwegian politics in the 1990s: the major institutions, the political decisionmaking process, and the central political issues. Let us turn to an author with a more narrow, though still comparative, focus on contemporary institutions and processes. Arend Lijphart certainly has theoretical ambitions, but his major aim is to conceptualize and describe the variations of democratic systems as they operate today.[2] In his analysis of institutions and rules in thirty-six democracies, he finds that two major dimensions are crucial to capturing how these countries organize their politics: the majoritarian/consensual and the unitary/federal. Decisionmaking in majoritarian democracies is characterized by majority rules—through single-party majority governments, executive dominance in parliamentary relationships, two-party systems, and so forth. The traditional example of majoritarian democracy is the Westminster-style politics of the United Kingdom. Consensual democracies, on the other hand, are focused on broad compromises and include as many groups as possible in decisionmaking processes. These have institutional designs that promote multiparty coalition governments, strong parliaments, multiparty systems, and proportional electoral systems. Here Switzerland is a major example. Turning to the second dimension, strong centralized governments dominate unitary polities such as New Zealand. On the other side of the continuum, both the United States and Germany are fairly clear-cut federalist cases with strong local/regional government.

How does Norway fit along these two dimensions? The Norwegian system does not fall into an extreme position along either. In Lijphart's analysis, all Nordic countries can be found in the consensual/unitary group.[3] With the predominance of coalition and minority governments, its multiparty and proportional electoral system, it is not at all surprising to find Norway among the consensual countries. As early as in the 1950s, American political scientists noted—evidently with some surprise—that the Scandinavian countries had "working multiparty systems."[4] Some explanation may be needed to account for the unitary label given to the Norwegian polity. I have repeatedly stressed the importance of the center-periphery cleavage in Norwegian politics, indicating the strong impact of local and regional interests. Norway has a low score, however, on the federalist indicators in Lijphart's scheme. But Norway does not have a federalist institutional structure. A high share of taxes going to the central government and the absence of any real ethnic autonomy for the Sami (or any other) minority contributes to the low score on federalism. Furthermore, the bicameralism in parliament is very weak, constitutional protection of minorities is medium or weak in terms of amendment procedures and judicial review, and the score on central bank independence is extremely weak.[5] The argument in this book, however, has not been that the periphery is *institutionally* particularly strong in Norway, but rather that the districts have been *politically* strong in the decisionmaking process. At first glance, it may appear to be a paradox that the main reason for this strength has been the dominant position of the central state in the Norwegian society at large. However, the district politicians have repeatedly utilized the central political institutions to challenge the dominant perspectives and policies nurtured in the capital. The periphery has successfully used the strong state and the political instruments available at the center to promote the district interests.

Minority government and, even more intriguing, minority coalition government have been the dominant executive types during the past thirty years. In fact, minority government is today the dominant Scandinavian mode—shared by Sweden and Denmark. It is much less common on the European continent, not to mention Great Britain. Weak governments have triggered more powerful parliaments, and this has become increasingly visible during the 1990s in Norway. Disintegrating executive authority was the main argument given by the Labor prime minister when he left office after the 1997 election. He was not forced out, and his successor had even less parliamentary support, but he claimed that sound government of the country needed more executive authority.

A new comparative study challenges the view that the Nordic model also has given rise to a particular form of Nordic parliamentarism.[6] The scrutiny of a whole range of empirical indicators on parliamentary relationships and voter surveys revealed that only three characteristics turned out to be particularly Nordic in the sense that they were found in all five Nordic countries. There was an overwhelmingly positive attitude toward the view that parliamentarians should also reflect the social background of the voters and not only their political preferences. There were also strong preferences favoring cooperation between parliamentary parties. Finally, there was the view that major threats toward democracy in the future would come from internal rather than external forces. In most other respects, the Nordic parliaments reflected standard features of parliamentarian systems operating with proportional electoral systems.

Small, Egalitarian, and a Strong Periphery

At the outset three theses were presented about Norwegian politics. The arguments were implicitly all comparative, pointing to the political effects of small size, an egalitarian culture, and strong peripheries. With 4.5 million people, Norway is undoubtedly a small country. Robert Dahl, among others, has argued that size and democracy are tied together in a trade-off between impact and influence.[7] In small states, as in the Greek *polis* and the early New England towns, citizens have direct control over the decisions made. The trouble with democracy in a small state, however, is that the state controls so few of the forces affecting the lives of its citizens. These forces operate outside the reach of effective (small) state control. The larger the state, therefore, the more control the state can have over such forces. But the price of large size is a greater distance between citizens and the effective decisionmaking centers.

Another general argument based on size is that small countries, with small, open economies, develop a stronger corporate structure than countries less dependent on export and with a larger home market. Their economic prosperity depends in part on the ability to absorb sudden economic shocks in international markets.[8] Quick adjustments in income policies may, for example, be necessary to safeguard employment when prices fall in crucial markets. To achieve this without major industrial unrest, close corporate networks are necessary. We have also in this book met the argument that small states are stronger supporters of international law and organizations than the large and powerful ones. The reason is the fairly obvious one that strong international regimes may protect small countries from the arbitrary power politics of large ones.

Norwegian politics bears out arguments favoring all three propositions. Norwegian politicians themselves have pointed to the small state dependence on international organizations and regulations (Chapter 7). The strong, continuous support for the work of the United Nations and the elite argument in favor of EU membership illustrate the point. And the strong corporate structure has been a major theme in discussions about Norwegian politics at least since Rokkan launched his thesis about the numerical and corporate channels in Norwegian decisionmaking (Chapter 4). During the 1990s, this was also reflected in the compromise worked out in the solidarity pact, in which trade unions agreed to wage moderation in return for policies to decrease unemployment (Chapter 5). When it comes to the quality of internal democracy, much depends on the indicators selected. Surveys from the mid-1990s showed that most voters (80 to 90 percent) expressed satisfaction with the way democracy worked in Norway.[9] Danish and Norwegian voters were actually the most satisfied in the whole of Western Europe. So even though Norway has its share of (increasing) political alienation, its comparative position on voter satisfaction is still near the top of the list (Chapter 4). Lijphart, in his comparative study, examines several measures on the quality of democracy.[10] Among his indicators are women's representation, political equality, electoral participation, and voter satisfaction. These are all areas where the Norwegian score is comparatively very high. In general terms

Lijphart finds the consensus democracies to be the "kinder and gentler" form of democracy. These are more likely to be welfare states, to protect the environment, to put fewer people in prison, and to give more aid to developing nations.

Equality is part of the Norwegian self-image. In cultural terms, this is often seen as a Nordic trait: "the passion for equality."[11] Even within the Nordic area, Norway has a special history of strong egalitarian traditions. The Norwegian aristocracy disappeared during the Middle Ages. The new aristocratic influx during the four hundred years of Danish rule was extremely small, and titles were abolished soon after the secession in 1814. Compared to other European countries and to neighboring Sweden and Denmark, peasant society in Norway was traditionally highly egalitarian, both in terms of culture and economy—a characteristic that remains today. Modernization did, of course, produce an industrial bourgeoisie, but it is much smaller and less distinctive in its social characteristics than in the European countries in general (Chapter 2). Political equality developed early. Voting rights were given to close to half of all males as early as 1814, and both all-male and universal suffrage came early, before World War I.

The locks against populist floods have traditionally been weak in Norwegian politics. There were few institutional, social, and cultural defense works against successive waves of political mobilization from peasants, workers, and women. The main exception to this is the foreign policy area (Chapter 7). In foreign affairs, there has until quite recently been a rather closed, elitist milieu for debate and decisionmaking. This certainly does not make Norway an exception, but it deviates from the generally egalitarian politics. It is also a major point in Chapter 7 that this exclusiveness in terms of foreign policy making has been under major pressure and change since the 1970s, when the first referendum debate on EU membership took place. This debate showed that foreign policy was also domestic policy. The foreign-domestic divide proved increasingly difficult to uphold with later developments in the international economy. A report published by the Directorate of Public Management early in 2000 illustrated the point.[12] It claimed that 15 percent of all changes in laws during the past five years derived from international agreements, not from internal administrative or political processes. Most of these changes derived from the EEA agreement to adjust to the internal EU market.

Finally, the periphery continued to prove its political strength during the latter half of the twentieth century. Legendary speaker Tip O'Neill in the U.S. House of Representatives argued that "all politics is local," which is also a useful adage in the Norwegian context. That is not to say that the center-periphery cleavage is the only or the most important cleavage in Norwegian politics. As in most industrialized countries, the left-right conflict, as it relates to the role of the state in the economy, is usually the most decisive cleavage. But unlike most of these countries, the political power of the periphery repeatedly has proved its clout in Norwegian politics. The political district alliance has been decisive in two referenda on EU membership. In spite of all the societal changes between 1972 and 1994 and the renewal of the electorate during this period, survey researchers are still pointing to the stunning geographical stability of the voters' response. And this occurred despite the fact that this is the period that saw the rise of the "volatile" voters. Maps showing the geographical distribution of the "yes" and "no" vote reveal virtually no change in the twenty-two years between the two referenda. Historically, the economic interests of the primary sector—along with the cultural differences entrenched in the "countercultures"—not only triggered the formation of a district party like the Center Party but also made the interests of the periphery crucial in internal party coalition-building. Urban and cosmopolitan politicians within most parties always had to watch for "the peasants within our party," as a major Labor Party politician put it in the 1950s.[13]

The strong position of the district interests in Norwegian politics is also reflected in the way political institutions work (although this is not picked up in Lijphart's indicators): the strong local government, the decentralized nomination process for parliamentary elections, the greater weight of the peripheral vote in electing parliamentarians, and the informal regional quotas in governments. A strong political presence coupled with a strong state also made the parties' maintenance of their district vote easier. Centralization was fought vigorously through localization of industry and administrative and educational centers, through the "district policy" of maintaining favorable conditions for the primary sector and industrial development in the countryside, and through the building of public infrastructure, communications, and public services.

Continuity and Change During the 1990s

Norway entered the 1990s with a minority coalition government that included the Center Party, the Christians, and the Conservatives. The decade ended with a minority coalition that included the Center Party, the Christians, and the Liberals. The person who had been foreign minister in January 1990 became prime minister seven years later. In March 2000 the center government was succeeded by a minority Labor government of the same type that had been in power for most of the decade. On the face of it, it was hardly much of a change. However, two events, both of which preceded the decade, had significantly transformed the way parliamentary politics operated. One was the pivotal position of the

Progress Party established at the 1985 election. The other was the new development in the EU question that at executive level started with the EEA initiative of the Labor government in January 1989.

The traditional postwar parliamentary pattern of a two-bloc alternation in government ended with the election of two Progress Party representatives in 1985. For the first twenty years after World War II, there had been a left majority in parliament. In the following twenty years, from 1965 to 1985, the "bourgeois" parties of the center-right alternated with the "socialist" parties of the left in having a majority. Political issues, events, and personalities definitely made the process of government formation complicated, but these were both potentially majority blocs. The nature of government formation changed when neither bloc achieved a majority in parliament in the 1985 election. The Progress Party had been in parliament since 1973, but this was the first time they "controlled the balance." The party was not, however, an acceptable political partner for either bloc. The Willoch center-right government fell in 1986 as a result. In subsequent parliaments, the position of the Progress Party and the divisive character of the EU issue have made the old option of a center-right government much less likely. In fact, considering the institutional integration into EU through the EEA agreement, it would take close to a political miracle to bring the two antagonists—the Center Party and the Conservatives—back into the same government. After the 1972 referendum, the EU issue more or less disappeared—and made way for the Willoch government of the 1980s—precisely because there were no institutional mechanisms to keep it on the agenda. Today the EEA arrangements, as we have seen, produce a steady stream of political issues for the parties to decide, making the hurdle for the old bourgeois bloc extremely high. Of course, miracles do occasionally happen in politics. However, they rarely make stable constructions.

Up to 1985, it was *the voters* in elections that made the choice between the two governmental alternatives—although a lot could happen on the way to government formation. After 1985, the *Progress Party* held the balance—at least in the negative sense of being in a position to topple the government—which opened the arena for parliamentary party strategies. And during the second half of the 1990s, it gradually became clear that the Center Party would decide the government.

The Center Party was the architect behind the center government that came to power in 1997, and the party was—and still is—in a position to choose. Do they want to support a minority Labor government (as they did in 1990), or go for a continued center alternative after the next election in 2001 (as they did in 1997), or opt for a closer cooperation with the Labor Party (as they did in 1935)? The problem for the Center Party, however, is that Labor supports strong EU integration, preferably membership. A coalition between Labor and the Center Party is inconceivable unless the EU issue somehow is stabilized or disappears.

In March 2000 the center government fell in parliament on the issue of building new gas-fueled power plants. The government was hesitant (or against), while Labor and the Conservatives were more eager to press ahead (or in favor). These gas plants would use existing technology and causing large carbon dioxide emissions. The government wanted to wait until new technology was available that reduced emissions significantly. According to the proponents, this technology would not be economically viable in the foreseeable future, and the gas plants would pollute much less than imported electricity from coal-based power plants on the continent. The vote in parliament was historic, as it was the first time a Norwegian government had to leave office on an environmental issue. On this occasion it was the Conservative Party that had to choose—between a government of the center parties and Labor. Traditionally the Conservatives were the main opponents of Labor's "socialist" policies, but the two parties have increasingly found common ground during the latter decades of the twentieth century in policies dealing with industrial development (see also below) and particularly on the question of EU membership. The parliamentary vote was, however, not only about an environmental issue. It was also a strategic decision over how to position one's party in view of the coming parliamentary election in 2001. In this perspective the Conservatives probably saw better prospects for recreating a center-right bloc with the Labor Party in power.

A government coalition between the yes-to-EU parties—Labor and the Conservatives—is unlikely other than for a short period in exceptional circumstances. Their ideological instincts tell them to fight each other along the left-right cleavage. The only coalition that potentially might win a parliamentary majority and not be destroyed by subsequent political infighting is between Labor and the (at present) moderate no-to-EU Christians. But the voters would have to be very kind to both parties to give them a combined parliamentary majority. And it would take a lot of straight talking between party leaders and old activists in both parties. That leaves the most likely alternative, which is a continuation of the present system of minority government. It is also likely that the parties in the toppled center government will face the voters again in 2001 as a governmental alternative to Labor—without including the Conservatives.

At the parliamentary level the European Union issue has played a destabilizing role in Norwegian politics since 1970; it decisively marked the 1990s and it will figure prominently in the upcoming election. What about other and new political issues? The parliamentary election of 1989 was marked by two major themes: the environment and immigration.

Both are definitely still important both to the parties and to the voters. As mentioned above, the question of new gas-fueled power plants brought down the center government. No doubt the issue of "environmental friendliness" will be central in the 2001 campaign. The issue of immigration was debated in the 1999 local elections, possibly with less intensity than in previous campaigns, but attitudes toward immigration still guide many voters, particularly those with the Progress Party as their first choice.

In terms of continuity, the left-right cleavage is—just like the center-periphery cleavage—still central in Norwegian politics. There are important debates about the role of foreign capital in Norwegian financial and industrial companies, about the return of major banks to private ownership, and the privatization of state companies like the enormous (by Norwegian standards) oil company, Statoil. Even today about half the GNP is channeled through public budgets, and public ownership is extensive in some sectors. There is obviously much to fight about—taxes and public bureaucracy—between left and right, between Labor and the Socialist Left on the one side and the Conservatives, the Progress Party, and the tiny Liberals on the other.

But there is also another side to this: cooperation, compromise, and for polemical purposes, "the grand coalition." The latter points to the fact that the traditional antagonists in Norwegian politics—Labor and the Conservatives—increasingly have found common ground in economic policies. Actually the making of "broad" compromises has removed some of the politics from the public agenda. The fact that oil has made Norway one of the richest countries in the world in terms of GNP per capita has also removed much tension in the field of economic policies. It was, in fact, rather astonishing that the politicians reached a broad compromise to place large parts of the oil revenue in a fund for future needs when the oil and gas era ends. These and other funds have given the Norwegian state an economic base that will make it the major source of credit for Norwegian industrial development in the future. In fact, the Norwegian state is a formidable capitalist actor in the markets. Around 1990, it bailed out—and even took over—major banks threatened with bankruptcy. Increasingly, politicians find themselves as directors in a "state capitalist" system. This both makes the old left-right struggle less potent as a political divider and places the politicians in the challenging position of being actors and guardians of markets at the same time.

Are there "new" parties and "new" voters in Norway? Since the 1970s, two major changes have affected the political parties: They have lost members, and they have become more dependent on state finance. A third important development is that voters have become less loyal. Voter volatility has increased, and almost half of the voters in the last parliamentary election did not vote for their chosen party at the previous election. These changes have accelerated in the 1990s, but they started—as in many other European countries—in the 1970s. The focus on political leaders—their style, their personalities, their ties—has increased as well, helped along by the media. It would not be the whole story to say that affluence, ignorance, and apathy characterize the new voters. Nor would it be true to say that voters finally have begun to choose, that they finally have turned into genuine democratic citizens making up their minds on the basis of the issues at stake. Declining voting loyalties may, of course, have more than one cause, although the consumer perspective, including the option to abstain at elections, has become a more common trait among Norwegian voters during the 1990s. Or more precisely, *also* among Norwegian voters.

The National Question

Norwegians have long been aware that they belong to a small nation. Until 1905, they fought to leave the union with Sweden and to establish an independent state, knowing fair well that they would never gain parity with their Swedish brethren. The feeling was also strong that Norwegian history and culture, even the economy, gave the foundation and the need for an independent nation-state. The recent independence—almost within living memory—is sometimes taken as an explanation for why Norwegians were so reluctant to join another union in the 1990s. But that analysis would make it difficult to explain why the Irish are favorable toward the European Union (another young state), while the Swiss stubbornly refuse EU membership (old state). The debate over EU membership also drew part of its strength from the old center periphery conflict and the (declining) "countercultures" in Norwegian history (lay Christianity, New Norwegian language, and teetotalism). In this debate, there were elements of an old coalition in Norwegian political history, namely, the one between the rural districts and parts of the radical urban intelligentsia. Added to that was the anticapitalist resistance against the "moneycratie" of Brussels—rooted in parts of the trade union movement and reminiscent of socialism—and the defense of the traditional welfare state (especially female voters).

In some ways it may look odd that the national question should reemerge so explosively during the EU debate. The process of nation-building was successfully over long ago. Nation and state had merged into an institutionalized democracy—the labor movement was integrated into the nation as well as the state during the 1930s and 1940s.

Norway is even today basically an ethnically homogeneous country with comparatively few immigrants. About 6 percent of the Norwegian population are immigrants, in the sense that both parents were foreign citizens. Roughly half of these, however, came from Nordic, North European, or North American countries and do not deviate much from standard cultural patterns in Norway. Traditional minorities—like the Sami, which make up less than 0.01 percent of the population—are extremely small. Still it is important to note that—however small—these minorities challenge the strong institutional and cultural imperatives of treating everyone equally—in schools, at the workplace, in politics, and in civil society generally. Their presence is forcing politicians and voters to confront the dilemmas and challenges of the evolution of a multicultural society from a traditionally homogeneous nation—ethnically, culturally, and to a fair extent, socially.

However, the greatest challenge to the old project of nation-building, so eagerly pursued through the nineteenth and most of the twentieth century, has not been from inside but from the outside. And this challenge has not been primarily manifested in the economic and cultural fields, in spite of fashionable arguments about globalization, Americanization, and the communication revolution. The major challenge has been political, in the shape of the European Union. The success of the EU in terms of building a transnational institutional framework for economic and political cooperation among an increasing number of European states has forced politicians and voters alike to reconsider the very foundation of the Norwegian nation-state. The EEA arrangement locks Norwegian politicians and citizens into continuous debate on the sustainability of Norwegian democracy, security, economy, and culture. The "national question" today is not about secession, rebellion, or multinational state-building—as in nineteenth-century Europe. It is about building viable political, economic, and cultural arrangements to sustain democracy, prosperity, and a "Norwegian" way of life. Or in the shorter version: To be or not to be a member of the EU.

Elites on Trial

Political elites are always on trial in democracies. Their power may end abruptly at the next election or through parliamentary action. In this Norway is not special. On the basis of the presentation of Norwegian politics in this book, we may ask whether the alleged "primacy of politics" makes politicians particularly vulnerable in Norway?

In the first chapter, I presented the proposition that political forces had been crucial in shaping the Norwegian society and that this possibly had left a lasting legacy. The construction of "Norway" as a modern state and nation was, to a large extent, the work of a tiny nineteenth-century elite of politicians, bureaucrats, artists, and academics. These elites and the institutional defenses entrenched in the "official's state" were not, however, able to stem the tide of the peasants' movement in the 1880s. Actually the old elites were split, and some of them belonged to the new wave of challengers. Later—in the twentieth century—the rising labor movement toppled the new "bourgeois" power elites.

Contemporary Norwegian institutions do not make any solid defenses against new challenges. The complaint of the conservative elites of the 1880s was precisely that the plebiscitarian elements were not sufficiently restrained in the political process. There was no federalist structure, no first chamber in parliament, and no royal veto in legislative matters after 1884. Today the proportional electoral system and the decentralized party nomination of candidates for parliament give central elites few instruments in "guiding" the electoral process. The formidable power of the media is unpredictable. It is, of course, possible to argue that the fixed parliamentary term of four years constitutes an elite defense. But that argument may equally well be put the other way: The lack of dissolution power in the hands of the government removes another instrument from the elite's toolbox.

The strength of politics is evident in the public budgets and in the corporate networks. In spite of the strong impact on market ideology since the 1980s and the Thatcher-Reagan crusaders who have been active in Norway, more than 50 percent of the entire economy still goes through public budgets, and the state coffer is well filled. Although privatization and increased market exposure of public enterprises have been the dominant political trends during the latter decades, the state is no doubt still strongly entrenched in economic processes. A major issue in Norwegian politics at the turn of the twenty-first century is still—just as in the first two decades of the twentieth century—how to secure national interests in a changing, increasingly internationalized economy. Corporate structures are of major importance in a small, open economy like Norway's. The mix of public and private structures is still a central characteristic of the Norwegian society. Finally, the strong impact of politicians is evident in the public policies pursued in areas like welfare, health care, district concerns, and gender equality (Chapter 6).

The proposition that Norwegian politics is particularly important is, of course, difficult to prove and must remain a hypothesis. Politics is, on the face of it, not more important in Norway than in the neighboring welfare societies of Sweden and Denmark. Certainly the consorted industrial strategies of Germany, the consensual politics of the Netherlands and

Belgium—or the French *dirigisme* for that matter—are challenging cases confronting the argument of a unique Norwegian "primacy of politics."

Nevertheless, Norwegian elites may be more "on trial" than politicians are in many other comparable democracies. Undoubtedly, political institutions strongly expose them to voter judgments. That is not unique. Electoral participation is also consistently high. That is not unique either, although the combination of weak institutional defenses and high electoral exposure is less common. Add the ingredient of having a small population, and the potential for elite challenges increases. Yet, the most demanding factor for Norwegian elites during the 1990s has been the mismatch between elite and voter opinions on the European Union issue—the dominant elites in favor, the dominant electorate against. This leads to crossing political allegiances and antagonisms, which impedes the formation of stable parliamentary government in line with party programs and public opinion. This is not a "trial" of elites that is likely to trigger a major breakdown in Norwegian politics. The consensual elements in politics and culture are too strong to make that likely. The major challenge facing Norwegian democracy in the years ahead—outside or inside of the EU—will be that of accountability, to sustain a democratic system where the electorate might vote for *alternatives*—and where they can expect to get what they voted for.

Notes

1. Peter Flora, "Introduction and Interpretation," in Peter Flora with Stein Kuhnle and Derek Urwin, eds., *State Formation, Nation-Building, and Mass Politics in Europe: The Theory of Stein Rokkan* (Oxford: Oxford University Press, 1999), p. 11.

2. Arend Lijphart, *Patterns of Democracy: Government Forms and Performance in Thirty-Six Countries* (New Haven: Yale University Press, 1999).

3. Ibid., p. 248.

4. D. Rustow, "Scandinavia: Working Multiparty Systems," in S. Neumann, ed., *Modern Political Parties* (Chicago: Chicago University Press, 1956), pp. 169–193.

5. There is an argument that this has changed slightly since 1999, when the new director of the bank started to "interpret" his instructions from the Ministry of Finance more freely.

6. Peter Esaiassen and Knut Heidar, eds., *Beyond Westminster and Congress: The Nordic Experience* (Columbus: Ohio State University Press, 2000).

7. Robert A. Dahl and Edward R. Tufte, *Size and Democracy* (Stanford: Stanford University Press, 1973), and Robert A. Dahl, *Dilemmas of Pluralist Democracy: Autonomy versus Control* (New Haven: Yale University Press, 1982), ch. 2.

8. See, for example, E. Damgaard, R. Gerlich, and J. J. Richardson, eds., *The Politics of Economic Crisis: Lessons for Western Europe* (Aldershot, U.K.: Avebury, 1989);

P. J. Katzenstein, *Small States in World Markets* (Ithaca: Cornell University Press, 1985); and R. Gourevitch, *Politics in Hard Times* (Ithaca: Cornell University Press, 1986).

9. Bernt Aardal, *Velgerne i 90-årene* (Oslo: NKS-forlaget, 1999), p. 177.

10. Lijphart, *Patterns of Democracy*, ch. 16.

11. Stephan R. Graubard, ed., *Norden: The Passion for Equality* (Oslo: Norwegian University Press, 1986).

12. Report from Statskonsult quoted in *Aftenposten*, January 31, 2000.

13. Foreign Minister Halvard Lange; see Knut Einar Eriksen and Helge Øystein Pharo, *Kald krig og internasjonalisering, 1945–1965* (Oslo: Universitetsforlaget, 1997), p. 83.

Bibliography

Aftenposten (Norwegian newspaper)

Andenæs, Johs. *Statsforvaltningen i Norge*, 8th ed. Oslo: Tano, 1998.

Andenæs, Mads T., and Ingeborg Wilberg. *The Constitution of Norway: A Commentary*. Oslo: Universitetsforlaget, 1987.

Bailey, Jennifer Leigh. "Norsk fiskeripolitikk." In Torbjørn L. Knutsen, Gunnar Sørbø, Svein Gjerdåker, eds., *Norges Utenrikspolitikk*. Oslo: Cappelen, 1997.

Benum, Edgeir. *Overflod og fremtidsfrykt 1970-* , vol. 12 of *Aschehougs Norges Historie*. Oslo: Aschehoug, 1998.

Bjørklund, Tor. *Om folkeavstemninger. Norge og Norden 1905—1994*. Oslo: Universitetsforlaget, 1997.

Bjørklund, Tor. "Aksjon, demokrati, protest." In Ingerid Semmingsen et al., eds., *Underveis, mot nye tider*, vol. 8 of *Norges Kulturhistorie*. Oslo: Aschehoug, 1983.

Bowitz, Einar, and Ådne Cappelen. "Velferdsstatens økonomiske grunnlag." In Aksel Hatland, Stein Kuhnle, and Tor Inge Romøren, *Den norske velferssstaten*, 2nd ed. Oslo: Ad Notam Gyldendal, 1996.

Brothén, Martin. "International Networking." In Peter Esaiasson and Knut Heidar, eds., *Beyond Congress and Westminster: The Nordic Experience*. Columbus: Ohio State University Press, 2000.

Brundtland, Gro Harlem. *Dramatiske år 1986–1996*. Oslo: Gyldendal, 1998.

Christensen, Tom, and Morten Egeberg. "Noen trekk ved forholdet mellom organisasjonene og den offentlige forvaltningen." In Tom Christensen and Morten Egeberg, eds., *Forvaltningskunnskap*. Oslo: Tano 1997.

Christensen, Tom, and Morten Egeberg. "Sentraladministrasjonen–en oversikt over trekk ved departementer og direktorater." In Tom Christensen and Morten Egeberg, eds., *Forvaltningskunnskap*. Oslo: Tano, 1997.

Claes, Dag Harald. "Norsk olje- og gasspolitikk." In Knutsen, Torbjørn L., Gunnar Sørbø, Svein Gjerdåker, eds., *Norges Utenrikspolitikk*. Oslo: Cappelen, 1997.

Claes, Dag Harald, and Bent Sofus Tranøy, eds. *Utenfor, annerledes og suveren? Norge under EØS-avtalen*. Oslo: Fagbokforlaget, 1999.

Dagbladet (Norwegian newspaper).

Dahl, Hans Fredrik. "Massemedia." In Dag Bjørnland, Hans Fredrik Dahl, and Peter Sjøholt, *Vareflom og massemedia*, vol. 3 of *Det Moderne Norge*. Oslo: Gyldendal, 1982.

Dahl, Robert A. *Dilemmas of Pluralist Democracy: Autonomy versus Control*. New Haven: Yale University Press, 1982.

Dahl, Robert A., and Edward R. Tufte. *Size and Democracy*. Stanford: Stanford University Press, 1973.

Dahlerup, Drude, and Brita Gulli. "Kvindeorganisationerne i Norden: Afmagt eller modmagt?" In Elina Haavio-Mannila et al., eds., *Det uferdige demokratiet*. Oslo: Nordisk ministerråd, 1983.

Damgaard, E., R. Gerlich, and J. J. Richardson, eds. *The Politics of Economic Crisis: Lessons for Western Europe*. Aldershot, U.K.: Avebury, 1989.

Danielsen, Rolf. "Nye kilder til regjeringskrisen i januar 1928." *Historisk Tidsskrift* 57 (1978): 93–102.

Dølvik, Jon Erik, et al. "Norwegian Labour Market Insitutions and Regulations." In Dølvik and Arild H. Steen, eds., *Making Solidarity Work? The Norwegian Labour Market in Transition*. Oslo: Scandinavian University Press, 1997.

Eckhoff, Torstein, and Eivind Smith. *Forvaltningsrett*, 6th ed. Oslo: Tano, 1997.

Egeberg, Morten, and Jarle Trondal. "Innenriksforvaltningens og den offentlige politikens internasjonalisering." In Tom Christensen and Morten Egeberg, eds., *Forvaltningskunnskap*. Oslo: Tano, 1997.

Egeberg, Morten. "The Fourth Level of Government: On the Standardization of Public Policy Within International Regions." *Scandinavian Political Studies* 3 (1980): 235–248.

Egeland, Jan. *Impotent Superpower—Potent Small State*. Oslo: Norwegian University Press, 1988.

Eliassen, Kjell A. "Rekrutteringen til Stortinget og regjeringen, 1945–1985." In Trond Nordby, ed., *Stortinget og regjeringen, 1945–1985. Institusjoner–Rekruttering*. Oslo: Kunnskapsforlaget, 1985.

Eriksen, Knut Einar, and Helge Øystein Pharo. *Kald krig og internasjonalisering, 1945–1965*. Oslo: Universitetsforlaget, 1997.

Esaiasson, Peter, and Knut Heidar, eds. *Beyond Congress and Westminster: The Nordic Experience*. Columbus: Ohio State University Press, 2000.

Espeli, Harald. *Lobbyvirksomhet på Stortinget*. Oslo: Tano, 1999.

Fevolden, Trond. "Fylkeskommunen–fra hjelpeorgan til selvstendig forvaltningsnivå." In Tom Christensen and Morten Egeberg, eds., *Forvaltningskunnskap*. Oslo: Tano, 1997.

Fimreite, Anne Lise. "Samspillet mellom privat og offentlig sektor." In Anne Lise Fimreite, ed., *Forskerblikk på Norge*. Oslo: Tano, 1997.

Flora, Peter. "Introduction and Interpretation." In Peter Flora Stein Kuhnle and Derek Urwin, eds., *State Formation, Nation-Building, and Mass Politics in Europe: The Theory of Stein Rokkan*. Oxford: Oxford University Press, 1999.

Flora, Peter, Stein Kuhnle, and Derek Urwin, eds. *State Formation, Nation-Building, and Mass Politics in Europe: The Theory of Stein Rokkan*. Oxford: Oxford University Press, 1999.

Frydenlund, Knut. *Lille land—hva nå? Refleksjoner om Norges utenrikspolitiske situasjon*. Oslo: Universitetsforlaget, 1982.

Furre, Berge. *Norsk historie, 1905–1990*. Oslo: Det Norske Samlaget, 1992.

Førland, Tor Egil. "En empirisk bauta, et intellektuelt gjesp. Kritisk blikk på Norsk utenrikspolitikks historie 1–6." *Historisk Tidsskrift* 78 (1999): 214–236.

Gourevitch, R. *Politics in Hard Times*. Ithaca: Cornell University Press, 1986.

Graubard, Stephan R., ed. *Norden: The Passion for Equality*. Oslo: Norwegian University Press, 1986.

Grytten, Ola H. "Arbeidsledighetens omfang i mellomkrigstiden." *Historisk Tidsskrift* 71 (1992): 249–277.

Hatland, Aksel. "Trygdepolitikken ved et veiskille." In Aksel Hatland, Stein Kuhnle, and Tor Inge Romøren, *Den norske velfersstaten*, 2nd ed. Oslo: Ad Notam Gyldendal, 1996.

Hatland, Aksel, Stein Kuhnle, and Tor Inge Romøren. *Den norske velfersstaten*, 2nd ed. Oslo: Ad Notam Gyldendal, 1996.

Heidar, Knut. "Civil Society and the Mobilization of Bias: Comparing Political Participation in the U.S. and in Norway." Working Paper 5/1999, Department of Political Science, University of Oslo.

Heidar, Knut. "The Polymorphic Nature of Party Membership." *European Journal of Political Research* 25 (1994): 61–86.

Heidar, Knut. "The Norwegian Labour Party: 'En attendant L'Europe.'" In Richard Gillespie and William E. Paterson, eds., *Rethinking Social Democracy in Western Europe*. London: Frank Cass, 1993.

Heidar, Knut. "Should the Parties Be Incorporated in the Written Constitution?" In Carsten Smith et al., eds., *The Role of the Constitution in a Changing Society: Joint Polish-Norwegian Conference, Oslo, May 14–16, 1991*. Oslo: Norwegian Academy of Science and Letters, 1991.

Heidar, Knut. "Norway: Party Competition and System Change." In Peter Mair and Gordon Smith, eds., *Understanding Party System Change in Western Europe*. London: Frank Cass, 1990.

Heidar, Knut. "Staten, politikken og det sivile samfunn." In Lars Alldén, Natalie Rogoff Ramsøy, and Mariken Vaa, eds., *Det norske samfunn*, 3rd ed. Oslo: Gyldendal, 1986.

Heidar, Knut, and Lars Svåsand, eds. *Partier uten grenser?* Oslo: Tano, 1997.

Heidar, Knut, and Lars Svåsand, eds. *Partiene i en brytningstid*. Bergen: Alma Mater, 1994.

Heidar, Knut, et al. "Nordic Parliamentary Design: Five Most Similar Systems?" In Peter Esaiasson and Knut Heidar, eds., *Beyond Congress and Westminster: The Nordic Experience*. Columbus: Ohio State University Press, 2000.

Hellevik, Ottar. *Stortinget–en sosial elite?* Oslo: Pax Forlag, 1969.

Hellevik, Ottar, and Tor Bjørklund. "Velgerne og kvinnerepresentasjon." In Nina C. Raaum, ed., *Kjønn og politikk*. Oslo: Tano, 1995.

Hernes, Gudmund, and Kristine Nergaard. *Oss i Mellom*. Oslo: FAFO, 1989.

Hernes, Gudmund. "Hva styrer styrerne?" In Gudmund Hernes, *Økonomisk organisering*. Oslo: Universitetsforlaget, 1985.

Hernes, Gudmund. "Mot en institusjonell økonomi." In G. Hernes, ed., *Forhandlingsøkonomi og blandingsadministrasjon*. Oslo: Universitetsforlaget, 1978.

Hernes, Helga. *Welfare State and Woman Power: Essays in State Feminism*. Oslo: Norwegian University Press, 1987.

Historical Statistics 1994. Oslo: Statistics Norway, 1995.

Hodne, Fritz. *Norges økonomiske historie, 1915–1970*. Oslo: Alma, J. W. Cappelen, 1981.

Hodne, Fritz, and Ole Honningdal Grytten. *Norsk Økonomi, 1900–1990*. Oslo: Tano, 1992.

Hveem, Helge. *Internasjonalisering og Politikk*. Oslo: Tano, 1994.

Hveem, Helge, Sverre Lodgaard, and Kjell Skjelsbær. *Vår plass i verden*, vol. 7 of *Det Moderne Norge*. Oslo: Gyldendal, 1984.

Høyer, Svennik. *Pressen, mellom teknologi og samfunn*. Oslo: Universitetsforlaget, 1995.

Jansen, Alf-Inge. *Makt og miljø. Om utformingen av natur- og miljøvernpolitikken i Norge*. Oslo: Universitetsforlaget, 1989.

Jansen, Alf-Inge, and Per Kristen Mydske. "Norway: Balancing Environmental Quality and Interest in Oil." In Kenneth Hanf and Alf-Inge Jansen, eds., *Governance and Environment in Western Europe*. Harlow: Longman, 1998.

Jensen, Torben. "Party Cohesion and Cooperation Across Party Lines in Nordic Parliamentary Parties." In Peter Esaiasson and Knut Heidar, eds., *Beyond Congress and Westminster: The Nordic Experience*. Columbus: Ohio State University Press, 2000.

Jenssen, Anders Todal, Ola Listhaug, and Per Arnt Pettersen. "Betydningen av gamle og nye skillelinjer." In Anders Todal Jenssen and Henry Valen, eds., *Bryssel midt imot. Folkeavstemningen om EU*. Oslo: Ad Notam, 1995.

Karvonen, Lauri, and Per Selle. *Women in Nordic Politics: Closing the Gap*. Aldershot, U.K.: Dartmouth, 1995.

Katzenstein, P. J. *Small States in World Markets*. Ithaca: Cornell University Press, 1985.

Kjellberg, Anders. "Fagorganisering i Norge og Sverige i et internasjonalt perspektiv." In *Årbok for Arbeiderbevegelsens Arkiv og Bibliotek*. Oslo: Arbeiderbevegelsens Arkiv og Bibliotek, 1999.

Knudsen, Olav Fagerlund. "Beslutningsprosesser i norsk utenrikspolitikk." In Torbjørn Knutsen, Gunnar Sørbø, and Svein Gjerdåker, eds., *Noregs Utenrikspolitikk*. Oslo: Cappelen, 1997.

Knutsen, Oddbjørn. "The Priorities of Materialists and Post-Materialists Values in the Nordic Countries: A Five-Country Comparison." *Scandinavian Political Studies* 12 (1989): 221–244.

Knutsen, Oddbjørn. "Partipolitiske skillelinjer i avanserte industrisamfunn." *Tidsskrift for samfunnsforskning* 29 (1988):155–175.

Knutsen, Thorbjørn L. "Norsk utenrikspolitikk som forskningsfelt." In Torbjørn L Knutsen, Gunnar Sørbø, and Svein Gjerdåker, eds., *Norges Utenrikspolitikk*. Oslo: Cappelen, 1997.

Kortner, Olaf, et al., eds., *Store Norske Leksikon*, vol. 9. Oslo: Kunnskapsforlaget, 1986–1989.

Kuhnle, Stein. "Velferdsstatens politiske grunnlag." In Aksel Hatland, Stein Kuhnle, and Tor Inge Romøren, *Den norske velfersstaten*, 2nd ed. Oslo: Ad Notam Gyldendal, 1996.

Kuhnle, Stein. "Finansiering av velferdsstaten," In Stein Kuhnle and Liv Solheim, *Velferdsstaten–vekst og omstilling*, 2nd ed. Oslo: Tano, 1994.

Kuhnle, Stein. "Historisk oversikt." In Stein Kuhnle and Liv Solheim, *Velferdsstaten–vekst og omstilling*, 2nd ed. Oslo: Tano, 1994.

Kuhnle, Stein. "Mottakere og goder." In Stein Kuhnle and Liv Solheim, *Velferdsstaten–vekst og omstilling*, 2nd ed. Oslo: Tano, 1994.

Kuhnle, Stein. "Stemmeretten i 1814." *Historisk Tidsskrift* 51 (1972): 373–390.

Kuhnle, Stein, and Ola Listhaug. "Makropolitiske komparasjoner, partier og politisk atferd: Linjer, status og utfordringer i norsk statsvitenskap." *Norsk Statsvitenskapelig Tidsskrift* 13 (1997): 215–254.

Lafferty, William M. *Economic Development and the Response of Labor in Scandinavia.* Oslo: Universitetsforlaget, 1971.

"Langtidsprogrammet 1998–2001," *Stortingsmelding* 4 (1996–1997), special attachment. Oslo: Finans- og tolldepartementet, 1997.

Larsen, Helge O. "Kommunene som forvaltnings- og selvstyreorgan." In Tom Christensen and Morten Egeberg, eds., *Forvaltningskunnskap.* Oslo: Tano, 1997.

Lie, Einar. *Ambisjon og tradisjon. Finansdepartementet, 1945–1965.* Oslo: Universitetsforlaget, 1995.

Lijphart, Arend. *Patterns of Democracy: Government Forms and Performance in Thirty-Six Countries.* New Haven: Yale University Press, 1999.

Listhaug, Ola. *Citizens, Parties, and Norwegian Electoral Politics, 1957–1985.* Trondheim: Tapir, 1989.

Listhaug, Ola, Art Miller, and Henry Valen. "The Gender Gap in Norwegian Voting Behaviour." *Scandinavian Political Studies* 8 (1985): 187–206.

Listhaug, Ola, Beate Huseby, and Richard Matland. "Valgatferd blant kvinner og menn, 1957–1993." In Nina C. Raaum, ed., *Kjønn og politikk.* Oslo: Tano, 1995.

Lundestad, Geir. "Hovedtendenser i norsk politikk, 1945–1965." In Trond Bergh and Helge Ø. Pharo, eds., *Vekst og velstand.* Oslo: Universitetsforlaget, 1977.

Maddison, Angus. *The World Economy in the 20th Century.* Paris: OECD, 1989.

Mjøset, Lars. "Norge og Den europeiske union." In Torbjørn L. Knutsen, Gunnar Sørbø, Svein Gjerdåker, eds., *Norges Utenrikspolitikk.* Oslo: Cappelen, 1997.

Moses, Jonathan W., and Bent Sofus Tranøy. "Norge i den nye verdensøkonomien." In Torbjørn L. Knutsen, Gunnar Sørbø, Svein Gjerdåker, eds., *Norges Utenrikspolitikk,* 2nd ed. Oslo: Cappelen Akademisk Forlag, 1997.

Nage, Anne-Hilde. "Politiseringen av kjønn: Et historisk perspektiv." In Nina C. Raaum, ed., *Kjønn og politikk.* Oslo: Tano, 1995.

Nagel, A.-H. "Politisering av kjønn—et historisk perspektiv." In Nina C. Raaum, ed., *Kjønn og politikk.* Oslo: Tano, 1995.

Narud, Hanne Marthe. "Nominasjoner og pressen." In Knut Heidar and Lars Svåsand, eds., *Partiene i en brytningstid.* Bergen: Alma Mater, 1994.

Narud, Hanne Marthe, and Henry Valen. "Does Background Matter?" In Peter Esaiasson and Knut Heidar, eds., *Beyond Congress and Westminster: The Nordic Experience.* Columbus: Ohio State University Press, 2000.

Narud, Hanne Marthe, and Henry Valen. "Mass and Elite Attitudes Toward Future Problems in the Nordic Countries." In Peter Esaiasson and Knut Heidar, eds., *Beyond Congress and Westminster: The Nordic Experience.* Columbus: Ohio State University Press, 2000.

Neumann, Iver B., and Ståle Ulriksen. "Norsk forsvars- og sikkerhetspolitikk." In Torbjørn L Knutsen, Gunnar Sørbø, and Svein Gjerdåker, eds., *Norges Utenrikspolitikk,* 2nd ed. Oslo: Chr. Michelsens Institutt/Cappelen Akademisk Forlag, 1997.

Olsen, Johan P. *Organized Democracy—Political Institutions in a Welfare State: The Case of Norway.* Oslo: Universitetsforlaget, 1983.

Olsen, Johan P., and Harald Sætren. *Aksjoner og demokrati.* Oslo: Universitetsforlaget, 1980.

Opsal, Torkel. "The Changing System of Social Values and the Written Constitution." In *The Role of the Constitution in a Changing Society: Joint Polish-Norwegian Conference, Oslo, May 14–16, 1991.* Oslo: Norwegian Academy of Science and Letters, 1991.

Riste, Olav. "Forord." In Narve Bjørgo, Øystein Rian, and Alf Kaartvedt, eds., *Selvstendighet og union. Fra middelalderen til 1905,* vol. 1 of *Norsk utenrikspolitikks historie.* Oslo: Universitetsforlaget, 1995.

Rokkan, Stein. *Stat, Nasjon, Klasse.* Oslo: Universitetsforlaget, 1987.

Rokkan, Stein. *Citizens, Elections, Parties.* Oslo: Universitetsforlaget, 1970.

Rokkan, Stein. "Nation-Building, Cleavage Formation, and the Structuring of Mass Politics." In Stein Rokkan, *Citizens, Elections, Parties.* Oslo: Universitetsforlaget, 1970.

Rokkan, Stein. "Norway: Numerical Democracy and Corporate Pluralism." In Robert A. Dahl, ed., *Political Oppositions in Western Democracies.* New Haven: Yale University Press, 1966.

Rokkan, Stein, and Angus Campbell. "Citizen Participation in Political Life: Norway and the United States of America." *International Social Science Journal* 12, no. 1 (1960): 69–99.

Rommetvedt, Hilmar. "Stortinget–Fra konsensus til konflikt." *Norsk Statsvitenskapelig Tidsskrift* 4 (1988): 5–22.

Rustow, D. "Scandinavia: Working Multiparty Systems." In S. Neumann, ed., *Modern Political Parties.* Chicago: Chicago University Press, 1956.

Ryssevik, Jostein. *I samfunnet 3.* Oslo: Universitetsforlaget, 1994.

Rødseth, Asbjørn. "Why Has Unemployment Been So Low in Norway?" In Erik Dølvik and Arild H. Steen, eds., *Making Solidarity Work?* Oslo: Scandinavian University Press, 1997.

Raaum, Nina C. "Introduksjon–kjønn og politikk." In Nina C. Raaum, ed, *Kjønn og politikk.* Oslo: Tano, 1995.

Raaum, Nina C. "Politisk representasjon." In Nina C. Raaum, ed., *Kjønn og politikk.* Oslo: Tano, 1995.

Sars, Ernst. *Norges Politiske Historie.* Kristiania: Oscar Andersens Bogtrykkeri, 1904.

Schmitter, P. C. "Still the Century of Corporatism." In P. C. Schmitter and G. Lehmbruch, eds., *Trends Towards Corporate Intermediation.* London: Sage, 1979.

Schwebs, Ture, and Helge Østbye. *Media i samfunnet,* 3rd ed. Oslo: Samlaget, 1995.

Seip, Anne-Lise. *Sosialhjelpstaten blir til: Norsk sosialpolitikk, 1740–1920,* 2nd ed. Oslo: Gyldendal, 1994.

Seip, Anne-Lise. *Veier til velferdsstaten: Norsk sosialpolitikk, 1920–1975.* Oslo: Gyldendal, 1994.

Seip, Jens Arup. "Fra embedsmannsstat til ettpartistat." In *Fra embedsmannsstat til ettpartistat og andre essays.* Oslo: Universitetsforlaget, 1963.

Sejersted, Francis. "From Liberal Constitutionalism to Corporate Pluralism." In Jon Elster and Rune Slagstad, eds., *Constitutionalism and Democracy.* Cambridge: Cambridge University Press, 1988.

Sejersted, Fredrik. "The Norwegian Parliament and European Integration: Reflections from Medium-Speed Europe." In E. Smith, ed., *National Parliaments as Cornerstones of European Integration*. London: Kluwer Law International, 1996.

Skjeie, Hege. *Vanens makt. Styringstradisjoner i Arbeiderpartiet*. Oslo: Ad Notam, 1999.

Skjeie, Hege. "The Uneven Advance of Norwegian Women." *New Left Review* 187 (1991): 79–102.

Smith, Eivind. *Høyesterett og Folkestyret*. Oslo: Universitetsforlaget, 1993.

Sosialt Utsyn 1993. Oslo: Statistics Norway, 1993.

Statistisk Årbok 1998. Oslo: Statistics Norway, 1998.

Statistisk Årbok 1997. Oslo: Statistics Norway, 1997.

Statskonsult. *Statråden som departementsleder*, 1997.

Stavang, Per. *Parlamentarisme og maktbalanse*. Oslo: Universitetsforlaget, 1964.

Svåsand, Lars. "Partienes finansieringsmønster." In Knut Heidar and Lars Svåsand, eds., *Partiene i en brytningstid*. Bergen: Alma Mater, 1994.

Sørbø, Gunnar M. "Norsk bistandspolitikk." In Torbjørn L Knutsen, Gunnar Sørbø, and Svein Gjerdåker, eds., *Norges Utenrikspolitikk*. Oslo: Cappelen, 1997.

Tamnes, Rolf. *Oljealder, 1965–1995*, vol. 6 of *Norsk utenrikspolitiske historie*. Oslo: Universitetsforlaget, 1997.

Topf, Richard. "Beyond Electoral Participation." In Hans-Dieter Klingemann and Dieter Fuchs, eds., *Belief in Government*, vol. 1 of *Citizens and the State*. Oxford: Oxford University Press, 1995.

Tvedt, Terje. "Norsk utenrikspolitikk og de frivillige organisasjonene." In Torbjørn L. Knutsen, Gunnar Sørbø, and Svein Gjerdåker, eds., *Norges Utenrikspolitikk*. Oslo: Cappelen, 1997.

Ukens Statistikk, no. 6. Oslo: Statistics Norway, 1998.

Vagstad, Steinar. "Næringspolitikk." In Anne Lise Fimreite, ed., *Forskerblikk på Norge*. Oslo: Tano, 1997.

Valen, Henry. "Norway." In Mark N. Franklin, Thomas T. Mackie, Henry Valen et al., *Electoral Change: Responses to Evolving Social and Attitudinal Structures in Western Countries*. Cambridge: Cambridge University Press, 1992.

Valen, Henry. "Norway: Decentralization and Group Representation." In Michael Gallagher and Michael Marsh, eds., *Candidate Selection in Comparative Perspective: The Secret Garden of Politics*. London: Sage, 1988.

Valen, Henry. "Partiforskyvninger ved stortingsvalget i 1965." In Henry Valen and Willy Martinussen, *Velgerne og politiske frontlinjer*. Oslo: Gyldendal, 1972.

Valen, Henry. "The Recruitment of Parliamentary Nominees in Norway." *Scandinavian Political Studies* 1 (1966): 121–166.

Valen, Henry, and Stein Rokkan. "Conflict Structure and Mass Politics in a European Periphery." In Richard Rose, ed., *Electoral Behavior: A Comparative Handbook*. New York: Free Press, 1974.

Wängnerud, Lena. "Representing Women." In Peter Esaiasson and Knut Heidar, eds., *Beyond Congress and Westminster: The Nordic Experience*. Columbus: Ohio State University Press, 2000.

Wängnerud, Lena. *Politikans andra sida*, Göteborg Studies in Politics 53. Göteborg: Gøteborgs universitet, 1998.

Wyller, Thomas C. *Skal folket bestemme? Folkeavstemning som politisk prosess.* Oslo: Universitetsforlaget, 1992.

Østerud, Øyvind. *Agrarian Structure and the Peasant Politics in Scandinavia.* Oslo: Universitetsforlaget, 1978.

Østerud, Øyvind. *Globaliseringen og nasjonalstaten.* Oslo: Ad Notam Gyldendal, 1999.

Øyen, Ørjar. "Norges befolkning." In Natalie Rogoff Ramsøy and Mariken Vaa, eds., *Det norske samfunn,* vol. 1. Oslo: Gyldendal, 1975.

Aagedal, Olaf. "Religionen." In Hans Fredrik Dahl and Arne Martin Klausen, eds., *Tro, tanke, form,* vol. 4 of *Det moderne Norge.* Oslo: Gyldendal, 1983.

Aardal, Bernt, Henry Valen, Hanne Marthe Narud, and Frode Berglund. *Velgerne i 90-årene.* Oslo: NKS-forlaget, 1999.

Aardal, Bernt, and Henry Valen. "The Stortings Elections of 1989 and 1993: Norwegian Politics in Perspective." In Kaare Strøm and Lars Svåsand, eds., *Challenges to Political Parties: The Case of Norway.* Ann Arbor: University of Michigan Press, 1997.

Aardal, Bernt, and Henry Valen. *Konflikt og opinion.* Oslo: NKS-forlaget, 1995.

Aardal, Bernt. "Hva er en politisk skillelinje." *Tidsskrift for samfunnsforskning* 35 (1994): 218–249.

Aardal, Bernt. *Energi og miljø,* report 93:15. Oslo: Institute for Social Research, 1993.

Index